Merseyside Mountaineers & Explorers

Allan McDonald

Published by

mi view dle

an imprint of
Avid Publications, Middleview
New Road, GWESPYR
Flintshire UK
CH8 9LS
Tel: (44) 01745 886769
e-mail: info@Middleview.co.uk.
www. AvidPublications.co.uk

CONTENTS

APPENDICES

ACKNOWLEDGEMENTS

I would like to thank the Alpine Club for permission to use the photograph of the Walker Family and their guides on the front cover. Also thanks to the Wayfarer's Club for permission to use the photograph from their archives of Colin Kirkus. Additional thanks must also be given to the Royal Geographical Society for image permission.

I would also like to thank the following for their support, guidance and encouragement. In no particular order and, sincere apologies to those I may have inadvertently missed out, Hollie McDonald, Bob Burton, Keith Colwell, Geoff Brierley, Neil Metcalfe, Carol Roberts, John McDonnell, Phil Earl, Rob Platt, Mal Bonner, Carol Boothroyd, Andy Odger, Dave Gray, Adrian Dolan, Helen Avison, Lin Jensen, Peter Vaughan, Andy Chapman, John Huxley, Steve McNally, Steve and Jane Davis, Dave Woodcock, Leon Winchester.

Finally thanks also to my dad who introduced me to the mountains as a teenager in the hope that I would find something that would interest me other than fishing and my train set........... you succeeded and though had I been left to my own devices I may have achieved great things, I would not change a thing.

Allan McDonald 2011

INTRODUCTION

I t may come as something of a surprise to the casual reader that Merseyside has a very long and distinguished history of mountaineers, rock climbers and explorers emanating from what we now call Merseyside. The county only came into being in 1974 and covers an area previously administered under the Cheshire and Lancashire authorities. The men and women mentioned in this book came from these districts rather than our own Merseyside and so I crave the readers forgiveness if I stray a few miles beyond the present boundary while discussing these eminent people.

Some of those mentioned may have been born within our boundary while others may have settled here in business; others may have only spent a short time here but carried out their greatest exploits while residing in the district. I will let the reader judge for themselves whether I have overstepped the mark!

I have tried to avoid being too technical in my descriptions of the people and the mountains / climbs they have completed so that the book will hopefully appeal to non mountaineers as well as the hardened expert.

In Victorian times Liverpool was a thriving, wealthy city with its fair share of rich merchants, ship owners and business men, so really it is not that surprising that some of them, given that the newly developed sport of mountaineering was a rich man's pursuit, took to the mountains of the European Alps in search of some novel exercise and uplifting of the soul by the sight of the dramatic and picturesque.

They climbed many peaks and snowy passes never before trod by man, they ventured further afield and climbed extinct volcano's, they were among the earliest westerners in such modern times to visit Tibet and came within a few days march of the much desired city of Lhasa before being turned back by the Tibetan army. In short, they were true adventurers and pioneers.

St George Littledale, the son of the Lord Mayor of Liverpool, was a prodigious hunter and explorer who with his wife made many trips to Central Asia gathering specimens for our superb museum as well as the Natural History Museum in London. They did not need nor seek publicity and it is only recently that a meticulously researched book was written about them thus shining a light on a chapter of exploration in Asia that had been overlooked by many.

It was not just mountainous areas outside the UK which drew their attention either. The little hills of Snowdonia, Lake District and the wonderful Isle of Skye caught their imagination and they were among the first to venture into the deep gullies and steep cliffs in a then new sport we now know today as Rock Climbing.

In time, due to many social and economic changes, more and more people, from differing backgrounds, took to the hills and mountains of the UK advancing standards and finding a release from the confines and hardships of the city without the expense and time needed for a long trip to foreign lands.

In the early to mid 20th Century one man in particular led such an incredible life of adventure, both in war, mountains and high seas that he has become something of a legend in the mountaineering and sailing community. Harold William Tilman deserves special mention and his many books, all of which are well worth reading, are listed at the Bibliography at the end of the book.

H. W. (aka Bill) Tilman was born and lived for many years in Wallasey and I end the book with another Wallasey man, Alan Rouse, who died on K2, the second highest mountain in the world and arguably one of the hardest, in 1986. A supremely talented rock climber and mountaineer who really helped push the standards of Britsh rock climbing to new levels in the 1970's with many of his climbs still being big undertakings today.

Today many thousands of Merseysiders head to the hills of the UK in search of steep rock, a high mountain or just a pleasant ramble to a country pub. In their own way they are doing just what our forefathers have done during the last century and a half. There is a distinct pleasure in escaping the seeming dreariness of our city even if only for a few hours and we should take pride in the fact that some of our local men and women of the past have helped contribute to the rich history of mountaineering and exploration.

In the Appendix at the rear of the book I have made mention of a number of mountaineering clubs operating within Merseyside who have helped, in no small measure down the years, to get many Merseysiders out into the mountains. They are still going strong and always welcome new members. So if this book entices the casual reader out into the hills and mountains to experience them for themselves then it will have more than served its purpose.

The Victorian Pioneers

I f you go into any outdoor shop today you will see a wide range of specialist clothing and equipment utilising the latest lightweight and waterproof, breathable fabrics. There are short Ice Axes and Crampons that clip onto your warm breathable boots with the simplest of ease. There is a wide array of brightly coloured, ultra efficient warm clothing and an untold medley of gadgets all designed to make life easy in the mountains.

However this has not always been the case.

In the early to mid 19th Century mountain climbing became a popular activity for a certain number of wealthy people from the UK and the rest of Europe. Yet as it was a relatively new pastime little was known of the effects of cold, wind, snow and the thin air of the high mountains on the individual. Clothing was rudimentary at best relying on the layer principle and the materials used, while probably pretty windproof, were certainly not waterproof. Wool and Cotton were a staple material with heavy Tweed jackets and Norfolk breeches being common. For women it was even worse as it was not becoming for a woman to be seen in trousers and so large voluminous skirts had to be worn, though the more enterprising women mountaineers dispensed with such niceties once the last village had been passed on the ascent of a peak or snowy pass.

Boots and shoes were of heavy leather often only sparsely nailed and once wet conducted heat from the foot and took an eternity to dry. Ice Axes were unheard of, a long wooden pole (Alpenstock) with an Iron spike in one end sufficed for the crossing of gaping crevasses and support on a weary ascent. Rucksacks were not developed until the late 19th century and often the climbers took only a small satchel of essentials and left the poor porters to carry heavy loads of food and blankets in wicker baskets.

It was by the beginning of the 19th Century that some of the local peasants in the Alpine villages began to lead or guide the wealthy clientele in the mountains. They were often very poor people, Shepherds, Chamois or Crystal hunters who were looking to take these wealthy foreigners into the mountains to supplement an otherwise pretty meagre existence. To them the mountains were a fearful place, it was only after all in the 18th century that Dragons were finally proven not to exist in the threatening and imposing glaciers though many locals still believed them to do so.

Initially the climbing of mountains was considered as only worthwhile if one was contemplating making some scientific observations, perhaps the study of glaciers or the measurement of air pressure on the summits. To this end the poor porters had to carry a wide range of heavy and unwieldy barometers, thermometers, kettles (for boiling water), telescopes etc as well as a vast array of food and provisions. Whole Chickens, Mutton, Veal, Bread, Chocolate, Sugar, Wine, Brandy, Champagne, Truffles, Cake, you name it they took it – travelling light was not in vogue

In time however, especially towards the middle of the 19th Century, mountain climbing came to be seen as pleasurable in its own right and the need for scientific observations became less and less desirable. The British were to play a prominent part in the development of mountaineering in the European Alps and elsewhere and in 1854 Alfred Wills climbed the Wetterhorn, a stunning peak, looming over Grindelwand, a delightful Alpine village dominated by the imposing North Face of the Eiger. This ascent heralded the start of what is known as the as the Golden Age of Alpine Climbing. It is at this point where our story largely begins.

The Walker Family.

An aptly named family one may think but this wealthy family were to prove no mean mountaineers in their day. Their great wealth came from the Walker & Parker Lead merchant business based at Mann Island in Liverpool and on the banks of the River Dee in Chester. The father, Frank Walker (1808-1872) took to the Alps, after finishing his education at Charterhouse and en-route to the forward looking Pestalozzi's School in Switzerland, for the first time in 1825 where he crossed both the Oberaajoch and the Theodule Passes, the latter lying high above the Swiss village of Zermatt. It lay in the shadow of that most famous of Alpine Peaks, the Matterhorn, and surely that incredible obelisk of unclimbed rock, ice and snow inspired him. However it was to be nearly fifty years later before he would ascend this mighty peak himself.

There then followed a lull in his Alpine excursions, which one must assume that he took to develop his business and start a family. The family finally settled at South Park Lodge on Belvidere Road in the south of the city, a large beautiful house overlooking the delightful Princes Park. He returned again to the Alps in 1858 where he climbed the Theodule pass for the second time and ascended Monte Moro (2985m) with his son and daughter, of which more, later. For the next thirteen years he made an annual pilgrimage to the European Alps, often with his family and a local guide, where he acquired a fine record of climbs.

Frank Walker made many notable climbs, some for the first time and many second ascents, throughout the Alps. Most notable of his climbs for the period were Monte Rosa(4634m) in 1862 and the monarch of them all, Mont Blanc (4810m), in the same year. In 1865, the year in which the Matterhorn was finally climbed, he made the first ascent of Mont Blanc via the formidable Brenva ridge. This stupendous bastion of rock and ice proved a daunting prospect and a much harder climb than the ascent from the village of Chamonix by the tourist route.

In 1871, his final alpine year, he climbed the Matterhorn (4478m), the incredible looking peak dominating the small Swiss village of Zermatt. It was first climbed in 1865 and on the descent four of the successful party fell to their deaths adding to the mountain's reputation as a difficult peak. Frank Walker died the following year in April 1872 after a short period of Ill health, however his son and daughter were to go and make a greater name for themselves in this new found pastime of mountaineering.

Horace Walker

Horace was the son of Frank Walker and though born in Canada, privately educated in Switzerland and Germany. He ultimately came back to Liverpool and settled into the now well established family firm of Walker Parker & Co and took over full control when his father died.

His first trip to the Alps was in 1855 when he ascended Mount Velan (3734m) in the Pennine Alps. He returned again to the Alps in 1858 where with his father and sister crossed the Theodule Pass and climbed Monte Moro. He came again to the Alps in 1859, then nearly every year thereafter till 1905 when old age curtailed his Alpine wanderings. Whereas many British Alpinists preferred to hire a guide for a journey or ascent Horace Walker was not afraid to climb without, often preferring a choice companion who he got on with rather than a guide of often unknown worth or ability. He also became one of the first Alpine Club (an old and venerable club, the first of its kind in the world, established to promote mountaineering though principally for the well to do) members to climb in the UK.

In the years 1864 and 1865 Horace Walker became one of the greatest Alpinists of the day making many first ascents including the Barre Des Ecrins (4102m) with Mr A W Moore and, the eventual conquerors of the Matterhorn, Edward Whymper and Michael Croz. This magnificent ascent has been so well told by Mr Moore and Mr Whymper that I dare not try to repeat it here for fear of doing it an injustice. A month later with his father and sister they climbed the Balmhorn (3698m) in the Bernese Alps.

In 1865 Horace had his best year, as far as first ascents were concerned, when with Mr A W Moore and the guide Jakob Anderegg he climbed the highest point of Piz Roseg (3937m), the Ober Gabelhorn (4063m) as well as the Pigne d'Arolla(3796m). If that was not enough he then played a leading part in the ascent of Mont Blanc by the Brenva ridge with his father and others as mentioned previously. This was considered a major achievement at the time. Thirty years later one of the leading climbers of the day, Capt. J. P. Farrar, a one-time president of the Alpine Club, wrote 'this climb involved the most continuous step cutting in hard steep ice I have ever seen' (step cutting is where the Adze of an axe is used to chop a foothold / handhold in the ice to enable progress). What must be remembered is that none of the party had an Ice Axe or Crampons, how they managed such an ascent is anyone's guess.

Though he made many other ascents over a total of 39 Alpine seasons two of his most well known, amongst mountaineers that is, are the first ascent of the highest point of the Grandes Jorasses (4208m) in the French Alps and Mount Elbrus (5642m) in Russia – an extinct Volcano and the highest summit in Europe.

The Grandes Jorasses is a stunning peak lying on the border between France and Italy, it is still one of the most sought after mountains to climb in the Alps as it breaks through the 4000m barrier. The highest point was named Pointe Walker in honour of its first ascentionist who climbed it on the 30th June 1868 with the guides Johann Jaun & Melchior Anderegg, who was to become a close friend and family favourite.

Horace was the 'leader' of the trip with Johann Jaun & Melchoir from the Swiss village of Meyringen employed as the guides. Julien Grange from the Italian village of Courmayeur was the porter carrying the provisions which would have been substantial as they had to spend one night on the mountain prior to an early Alpine start. They passed the first night on some rocks near the foot of the mountain and about 4 ½ hours out from Courmayeur. This was in the days before tents and sleeping bags were widely used so the early pioneers used to look for a convenient overhanging boulder and some thick blankets as protection from the elements.

An early start is essential in the Alps to make the best of the snow which hardens in the night frost and makes for easier going underfoot. Later in the day soft snow, after the sun has done its work, does not just make for harder going but also is much more dangerous with the attendant peril of possible avalanches. They awoke early and followed the route taken by Edward Whymper, the 'conqueror' of the Matterhorn, who had passed this way while climbing to a lower summit of the Grandes Jorasses a few years previously. They climbed up to cross a steep ridge which led to a dangerous looking hanging glacier, this had to be crossed with difficulty to join yet another ridge which would eventually lead to the summit on good hard snow. Thus the highest point of the Grandes Jorasses had now been reached and in time another way would be found up this pinnacle by the famous Italian mountaineer, Riccardo Cassin, in his ascent of the Walker Spur. This is still one of the most coveted routes in the whole of the Alps and forms one of the classic North Face Grandes Courses which are the aim of any aspiring young Alpinist.

Mount Elbrus in the Russian Caucasus, while not a technically demanding problem, proved a difficult peak to ascend given the greater altitude to be gained and much colder temperatures than they had previously experienced in the Alps. The peak was ascended in 1874 by Horace Walker, Frederick Gardner (another Liverpool man!), F. Crauford Grove and Peter Knubel (a Swiss guide brought especially for the purpose!).

Travelling to the Caucasus became easier as the railways improved dramatically in the 19th Century making getting there more feasible in a shorter period of time than required for the Himalaya or other greater ranges, indeed the Caucasus were being seen as a sort of halfway house to the Himalaya or south American giants.

The trip to Elbrus was organised by Mr Crauford Grove and Horace's long standing friend Mr A W Moore who had been there a few years previously and who had then managed to climb the lower Eastern Summit, clearly he felt he had a score to settle.

The local people of the Caucasus had not yet adapted to the requirements demanded by these wealthy foreign mountaineers and as such they suffered a poor monotonous diet of boiled mutton and bread with the occasional Goat or Bharal (wild sheep) thrown in for good measure when they could be shot. The 'comforts' of the Alps must have seemed a long distant memory at times and they were forced to rely more on their own resources and abilities to a much greater extent than normal.

The area was not as well mapped as the Alps either and so they had to find their own way eventually espying their mountain after ascending a small peak near to the village of Uruspieh where they were staying. A plan of attack was formulated and after finally procuring enough bread and other morsels of sustenance they set out to spend the night in the forests of the Upper Baskan valley where they enjoyed a rare treat of potatoes with their evening meal. The next day they moved on towards the mountain and chose to spend the night in a lower camp than that used in the previous attempt at a height of 11,400ft. They made their camp and planned for a 1.00am start for the summit.

At midnight they arose and the leader, Mr Moore, decided to await the arrival of his two Russian friends to a lamentable cost as the weather turned the next day and so he suffered one of the bitterest blows of his mountaineering career by missing out on the highest summit of the Caucasus.

They started at 1.00am forcing their feet into frozen boots and marched upwards through the snows in a deathly cold. The moon clearly highlighted the twin peaks of Elbrus and although the wind was very strong it did not hinder them and they continued upwards on good snow eventually reaching the col between the two summits where the rising sun in the East announced a brilliant Oriental sunrise while to the west the shadow of Elbrus itself was cast wide upon the sky above. With elated spirits and the warmth of the rising sun they toiled upwards, stopping often to gasp for air, Frederick Gardiner noticed that Horace's nose had begun to bleed – an indication of the great height they were now at.

The summit itself is a small peak on the western side of the circular ridge which formed the lip of the crater of this now extinct Volcano and after crossing a small though tiresome snowfield they finally reached the highest summit of Elbrus at 10.40am on the 27th July 1874.

For many people Mont Blanc is not the highest mountain in Europe, that honour should belong to Mt Elbrus and those mountaineers completing the Seven Summits challenge today (the highest summit on each of the seven continents) consider Elbrus as the more desirable of the two mountains.

Horace Walker continued to climb regularly in the Alps and also on our own home mountains, organising Alpine Club trips to the Lake District and Skye. He climbed the Inaccessible Pinnacle and many of the great Skye mountains, he was also on the first ascent of Clach Glas, that most beautiful of rocky peaks on the magical isle. In 1892 he made an early ascent of the most well known of rock climbs, Napes Needle, in the Lake District and also the Needle ridge with the Birkenhead solicitor, Godfrey Solly amongst others. In the same year he made the second ascent of Pillar Rock by the North Face and so there can be no doubt that Horace was as much a rock climber as a mountaineer.

Horace Walker achieved many things in his life, inter alia, he became a fellow of the Royal Geographical Society, a president of the Alpine Club, a trustee of the Liverpool Savings Bank, he was also the longest serving member of the Liverpool Committee of the RSPCA serving for over 35 years.

He died aged 69 on the 1st January 1908 after a long illness and after a short service at St Paul's Church near Princes Park he was interred at St James Cemetery, thus leaving one surviving family member, his beloved sister Lucy.

Lucy Walker

Lucy Walker was the eldest child of Frank Walker and suffered terribly from rheumatism as a young woman for which her doctor prescribed a remedy of good long walks, given what she achieved later in life I am sure her doctor would have been very impressed at her rapid cure. Ms Walker was the first woman to climb regularly in the Alps, season after season, with her father, brother and also the family guide Melchior Anderegg to whom she attached an especial fondness. She never married and when asked why she replied "I love mountains, and Melchior already has a wife", one can only imagine the constraints imposed on her feelings by Victorian dogma and while she could do nothing over Melchior she could satisfy her first love and her record in the mountains was impressive.

Her alpine career started modestly enough when with her father and brother she crossed the Monte Moro and Theodule passes. However by 1862 she had climbed the Finsteraarhorn (4274m), Monte Rosa and Mont Blanc and in the following years she made ascents of other Alpine giants such as the Weisshorn (4505m) and the fourth ascent of the mighty Eiger (3970m). She was on the first ascent of the Balmhorn in 1864 and she was the first woman to ascend the beautiful Wetterhorn in 1866, the Lyskamm (4527m) in 1868 and Piz Bernina (4049m) in 1869.

Lucy was, apparently, a large bespectacled young woman, who climbed on a diet of sponge cake and Champagne. On her early climbs she wore a simple white print dress which caused her many problems on her return to civilisation as it was difficult to get back into shape and stains were difficult to remove.

Her greatest achievement, and one that astounded the establishment at the time, was her ascent of that most impressive and daunting of Alpine peaks, the Matterhorn in 1871, the ascent with her father and Melchior was the first by a woman. Surprisingly, by modern standards, she received some criticism for this feat as some thought that ladies should stick to the valleys and leave the dangerous summits to the men. She was celebrated though in Punch with the following verse :

'A Climbing Girl'
A lady has climbed to the Matterhorn's summit,
Which almost like a monument points to the sky;
Steep not very much less than the string of a plummet
Suspended, which nothing can scale but a fly.

This lady has likewise ascended the Weisshorn,
And, what's a great deal more, descended it too,
Feet foremost; which, seeing it might be named Icehorn,
So slippery 'tis, no small thing is to do.

No glacier can baffle, no precipice balk her,
No peak rise above her, however sublime,
Give three times, three cheers for intrepid Miss Walker,
I say, my boys, doesn't she know how to climb !

In 1872 Frank Walker, her father, had died though by 1873 she was back in the Alps with her brother and great friend Melchior where they climbed the Jungfrau (4158m), the difficult Taschhorn (4491m) and the Weisshorn again. She visited the Alps nearly every year, climbing new peaks and crossing untold passes, till 1879 when her doctor advised her to give up such long expeditions as they were proving detrimental to her health. She did however continue to walk in the Alpine valleys with her many friends and Melchior, she is widely acknowledged as a true pioneer for women climbers throughout the world making a total of 98 expeditions throughout the Alps. In 1909 she joined the newly formed Ladies Alpine Club (the Alpine Club being a male only preserve to this day!) and she became the club's second president in 1913.

Away from the mountains, Lucy Walker led the life of a typical cultured lady of the time, she was apparently a charming hostess, an expert needlewoman and fluent in several languages.

Her brother, Horace, had now gone and so she spent the last few years of her life alone, and largely infirm, in the grand family home of south Park Lodge. Lucy died in her eighty first year and was the last member of the Walker family. Their large house still stands at the corner of Belvidere Road and Ullet Road and sadly there is no official city record or memorial to the remarkable family that once lived there.

Mr Frederick Gardiner

Frederick Gardiner was born in 1850 to a well heeled shipowning family whose business operated from south Castle Street in premises now long since demolished. The family lived in a grand house called 'Roselle' at 11 Croxteth Road, a short walk from Sefton Park and near neighbours to the Walker family not five minute's walk away. Frederick was a tall, strong and good looking man, occasionally compared to Lord Byron in appearance and with a good tenor voice which he apparently liked using 'to awaken the mountain echoes' with his yodelling. He was very well thought of by the Alpine locals, good natured and he took the trouble to learn their language.

His first visit to the Alps was in 1868 though what he climbed is not recorded, however he made some minor ascents in the following two years before meeting up with his near neighbours from Liverpool, the

Walkers, in Zermatt where he climbed the Matterhorn with Frank and Lucy in 1871. In 1872 he returned to the area and climbed the Breithorn (4165m), now surely the easiest 4000m peak in the Alps thanks to the cable car. Next he climbed the nearby Pollux (4092m) and received a bit of a shock when he found a dead body on the Verra glacier. He climbed the impressive Dom (4545m) the third highest mountain in the Alps, before completing a traverse from Zermatt to Breuil in Italy over the Matterhorn itself.

In 1874 he was on the Mt Elbrus expedition with Horace Walker and at 24 was much the youngest member, he always looked back on that trip with great pride and often liked to recall, how, on nearing the top of Elbrus, the others said : 'Let the young one go first, it means more to him'.

Peter Knubel, the expert Swiss guide was with him for many of his early climbs and under his tutelage he became an expert in judging snow conditions and how to deal with them. Peter Knubel once said that he had never climbed with any other 'Herr' who was so capable and with unexcelled staying powers, he was, apparently, simply marvellous.

In 1876 he made an ascent of Monte Rosa without guides and perhaps it was this ascent that awakened in him the possibilities of what the future may hold for mountaineering. He loved to explore the less frequented parts of the Alps such as the Dauphine with the Pilkington's in 1878, he proved a meticulous organiser (the Dauphine were particularly undeveloped for mountaineers in those days) and once he even had the foresight to hide a bottle of Champagne in the snow for when they returned from an ascent.

Frederick Gardner was methodical in his approach to visiting mountainous areas, he would visit a district at time and work his way through the peaks before moving on to another area. He climbed the Jungfrau in the Swiss Alps with his son, George, in a very fast time when he was fifty years of age though George was called before his time and died young.

His climbing record would fill a book in itself and he made over 1200 ascents in the mountains many of them guideless (after 1878 he never climbed with a guide again) which while initially incurring the wrath of some Alpine Club elders was by the 1880's becoming more the norm. The cost of a guide was not cheap and the Chamonix guides were especially expensive with minimum numbers of guides and porters being designated for any particular excursion. It is perhaps his attitude to climbing which is

Frederick Gardner's greatest legacy as he was one of the first competent climbers to consider attempting serious climbs without the support and assistance of a local guide.

In the Alps today a tiny percentage of climbers use the services of a local guide, true, the mountains are better mapped and there are many guidebooks to point us in the right direction but to take that first step was no doubt a daunting prospect given the weight of tradition on his shoulders and perhaps the modern alpinist is a vindication of Frederick Gardiner's ideals and principles.

Like Horace Walker, Frederick Gardiner also had a fondness for the British mountains and in 1872 he was with Mr Pendlebury (yet another Liverpool man!) on his eponymous traverse on Pillar Rock in the English Lake District. Unfortunately few records remain of his excursions though he did state in 1878 that he was 'in the habit of wandering [with the Pilkington's et al] among the hills of Cumberland and westmorland at all periods of the year, but more especially in the winter season', gaining thereby 'considerable knowledge of rock-work'.

In 1913 Frederick Gardiner made his last trip to the mountains when he visited Darjeeling in India, he was too old now for any strenuous walks though he contented himself with the view of Everest and Kangchenjunga from Tiger Hill, the well known view point above the hill town.

His later years were most troublesome health-wise and he suffered terribly with Rheumatic Gout. The First World War was also a worrying time for him personally as his sons were away fighting in Europe and although he lived to see them return on the 28th March 1919 he died suddenly at the family home 'The Gables' on Vale Road in Woolton.

His funeral, which was well attended by family and servants alike, took place at All Hallows Church, Allerton and thereafter he was taken for burial in Allerton Cemetery. His grave is well marked and is near to the ruined Chapel where he is interred with his wife and sons the last of whom died in 1976.

Charles & Lawrence Pilkington

Charles and Lawrence were two sons of Mr. Richard Pilkington of Windle Hall near St Helens and while many will consider them glass manufacturers, that was mainly their father's business, they were more concerned with Coal Mining, an industry now long gone but at the time was a considerable employer throughout the North of England.

Charles was born in 1850 and from an early age had a love of the open air. After leaving school he began work in the Cotton industry but soon abandoned it for life as a Colliery Engineer in Haydock. Apparently many a good Ice Axe was manufactured in the Colliery workshops and merry week-end gatherings at his house nearby were had with his Alpine Club friends.

It would appear that he first started climbing mountains in the UK rather than the Alps as in 1869 he climbed the Pillar Rock and it is known that he climbed regularly in the Lake District throughout the 1870's. He was one of the first climbers to appreciate and realize the incredible possibilities offered to climbers and mountaineers by the Misty Isle of Skye. He made the first ascent of the Inaccessible Pinnacle of Sgurr Dearg with the climbing photographers 'The Abraham Bros'. This pinnacle ridge of rock is the hardest of all the Munro's to climb (a 'Munro' being a peak in Scotland over 3000ft, they were listed and named by Sir Hugh Munro – though he did not climb them all himself !) and is a daunting prospect to a non climber even today. Charles was also in the party that made the first ascent of that most shapely of Skye peaks, Clach Glas and Sgurr Mic Choinnich. He made many ascents and rock climbs in Skye, the peak of Sgurr Thearlaich was named after him, and the Lake District with his brother Lawrence, Horace Walker as well as the Birkenhead Solicitor Godfrey Solly.

His first Alpine trip was in 1872 when he crossed the Col De Geant and climbed the Wetterhorn, Monte Rosa and several other peaks with his brother Lawrence. An amusing footnote appears in Lawrence's Obituary for his brother where he describes a game they played as to who could lie down the longest in a glacier stream. Apparently the game was curtailed when Charles cut his heel and they had to descend from Zermatt after treatment by a friendly hotelier 'in the biggest slipper they could find 'in the village. He visited the Alps again in 1874 and in 1876 where with Frederick Gardiner he ascended the Gabelhorn (4063m). For the next four years he was with Gardiner on his many climbs most notably The Meije in the Ecrins (3984m) which was the last major summit in the Alps to be climbed due to its location and difficulty. This they did in 1879. In 1882, with his brother Lawrence again, they made the first guideless ascents of Piz Kesch (3418m), Piz Roseg and the Mont della Disgrazia (3678m) by a new route. They also made the second guideless ascent of the peerless Piz Bernina (4049m).

Charles, with his wife and the seemingly ever present Walkers, made a number of trips to the Dolomite mountains of the Tyrol / Northern Italy area of Europe. They are not quite so high as the western Alps and there are fewer glaciers, however they are, generally speaking, more precipitous and shapely mountains. In 1893 they climbed Monte Cristallo (3221m), Cima di Brenta (3155m)and the Konigspitze (3851m) as well as many other peaks throughout the Graian , Ortler and other 'lesser' known areas of the Alps.

Charles was a firm proponent of guideless climbing in the Alps and save for one or two exceptions from 1878 to his last Alpine season in 1911 he never climbed with a guide again.

Lawrence Pilkington was born in 1855 and he also became a mining engineer like his elder brother, he developed a deep affection for high mountains and mountaineering. However in 1884 he was crushed by a fall of stones while climbing on Piers Ghyll near Scafell in the Lake District which sadly put a stop to his climbing for several years.

Lawrence was also a major figure in the approach to guideless climbing and made many ascents with his brother, Frederick Gardiner and the Walkers both in the UK and Alps. In later life he moved to the middle class haven of Alderley Edge, his life there is chronicled in a lovely book 'Manchester Made Them' by Katherine Chorley. Lawrence was a talented artist and wrote a couple of books on Lancashire Colliery Life in Victorian times and a book of poetry 'An Alpine Valley and other Poems'.

In this country, at least, they are and should be remembered for their ascent of the Inaccessible Pinnacle or 'Inn Pin' as it as affectionately known, as being, the only mountain in these Isles where hands are needed as well as feet to reach the top.

The Parker Brothers

Alfred and Samuel Parker were both born in 1837 and while their Alpine career was short they achieved much and showed some vision and foresight at least where one, rather large mountain, was concerned.

Alfred Traill Parker was educated at Harrow and Oxford before returning to Liverpool to become a partner in the family firm of Ship

Owners and General Merchants. He took to the Alps with an elder brother, Charles Stuart Parker, in 1857 and climbed the Weisstor (3535m) and some time before 1860 he made an early ascent of Sgurr nan Gillean on Skye.

In 1860 with Samuel and Charles he went to the Alps yet again and, climbing without guides, made many superb ascents. Notable among which was an early, indeed the first ever recorded, attempt on the Matterhorn from the Swiss (Zermatt) side. This was the side of the mountain from which the peak was eventually climbed by Edward Whymper in 1865 despite its ominous and imposing appearance. It is a considerably easier climb than it looks and only the last few hundred feet are really steep, one can only wonder why Mr Whymper, Tyndall etc did not study this side of the mountain closer rather than make repeated attempts from Breuil on the Italian side of the mountain. It was not the technical difficulties of the climb that defeated the brothers but rather the weather, they hoped to come again........

Their next, and final, visit to the Alps was in 1865 when again, climbing without any guides, they made inter alia the first guideless ascent of that giant of the Bernese Alps the Finsteraarhorn (4273m) and also crossed a new and unnamed pass. They did intend to make a further attempt on the Matterhorn, however they had heard of the tragic accident and never returned to the peak again.

And that was it ! Both brothers then seemed to have immersed themselves in their various commercial concerns, including the Mersey Docks & Harbour Board, Liverpool, London & Globe Insurance Co. and Bank of Liverpool, and they never climbed, so far as is recorded in the Alpine Club records again.

Alfred Parker died suddenly at 10 Fulwood Park, Aigburth, his home for over twenty years, in 1900 and Samuel died while out on a shooting trip in 1905.

James Eccles

James Eccles was born in Liverpool in 1838 and made his first trip to the Alps in 1865 when he climbed Mont Blanc. In 1869 he made an early ascent of the Matterhorn and walked the High Level Route from Zermatt to Chamonix. While there he attempted the first ascent of the magnificent

Aiguille Du Plan – eventually he did manage the first ascent of this glorious peak in 1871. He visited the Alps again in 1873 and 1875 and in 1876 he attempted the ascent of Mont Blanc in Winter where he managed to get as far as the Grand Plateau high above Chamonix before retreating due to the deep snow and excessive coldness.

His best year came in 1877 when he made a new route up Mont Blanc via the Brouillard and Fresnay glaciers and made the first ascent of Mont Blanc De Courmayeur (4748m). There are now a couple of bivouac huts named after James Eccles on this Italian side of Mont Blanc. As if this major ascent was not enough he made the first passage of the Col De Rochfort and the third passage, with a new variation, on the Col De Trelatete. In 1878 he made a trip to the Rocky Mountains in the USA and made an early ascent of Wind River Peak (4021m) and the Fremont's Peak (4189m). It was on this trip that James Eccles really began to appreciate Geology and its importance, he wrote an important paper for the time on the volcanic rocks Montana.

In 1880 he made the first ascent of Aiguille Du Tacul (3438m) with another Liverpool Alpinist Mr F C Hartley and if the weather had not been so bad they would have managed an early ascent of the magnificent Aiguille Verte (4122m). In later years he made a number of first ascents and difficult climbs throughout the Alps and began climbing with Professor Bonney the well known Naturalist and Geological expert of the Alps. Finally age and ill health caught up with him and while he still continued to visit the Alps he kept his expeditions 'below the Snowline'.

James Eccles was an accomplished artist and photographer and a large number of his slides and negatives were left to the Alpine Club on his death in 1915.

Francis and James Hartley

These two men were the sons of Mr John B Hartley who produced the plans for the docks near to the landing stage at the Pier Head.

The two Liverpool brothers first took to the Alps in 1873 and climbed the Wetterhorn, Eiger and its near neighbour the Monch (4107m). The next year saw them attempt the North East ridge of the Eiger and they were the first climbers to ever cross the Mittellegi pass which now lends its name to this magnificent ridge on probably the most famous mountain in the whole alpine chain.

The most well known ascent for James Hartley however, was to be on the first ascent of the incredible Aiguille Du Dru (3754m) in 1878. This is one of the most impressive peaks in the whole of the Alps, rising almost from the foot of the Mer De Glace it soars into the sky like a skyscraper. It was made with the determined Victorian Surgeon / climber, Mr Clinton Dent, who was on his eighteenth attempt on the mountain. He wrote the following about their climb :-

'Those who follow us, and I think there will be many, will perhaps be glad of a few hints about this peak. Taken together, it affords the most continuously interesting rock climb with which I am acquainted. There is no wearisome tramp over moraine, no great extent of snow fields to traverse. Sleeping out as we did, it would be possible to ascend and return to Chamonix in about 16 to 18 hrs. But the mountain is never safe when snow is on the rocks, and at such times stones fall freely down the couloir leading up from the head of the glacier. The best time for the expedition would be, in ordinary seasons, in the month of August. The rocks are sound and are peculiarly unlike those of other mountains. From the moment the glacier is left, hard climbing begins, and the hands as well as the feet are continuously employed. The difficulties are therefore enormously increased if the rocks be glazed or cold; and in bad weather the crags of the Dru would be as pretty a place for an accident as can well be imagined.'

They enjoyed several more Alpine seasons climbing many peaks, occasionally without guides and often in the company of esteemed Alpinists Mr W E Davidson and, Virginia Woolfe's father, Leslie Stephen. In 1883 they made the fifth ascent of the magnificent rocky pinnacle of the Aiguille Du Geant (4013m) and the second Ascent of the Petit Aiguiile Du Dru (3733m) which marked the last of their major Alpine excursions.

It is assumed that they then began to concentrate their efforts on a career with Francis Hartley becoming an Inspector with the Scottish Education Department and James Hartley, a Barrister on the Northern Circuit, latterly becoming an Inspector of Technical Institutes and Evening Schools under the Board of Education.

Richard Pendlebury

Richard Pendlebury was educated at the Liverpool Collegiate before studying Mathematics at St John's College, Cambridge. However his increasing deafness prevented further progress as a teacher, and a weakening of his eyesight cut short a promising Alpine career.

In 1870 he made his first visit to the Alps completing a number of minor ascents including inter alia the fifth ascent of the Wildspitze (3774m), the second highest mountain in Austria. In 1872 with Rev. C Taylor he made the first ascent of Monte Rosa from Macugnaga via the Marinelli Couloir, a route so difficult and dangerous that he said :-

'If nothing came down on you it was alright, but if anything did you would probably be wiped out!'

For the next eight years he visited the Alps every year, often with his brother William, and usually visiting the less frequented parts of the Alpine chain he began making many ascents including in 1874 the first ascent of the Dom (4545m) from the Nadeljoch and the first ascent of the Schreckhorn (4078m) from the North East.

On this peak he received a rather severe wound from a falling rock but not so severe as to inhibit his ascent. A first ascent of the Pic d'Olan in 1875 was shortly followed by an early attempt on one of the most impressive and fearful peaks in the Alps, the Aiguille Du Dru, which eventually succumbed in 1878 as previously described under the Hartley Brothers. With William in 1876 he made the first ascent of the Grivola (3969m) by the North ridge which was not repeated for nearly 20 years and in the same year the made the first ascent of the south Summit of the Aiguille De Blaitiere (3521m).

The following year he made the first ascent of the Pic Sans Nom as well as a number of new climbs in the Ecrins region of the French Alps.

Richard Pendlebury was also one of the earliest climbers in the Lake District as in 1872, with Frederick Gardiner, he made a new ascent of the Pillar Rock in Ennerdale by his eponymous traverse. He retired, rather early in life, to Keswick where he died suddenly, aged 55, from heart failure in 1902.

Godfrey Allan Solly

Although born in Congleton and educated at Rugby, for most of his adult life he lived and worked in Birkenhead as a Solicitor having offices in Hamilton Square and living in a quiet suburb of the town at 1 Grosvenor Place. He was made an Honorary Freeman of Birkenhead in 1933, in later years he was to become Mayor (at the time of the great scout Jamboree at Arrowe Park) and Alderman of Birkenhead and was present at the opening of the first Mersey tunnel in 1934.

His list of climbing achievements is impressive climbing as he did in the Alps, Caucasus and the Canadian Rockies though he is perhaps best known among mountaineers for a rock climb in the English Lake District that does not even reach the giddy height of 200ft. Its fame lies more in its difficulty rather than its height and even today Eagle's Nest ridge Direct can give food for thought to an inexperienced climber.

Godfrey Solly first visited the Alps in 1887 climbing with the Yorkshireman William Cecil Slingsby and in 1892 he was with Mummery on his audacious attempt on the Aiguille Du Plan (3673m). In 1893 & 1894 he visited the Caucasus and, climbing guideless, made an attempt on the south peak of Ushba (4710m), a mountain praised as the Matterhorn of the Caucasus and one that was not finally climbed until 1903. He made the first ascent of Bak Peak (3578m) and crossed many new passes, they would have achieved more however, had the weather been more favourable.

In 1895 he visited the Alps for a month but only climbed the Grand Paradiso (4061m) before an accident put paid to any further exploits. In the following years he made a number of guideless ascents in the Alps and for Godfrey Solly it was not just the peak itself that mattered but the difficulties encountered on the way that he derived his pleasure from. The earlier mountaineers chose to climb the mountain by any route possible however as the 19th century progressed mountaineers were now looking at different and harder ways up any given peak.

He climbed not just on the big foreign mountains either, I've already mentioned Eagles Nest ridge Direct climbed in 1892 and still graded Mild Very Severe. In 1894 he attended a Scottish Mountaineering Club Easter meet at Inveroran where, amongst other things, he climbed one of the most famous winter climbs in the world for the first time. Despite its seemingly diminutive height Ben Nevis is one of the world's great mountains. Seen from Fort William its appearance has often been likened to that of a hump backed whale however its real majesty lies on its North face which holds snow and ice well into the Spring and sometimes patches still last year round. Tower ridge had been descended before by the Hopkinsons some eighteen months previously however, they were unaware of this, and it had never been ascended before. It is now recognised as a truly impressive climb under full winter conditions. The climb is nearly 2000ft long and even today it catches slow parties unawares as darkness can overtake some who are then condemned to a cold bivouac till the dawn unfreezes their stiff limbs and allows them to cross the daunting Tower Gap and freedom.

In 1898 Godfrey climbed on Skye making a new route up the Pinnacle ridge of Sgurr nan Gillean, thereafter he was a frequent visitor to the Isle and a constant attendant at the SMC Easter Meets for many years. He was eventually to become Vice President of this august club and did much to promote a greater understanding with the English clubs, the Climbers Club and the Fell and Rock Climbing Club of the English Lake District.

He took a great interest in the younger climbers and their development taking a couple of holidays in the Alps to instruct in good Alpine technique, one such pupil. Bentley Beetham, went on to become a member of the ill fated 1924 Mount Everest expedition where Mallory and Irving disappeared high on the mountain to be absorbed into immortality.

In June 1924 aged 65 he walked up Great Gable in the Lake District to attend the unveiling of the War Memorial for lost members of the Fell and Rock Club killed in the First World War and he read the touchingly fitting Psalm121 'I will lift mine eyes up to the Hills' . In Birkenhead matters Godfrey was a staunch supporter of the local schools, in particular Birkenhead Grammar School and of the museums and galleries in Birkenhead.

Godfrey Solly continued to climb throughout his advancing years even climbing the magnificent Grepon high above Chamonix in his eightieth year. He died in February 1942 and is buried in Landican Cemetery on the Wirral.

There are many other early mountaineers who were born in the city but whose links are somewhat tenuous in later life, Claude Wilson was born in Wavertree in 1860. He was the younger brother of Francis Wilson with whom he did some of his early climbing. In 1879 they climbed the Matterhorn together and in 1882 he made the first ascent of the south face of the Weissmiss (4027m) in the Swiss Alps with his elder brother Herbert Wilson. Thereafter Claude continued climbing in the UK and the Alps well into the 1920's though by this time he had been living in Scotland for many years. He wrote a delightful book on mountaineering for the 'All England Series'. Sadly Francis died while only in his thirties, and Herbert died in a shooting accident in 1912.

Sir William Martin Conway was also a Liverpool resident, as the first professor of Art at Liverpool University. He lived for three years at 25 Princes Avenue and while here did much to organise an association for the advancement of Art and published a work entitled 'The Gallery of Art of the Royal Liverpool Institution' in 1885. He was a prolific mountaineer climbing throughout the Alps, the Andes and the mighty Himalaya as well as making the first crossing on foot of Spitzbergen.

John Garforth Cockin was a Liverpool barrister who after a number of Alpine seasons went to the Caucasus in 1888 and in a three week period climbed several 5000m peaks including the much coveted first ascent of Shkhara (5200m). The ascent proved desperately hard with, at one point, six hours continuous step cutting being required which resulted in some frostbite, their climb would not be repeated for another thirty years. In addition he climbed the very technical North peak of Ushba (4710m) and Jangitau (5051m). Cockin was a firm advocate of guideless climbing and died in 1900 in a fall from the Weisshorn (4506m) while attempting a guideless ascent.

What many may not be aware of is that W. H. Murray, the author of the classic 'Mountaineering in Scotland' was actually born in Liverpool, at the infirmary on London Road, in 1913. His father was killed at Gallipoli in 1915 and so his mother moved back to Scotland shortly afterwards to be nearer her parents.

Also, Ernest Baker, the prolific grit-stone climber and caver of the Peak District was for a number of years chief librarian at Wallasey Library and lived in the district.

The Littledales of Central Asia

Perhaps surprisingly a very emminent Victorian explorer hailed from the city of Liverpool and little was known about him and his equally much travelled wife until recently. They chose not to write any books and gave only a handful of lectures or written contributions to the Royal Geographical Society journals. Yet had they chosen to promote themselves they would now be lauded as true pioneering explorers of a little known part of the world and would have been rightly praised.

In 1851 Thomas Littledale was elected Mayor of Liverpool at the tender age of 33 and was thus the youngest Mayor in over a century. In the same year his wife Julia gave birth to a son who was christened Clement St. George Royds Littledale, he affectionately became known simply as St George Littledale. They lived at Highfield House in the Old Swan district of Liverpool in a large house which for many years became the atypical Victorian family home complete with all the attendant pomp and ceremony as expected from a prominent Liverpool merchant family. Sadly Highfield house was demolished in 1915 after falling into disrepair, the site is now occupied by the local School and even the two impressive gate houses on Prescot Road are now long gone.

St George was educated at both Rugby and Shrewsbury schools where he was decidedly 'average' in academic attainment though he did apparently show an aptitude for foreign languages. Physically St George was as determined as he was capable, in 1866 while on the Shrewsbury 7 mile 'Long Run' he passed out after finishing the race and remained unconscious for a full twelve hours. Overall his education gave him a good grounding and in 1870 he worked for a short while in a barrister's office, the following year saw him take a brief interest in business. Then he was off, travelling to Norway to indulge a passion for hunting and shooting.

Throughout his life St George collected many hunting specimens for the Natural History Museum in London as well as the Liverpool Museum. Even today there are a number of his exhibits still on display in the museum and St George became acknowledged as one of the greatest big game hunters of all time. This may seem somewhat inappropriate in the modern age but one must consider that exhibits were collected to develop our understanding of the many creatures that roam our world which at that time was a much bigger place. Edgar Barclay, the author of Big Game

Shooting Records wrote :

As a hunter of big game in the Northern Hemisphere, the name of Littledale must surely stand alone. His success in this sphere has never I think been equalled, most certainly never surpassed.

In 1872, when he became 21, St George gained some financial independence from his father's legacy which included a substantial income and the Oak Hill estate next to the family Highfield estate. It was the norm for any wealthy family in the 19th century to send their offspring on a grand tour to finish off their education. Initially this involved a visit to the main European Capital cities and perhaps also to Athens and other 'eastern' cities. With the burgeoning popularity and efficiency of the Steam Boats it became possible to travel further afield and so in 1874 St George made his way to the west Indies to see the family Sugar Plantations. New Orleans, New York, and Canada followed before he found himself in Japan.

He made an attempt on Mt Fuji (3776m) but had to retreat when only 200ft from the summit due to an oncoming powerful storm. There was an interesting incident shortly before this ascent where St George reacted angrily to an incident of overcharging in a rest house. He lashed out with his Alpenstock at the cook who seemed intent on charging double or treble the standard price. This was totally out of character for St George and there is no other record of his anger or passions overflowing again despite at times some rather justifiable opportunities to do so.

Not long after this episode he found himself in Yokohama waiting for a ship to Shanghai, he had to wait a week as he had missed his boat and as sometimes happens misfortune can be tainted with fate, the fate in this instance was a meeting with a certain Canadian woman called Mrs Theresa Scott who was globe- trotting with her Scottish husband William Scott, a Scottish ship-owner and a wealthy man.

It may be wrong to state that Theresa and St George had fallen in love at first sight however it is hard to believe otherwise when one considers what followed. William Scott was not a great traveller and frequently struggled with the ardousness of a long journey, however his wife, despite her being 12 years St Georges senior, seemed to revel in the difficulties and trials that came her way. In early January 1875 St George was away Big Game Hunting in India though by early March he had arranged to meet the Scott's in Calcutta. On his arrival the Scott's persuaded St George to visit Kashmir where the hunting was good. Together they made their way to the Astor region near the Himalayan giant, Nanga Parbat.

It was all proving too much for Willie Scott and when they finally left Bombay on the 30th May Willie was in terrible pain with typhoid, yet Theresa left her husband to spend time shopping with St George in Aden and upon her return he was even worse, his days were sadly clearly numbered and he passed away at sea a few days later. Problems arose in getting the body back to England though they managed to outwit the Suez authorities with a small bribe to allow the heavy lead coffin aboard the ship through. On the 6th July the ship Palestine arrived in Liverpool and eventually Willie was buried a few days later at Easthampstead Parish Church. Theresa was left a substantial fortune which made her subsequent life much easier as she was now financially independent to do as she wished, and what she desired more than anything was to travel with her beloved St George. Her family disapproved of St George, however they were powerless to stop her marrying the man she loved, the smitten couple were married at St George's Church, Hanover Square, London on the 27th February 1877. Immediately after the ceremony they left for Paris on what was to be the first stage of their first trip as a married couple to India.

Their honeymoon was spent in Kashmir & Ladakh where they travelled to Srinigar, Astor and Skardu, as they left Skardu heading up the River Indus towards Ladakh Teresa wrote 'we have been marching through the most barren country I ever was in. Nothing but mountains the 'Karakoram' range. They are very grand entirely composed of black and white granite. Not a blade of grass grows upon them but then one suddenly comes upon a village where there is water, and green is no name for it'. Teresa spent most of the day on her own while St George went hunting for sport and specimen collecting for the many museums. She never complained though and kept herself busy and once made 'Georgie' 6 pairs of linen Coolie drawers. Shortly afterwards they had to alter their plans as Teresa had developed altitude sickness, they made their way to Leh, the capital of Ladakh but in doing so they had to cross the perilous Zoji La, an infamous pass that sees more than its fair share of deaths as pilgrims and traders get overtaken by snow and storm.

From Leh they went back to Srinigar where they spent ten days shopping and sightseeing before attending a dinner with the Maharaja of Kashmir. After a good rest they went off for six weeks to hunt bear in Bandipur, the winter came early that year and had it not been for a troop of soldiers battling to keep the pass to Kashmir open they may have had to winter over. Eventually they made their way back to Calcutta where a near constant round of garden parties, dinners, balls, races and opera kept them occupied.

Teresa wrote during this time *'......there is a great charm in the gypsy sort of life'*... she had clearly adapted well to this almost nomadic temporal existence and when they returned to England in June 1878 their extended honeymoon had set the pattern of their lives for the next thirty years.

St George was now widely acknowledged as a class Big Game Hunter and was proving a great benefit to the museums to which he donated many of his specimens, most notably Liverpool Museum. St George never hunted in Africa, the continent did not interest him as there were no mountains where big horned game could be found. It was mountains that interested him as they held the big, rare, horned sheep and goats that he favoured, they often were to prove such hard and tough opponents that he clearly relished the chase. St George and Teresa went to the United States, mainly to see Teresa's family and to hunt in Alaska after receiving a request from Thomas Moore, a director of Liverpool Museum, to obtain a Rocky Mountain White Goat.

In March 1886 St George wrote to Thomas Moore *'We are thinking of making a little tour somewhere this summer, British Colombia, Japan, Mount Ararat & the Caucasus, have you any suggestions ? With your habitual modesty you will doubtless find a want'.* Travel in the 19th century was not always easy and permission often had to be sought from the government if one wanted to go to a sensitive area, the patronage of a Museum or other august body could often prove a great help. St George & Teresa knew what they were doing.

They decided upon Ararat & the Caucasus but given recent Russian expansionist policies the area was very sensitive and it was only through good strong diplomatic efforts that war was avoided with Russia. Although the Caucasus were away from the main troubles the natives were restless and mistrusting of foreigners, permits were needed from the British Foreign Office and with the scientific patronage of the Liverpool Museum they were usually granted. St George and Teresa landed at Odessa in July via Vienna where they met with St George's brother Alfred who was coming with them. They picked an interpreter up at Tiflis and were told that Mt Ararat was out of bounds due to fighting so they decided to visit the Northern Caucasus where apparently good game could be found.

They left Tiflis to cross the Caucasus over the Dariel Pass which Teresa described as the grandest pass she had ever seen though the fleas were awful, so bad where they that she chose to sleep in her fur coat rather than use the blankets provided in the rest houses. They eventually arrived at their base camp, in August, on the slopes of Mount Elbrus which had been climbed only twelve years earlier by fellow Liverpool men Frederick Gardiner & Horace Walker. St George shot some more rare game, but could find no trace of the elusive Auroch which was his main target, the whole party returned to Tiflis and he forwarded his specimens onto the Liverpool Museum, which was now becoming one of the better museums in the country with many rare specimens. Upon their return to England Thomas Moore was so impressed with the quality and scarcity of the specimens that he wrote a letter of commendation to Dr Albert Gunther at the National History Museum in London, this was an act of great generosity that was to open many doors for the Littledales and give a greater purpose to their future expeditions. St George was now considered a professional collector, he and Teresa took this seriously and, working as a team, they collected many items of flora and fauna for this distinguished organisation. A second visit to the Caucasus was made in 1887 and travelling by the same route as the previous year they arrived back at their old base camp. They again tried hard to find the Auroch without success though St George did manage to get some Tur, Ollen, Chamois and Bear which they shipped back to England. The whole party also tried to get to Mount Ararat again but there was still fighting and it was just too dangerous so by early November the Littledales were back in England. St George was deliberating as to which Museum should get what, Liverpool Museum held preference but he wanted to please Dr Gunther as well, it was important to ingratiate oneself with as many influential people as possible to have the best possible chance of obtaining permits, this was especially so as their next trips were planned to the Pamir, Altai and Alai areas of Russia an especially difficult area to visit as the stakes in the Great Game were moving ever higher.

St George need not have worried, his contacts and also his lack of desire to publicise his and Teresa's exploits would and could assuage almost any difficulty that came their way when dealing with both the Russian and British Foreign Offices. They were now well respected and highly regarded explorers and collectors and while permits could never be guaranteed they usually had little difficulty in getting to where they wanted to go.

On the 27th May 1888 the Trans-Caspian railway finally opened and thus the route from the Caspian Sea to Samarkand in Central Asia was now much easier and quicker to reach. A mere three days after its opening, St George and Teresa left England to arrive in St Petersburg on the 2nd June. They met Sir Robert Morier, the British Ambassador, who became a good and influential friend of the Littledales often smoothing their path through bureaucratic difficulties. They also met a reporter from the Pall Mall Gazette and St George gave a rare interview, though they were very cautious about divulging their plans for fear of upsetting their hosts and jeopardising any future plans for travel in this delicate area. St George and Teresa soon learned that on their two previous Caucasus trips the Russians 'had had detectives about us the whole time and really {they} knew more about us than we knew ourselves'. After taking a train to Moscow then a journey down the Volga to the Caspian Sea where a boat awaited them to take them to Usunada they finally boarded a train on the Trans-Caspian railway. A further 900 mile journey across the desert eventually brought them to the ancient city of Samarkand which lies on the old Silk Route from China to the Mediterranean. They took a room with, according to St George 'a supply of fleas proportionate to the heat'. It should be noted that Teresa was actually the first western woman to ever visit this ancient city.

They purchased more supplies and a Tarantass, a small horse drawn coach which can have its wheels removed and replaced with runners for travel on snow. A caravan of twelve horses then headed south up the Taldik river, crossing two high passes before arriving on the Alai plateau. They crossed the Kizil Art pass at over 14,000ft to reach the Kara Julga valley, this was to be their main hunting ground. It was a desolate country with scarcely a blade of grass, surrounded by lofty mountains, some over 20,000ft high. The hunting was good during the expedition and St George bagged many fine specimens for the museums. They eventually found themselves at the Kara Kul Lake where so few westerners had ever been and it is highly likely that Teresa was the first western woman ever to reach its shores.

They made their way back to Samarkand and despatched their many specimens back to England while St George and Teresa stayed a while longer in Russia specifically to thank Morier et al for his efforts in helping to secure the permits. St George was always at pains to show his gratitude to those who helped them and by the November they too were back in England. In 1889 they were back in Russia again this time heading for the Altai area of Mongolia. In St Petersburg St George had the good fortune to borrow a restricted map of the area and they made their way onward to the Tabagatai mountains on the border of Mongolia and modern day Kazakhstan. With camels, ponies and bullocks in their pack train they crossed into China up into the high ranges beyond the deserts and the stronghold of the mighty sheep.

The hunting was good and St George managed to procure some Mammoth bones and teeth for just a few shillings, he presented them to Thomas Moore at Liverpool Museum as well as giving some Ibex, Argali and some forty-seven different birds to the Natural History Museum in London.

Things were going well for the Littledales. Every year the Liverpool Museum held a soiree in St George's Hall, the building after which St George was named. In January 1890 the exhibit featured the Littledale contributions to the Museum. It must have been impressive. Fifty trophies of complete stuffed animals as well as mounted heads were placed on the orchestral platform. The display included Ollen, Stags, Bear, Chamois, Serow, Ibex and Bharal wild sheep from the recent Altai expedition. Apparently the most sensational exhibit was the Ovis Poli Marco Polo sheep shot at 15,000ft in the Pamirs in 1888. The Littledales were now very well known and trusted by the Museums, the Russian and British Foreign ministries and thus St George felt the time was right to push again for a big expedition with the aim of crossing the Pamir mountains in their entirety and right through to India.

The Pamir's

The Pamir's are a range of mountains reaching up to 20,000ft with high valleys that are sparsely populated even today. It was harsh terrain, the crossing of which would prove a much tougher prospect for the Littledales than they had previously encountered.

At such elevated altitudes there is an abundance of grazing but no real cultivation so 19th Century travellers had to go well prepared and carry everything they needed with them. There was also an increased risk from the local people who were hostile to foreigners as well as the political turbulence from the Great Game being played out by the Russians and the British. St George and Teresa thought that as they were a man and woman travelling together they would arouse curiosity perhaps but would not prove much of a threat to local and national sensibilities. British diplomats fought hard on behalf of the Littledales, St George even offering to do a little spying if it would help his cause and let them have their chance to travel and explore in this part of Central Asia. On the 7th March 1890 permission was finally granted, St George and Teresa were ecstatic as for the first time this was not primarily a hunting trip, Teresa wrote 'It is a big trip and I do not know whether we shall accomplish it. I hope we shall as it will be something to have done'.

They left England on the 10th April 1890 and at Odessa they boarded the SS *Tzarevna* which took them to Batum, where St George had to wait to sort out a number of problems with the Customs. Teresa made her way to Tiflis again to do some essential shopping for ox tongues, a staple of the Littledales travelling diet. They reunited a few days later and sailed across the Caspian Sea to join the now familiar Trans-Caspian railway to Samarkand. Such was their notoriety and perhaps fame that the authorities attached a special carriage onto the train solely for the use of the Littledales and their baggage.

At Samarkand another Tarantass was purchased and on the 8th May they were on their way to Margilan across barren country with only the occasional green oasis to catch the eye and break the monotony of a desolate landscape. St George noted that in the far distance there were huge snowy mountains which reminded him of the Vale of Kashmir. Once at Margilan further provisions had to be acquired and they bought five months worth of white flour, some potatoes and onions. Leaving that same day they travelled through the night to the small town of Osh some 500 miles beyond Samarkand.

A week had to be spent at Osh gathering further supplies and making improvements to their baggage, men and horses. Their experience from previous expeditions came to the fore and they took as little weight as possible though the equipment of the time was nothing like we have at present. Their tent alone weighed eighty pounds without the poles. Altogether their equipment, not including food and personal items, required three sturdy ponies to carry it all. Due to the lack of firewood on the Pamir's, the Littledales baked 2000 biscuits which they dried in the sun until they were as hard as stone and would last indefinitely. St George also bought a traditional local tribes felt tent called a Yurt, this proved much warmer and more practical than their own tent which they ended up draping over the Yurt to provide better insulation. Finally St George bought himself a sheepskin coat that reached down to his heels and Teresa a cape of Harris Tweed lined with lambskin.

On the 22nd May 1890 they were off, a huge caravan of horses, ponies and the Tarantass made their way out of Osh into the harsh semi desert, it was the start of a magnificent and now largely forgotten journey.

A few days out they encountered their first setback as one of the passes they hoped to cross was blocked by snow though they did have some good fortune in acquiring a six week old puppy from some local tribesmen which they trained to keep guard on their tent during the night. It worked too, as anyone who came near the Littledales tent awoke the puppy into a barking frenzy.

On the 3rd June they finally crossed the Taldik Pass and mounted onto the Alai plateau, all brown and desolate with barely a living creature save for the occasional marmot and great bustard. It proved exceedingly cold with frequent snow squalls and thunderstorms though in clearer spells the snowy peaks of the Trans Altai mountains came into view with Peak Communism standing proud above all others.

The Littledales wanted to cross another high pass, the Kizil Art, to reach one of their old camping grounds from a previous expedition on the Markan Su river and on the 7th June they managed to do so but the weather closed in again and, confined to the Yurt, Teresa complained that it was too big and not as warm as she had hoped it to be.

The next day with some Kirghiz and the local tribesmen, St George went hunting the Ovis Poli but they could not find any and upon returning to camp St George received news that another foreigner was hunting in the same district. Major Charles Cumberland came along to their camp where St George advised him of their plans to reach Kashmir by passing through the Chitral region, needless to say the Major tried to dissuade them from such an arduous undertaking as the region was still subject to surprise attacks from bandits. Teresa made an interesting entry in her journal which seems to confirm that St George was passing information onto British Intelligence.

They carried on through the Kara Julga, a valley almost completely devoid of vegetation, St George wrote ' This Central Asian scenery has a type of its own, quite different from the Swiss or Caucasian mountain scenes, where your eye when tired wanders from grand ice-fields above to a pleasant change of green pastures and the forests of pine below. Here, though the mountains are higher, the glaciers, owing to the small snowfall, are much more puny while below there is a picture of utter desolation that would be hard to match in any other part of the world'.

The Littledales had now arrived at the farthest point of their first Pamir trip, from here on in they were to be on totally new ground completely unknown to them or few westerners at all. On the 16th June they crossed the Tuyuk Pass at 14,300ft and reached the Murghab river the next day, to the east they could see the mighty peak of Mustagh Ata (24,750ft).

It was now becoming quite hot and a strong wind blew up sending dirt into their faces and making for hard going, they pitched camp not far from some Yurts where they managed to procure some milk from the herders – the days were getting steadily harder and more trying. They continued down the Alichur river and came close to Afghanistan territory where St George persuaded a Kirghiz chief to find them a guide. When questioned the guide promised to take them anywhere except Heaven or Hell, two days later the guide got lost.

The next morning over thirty of their horses were missing, this was becoming a regular problem and was increasingly frustrating for the Littledales. The horses belonged to two brothers except one which belonged to the caravan bashi's brother, the two brother's had bullied him into watching the horses all night. Clearly it is not possible to walk all day and keep watch all night, so he fell asleep and the horses wandered off. The horses were eventually rounded up but the owners were not happy and wanted more money or they threatened to take the horses away. St George said they could leave if they wished, however he had hired the horses for as long as he needed them and if they tried to remove them against his will he would shoot them one by one. Needless to say the problem was overcome and St George noted in his diary that these men were just like small children, one just had to be firm with them.

The following day was a long march over two very high passes, there was to be no grass for the horses to graze and so the Littledales decided to make a slight detour to Victoria Lake principally to do some hunting but also to allow the horses a good rest and feed before the long trying journey ahead. On the 27th June they reached the Lake perched at 14,000ft. Teresa was cold despite her furs though she was enchanted by the scenery and was overjoyed at being the first white woman ever to see the lake which had rarely been seen by any westerner. Yet in her moment of joy she knew that the most difficult and dangerous part of their journey lay ahead.

They left Victoria Lake after only a day and made their way to the Wakham River, a slight detour as their original route was impassable due to rivers swollen with glacier melt. Fuel and supplies were running low now and they only had four small pieces of sugar left out of a supply that was meant to last four months, they had used it all in only six weeks. The Littledales arrived at Teter Su and stayed for six days to allow St George an opportunity to go hunting. He managed to shoot but could not catch the largest Ovis Poli he had ever seen and it was with great regret he had to leave a wounded animal, he simply could not keep up with this monarch of the Pamir. The weather was continuously bad with heavy snowfall often necessitating a rising in the early morning to remove snow from the tent to avoid the ridgepole breaking. They headed south and used their last sticks of firewood to cook a meal before crossing the Andemin Pass climbing to over 15,000ft and which led eventually to the Little Pamir Lake where they could at last obtain some wood for fuel. St George had fashioned a net for catching trout in the many streams and rivers they crossed and for the first time they feasted on the delicious fish which provided a welcome change from their normal diet.

Beyond a place known as Bozai Gumbaz the track they were following became a narrow slash along the steep side of the mountain, Teresa elected to walk rather than risk being forced off her horse into the fast flowing and freezing water. She later wrote after a particularly awkward and hard day '.....the worst road we have ever been over, frightfully steep ascents and descents. At one place the road led down to the river edge over large boulders, really no path, and no room for the packs between the water and the rocks. The horses had been unpacked and St George and the men carried the packs on their backs along the river for a long distance and up a steep slippery rock.'

They made their way to the village of Sarhad and were delayed some days by armed Wakhis who were acting on instruction from the Afghan authorities. St George produced his Persian passport signed by Lord Salisbury and he explained that they did not wish to stay in Afghanistan but were intending to cross the Hindu Kush in Chitral which was only 20 miles away. They could not be 'released' from Sarhad till the head of the village had received permission from his chief stationed over 220 miles away. The local farmers, under orders, from their masters provided chickens, eggs and butter which the Littledales could not refuse but ate guiltily as they knew the local people had little and whenever they did require something they always sought the owner so that he could be recompensed. Finally permission came through and they could leave, they managed to hire six yaks and extra hands to help them cross the Hindu Kush. Ten days had been lost in Sarhad and the Littledales were anxious to make up for lost time, uncertain of the welcome they would receive in Chitral they took enough supplies to remain largely independent.

The caravan climbed slowly up the Baroghil Pass where St George managed to annoy the accompanying Afghans by photographing it, was it a case of a spy doing his duty one wonders. Once they had reached their first camp on the other side of the pass the Littledales bade farewell to their Afghan escorts and distributed presents, St George gave one man a silver watch and later that day he went to check his own gold watch only to find that it had been filched by one of the Afghans, he was more chagrined than angry though. They had not heard the last of the officials from Sarhad as they sent men to discourage the Littledales from going any further by threatening their guides and men. St George was as diplomatic as ever and managed to assuage his men's fears promising them extra pay if they stayed.

They were now anxious to put as much distance between themselves and Sarhad as possible and so marched on not stopping to camp till they reached the foot of another high pass which was covered in snow and ice. There was no room to pitch any tents so they had to sleep amongst the rocks in the open but not before feeding the horses barley and cutting steps in the ice for them to climb the pass the following morning. The next day started well but once the sun rose the snow became soft, both horses and men were sinking into the deep snow. St George began to wonder whether they would ever reach to the top or not however after a great effort they finally did so to be greeted by a stupendous view of the Himalayan giants and incredible glaciers. The descent of the pass proved perilous due to many hidden crevasses and difficult moraines that had to be crossed, they had to repeatedly unpack and pack the horses to allow them to negotiate such difficult terrain. One horse fell into a crevasse and they had terrible difficulty releasing it with the ropes and tent poles being put to great use. The angle of descent eventually eased and though they were still on bare ice for most of the way they finally made it off the glacier and were glad to finally make camp and rest, this last stage had proved to be the hardest by far.

The next day the Littledales were met by two men sent by the Mir of Chitral who explained the reasons for the delays encountered in Afghanistan. Quite simply the Afghans did not want to allow any English travellers through their territory for fear that the Russians would want the same privileges, such were the ever increasing stakes in the Great Game.

They made a short march to the village of Darkot where they were treated well by the rough looking but kindly inhabitants, another short march led to Mir Wali, a small village within a stone fort, which belied the feudal nature of the terrain they were now travelling through. They received their first apricots here, some of the finest in the world and a gift from the Mir of Yasin.

The next day they reached the village of Yasin and were met by the Mir himself who led St George into his home where both he and Teresa gorged themselves on more fresh fruit. They were treated well and respectfully and managed to engage some new, though somewhat lazy, men to replace their own who now chose to head back to their home country as they were frightened of entering Gilgit itself. The terrain now became much harder to travel along and the horses had to be frequently unpacked and packed to negotiate the narrow paths and steep gorges. They arrived at Khalti with a sense of dread, a rope bridge crossing awaited them the next day, Teresa especially was not looking forward to the crossing.

These nightmarish structures are a formidable hazard in the Himalaya, flimsy looking and occasionally collapsing without warning costing an unwary traveller their life. In the Littledales time they were even worse and very much ramshackle affairs cobbled together by the local peoples with bits of twig and twine. If it failed death was certain by dropping hundreds of feet into the gorge below, thankfully it held for Teresa and Co, but the horses had to be led to a deep crossing of the river which took many hours and more than once a horse was nearly lost.

As soon as they reached the next village Teresa went straight to bed in a small rest hut such was her distress at the day's exertions.

The following day they wandered along a very rough path, and again frequently had to unpack and re-pack the now mostly unshod horses who suffered terribly. There was no village and no grazing so they camped out under the stars. The horses were clearly getting worse and struggled to carry their loads so the porters had to carry the essential supplies. They made a camp at Gakuch and such was their state of exhaustion that the Littledales spent the best part of a full day resting in bed. Thankfully the British Agent in Gilgit heard of their plight and sent a local runner with horseshoes and nails to aid the horses.

The next day they rose at 3.00am for the long march to Gilgit, passing another rope bridge which twelve years earlier had collapsed killing fifteen people who happened to be crossing at the time. On the 7th August they marched tired and exhausted into Gilgit to take up a temporary residence in the British Agency house. Their journey was now at an end, they had finally crossed the Pamir's and were the first westerners ever to do so.

The Littledales now found themselves on familiar ground, the path to Srinigar was known to them from one of their previous expeditions. They left on the 10th August and two days later Theresa celebrated her 51st birthday with a basket of fresh fruit provided by the British Agent from Gilgit who had forwarded these much needed luxuries onto their camp by runner. St George managed to indulge his passion for hunting for another week before two weeks of tough going saw them arrive in Srinigar and eventually the long journey home to England via Bombay.

Six months later they made their third visit to the wonderful Caucasus in a search for the elusive Aurochs, it was as though they could never remain in one place for too long before the urge to travel took hold again. They took a new travelling companion, Tanny, a young fox terrier who was to prove a good and loyal watchdog for the Littledales, Teresa commented on how well he took to travel and was such good company when St George was out hunting.

On this trip St George finally got his Auroch, however an incident occurred that greatly impressed the hunting community, he wrote:

.....I found myself face to face with the grand old bull, bigger than my first victim. We were hidden in the bush and he stood in the open wood, and grand indeed he looked. I laid my rifle down, for the temptation was great, and I would not have slain him for £1000. I took my cap off to him out of respect for a noble representative of a nearly extinct species. I had got what I wanted, and mine should not be the hand to hurry further the extermination of a fading race for mere wanton sport.

St George had a great respect for the animals he hunted and presented the two Auroch he did shoot to the British Museum when he returned to England in October 1891. He then began to fret over the reading of his paper on the Pamir trip to the Royal Geographical Society, he was extremely anxious to avoid any political reference as he did not want to write anything that could be used against him on his future travels. He need not have worried as the Littledales were too well respected and as Douglas Freshfield read out his paper, although St George was present he chose not to read his own paper, the Russian guests from the Embassy were greatly impressed and received great thanks from all present for the help and assistance afforded to the Littledales on their arduous journey.

A further trip to the Caucasus was planned for 1892, however an outbreak of cholera put paid to that and they had to spend a whole year at home. St George did not waste his time and spent the year learning how to make maps so that he could provide even greater knowledge to the geographical and intelligence agencies who had sponsored and supported them both on their previous trips.

A new trip was thus planned, one even more difficult than their Pamir journey. St George wanted to obtain the Bactrian Asian Wild Camel for the Natural History Museum. It had only been discovered in 1887 and was an incredibly rare creature, it afforded a fine excuse for another long trip, this time from west to east across Russian & Chinese Central Asia all the way to Peking.

St George applied for the necessary permits which were granted without any real difficulty, such was the Littledales status, by the Russian and Chinese governments. This trip would be hard as they had to begin their journey again crossing Russian Central Asia but this time in the depths of winter where the wind and cold would prove as tough an enemy as the unforgiving barren terrain.

West to East across Asia

The trip got off to a bad start as St George had developed a rather severe back pain and so the packing and much of the planning fell onto Teresa which left her exhausted. One thing she did insist upon however was for little Tanny to come along on this demanding trip, St George knew only to well how much the dog meant to Teresa to object.

They finally left London on the 31st January 1893 and Teresa wrote:

'We are...... on our way to explore the interior of Thibet & China and expect to return with Pigtails and old Manuscripts.'

It proved an exceedingly cold journey to Russia on the Orient Express, Teresa often had to wear two thick fur coats and the train at one point became frozen to the track necessitating two hours hard labour with pick axes and brute force to free the train from the rails. They met Lord Dunmore at Samsun on the shores of Turkey and he recommended his servant, Ramzan, who had just accompanied him on his journey from Kashmir to Kashgar. It was a fortunate meeting as Ramzan agreed to join the Littledales for the princely wage of 20 Rupees a month, he proved a great asset to them during the coming months.

The party of travellers all arrived at Tiflis to spend several days buying ox tongues and lemons as well as other essential supplies. They made their way to Baku but their baggage didn't and a delay was inevitable but such was the Littledales influence in the area that they managed to persuade the general in charge of the Trans-Caspian Railway to delay their trains departure by a whole day. There were clearly advantages to travelling as 'the emperor's personal friends'.

They reached Samarkand on the 25th February and it proved to be even colder than anywhere else they had been, as a consequence their sightseeing was cut short. They made their way to Margilan by tarantass and were fortunate to re-employ many of their old servants from previous trips, this re-assured Teresa as they would all be aware of each other's foibles and thus a more harmonious and stress free trip would hopefully follow.

On the 9th March they left Margilan for the 248 mile long trade route to Kashgar, it was so cold that during a meal taken in their Yurt a glass of water would freeze before they could drink it. Two relatively easy marches from the village of Gulcha took the Littledales past Sufi Kurgan where they had separated from the main trail in 1890 to head south across the Pamirs. From here onward they would be travelling through new and unfamiliar country and thus the real journey began.

It was tough going, bitterly cold and although most of the snow had melted on the passes it had re-frozen into hard ice which made for treacherous conditions underfoot. They reached the top of the Terek Dawan pass which at 13,350ft proved a tough proposition especially for poor Tanny who became increasingly tired and grateful for the rest stops each night. They descended ten miles to reach Kok Su and a delightful, but cold, camp in perfect Ibex country. The next day they reached the Russian border and crossed into China to follow the Kashgar River for several days to finally and gratefully reach the substantial Chinese frontier fort of Ulukchat. Ramzan eased their passage through the border where they continued down the Kashgar River through arid country to reach a small village after a further 26 miles. It started to snow the next day and they soon entered a narrow winding gorge between vertical walls of compact clay hundreds of feet high, the path narrowed to that of the width of a single horse, it was hard to believe that this was the main trade route from Osh to Kashgar.

After several more days of hard going they finally made it to the large city of Kashgar where the British Agent, George Macartney, offered the Littledales his own personal rooms in his residence. Kashgar is the capital of Chinese Turkestan and is surrounded on three sides by mountain ranges. The Tien Shan to the north, the Pamirs to the west and the Kun Lun to the south, to the east lay the massive, barren Gobi Desert. The Tarim basin covers most of the southerly portion of today's Xinjiang province and consists almost entirely of one of the most desolate portions of desert in the world, the Taklamakan, around which are a string of oases at the foot of the surrounding mountains which provide water from melting snow and glaciers. These oases make possible the trade route known as The Silk Road and Kashgar's location has made it a hub for trade in every direction for many centuries, thus Kashgar is truly the greatest of crossroads in Central Asia.

Teresa was not impressed with the town and described it as a dirty place and one that would be intolerable to live in for any great length of time. St George reported to George Macartney details of his trip through Turkestan which were then forwarded to British Intelligence in Srinigar, this was a rather delicate period in the Great Game and the British feared a Russian invasion of India was becoming increasingly likely.

The Littledales spent their time in Kashgar wisely buying silver (for future purchases on their journey), exchanging interpreters and buying some Chinese clothes which Teresa especially enjoyed though St George could not get any boots big enough to fit. They had dinner with the Russian Consul, Nikolai Petrovsky, who gave them much assistance and information about the country they would be travelling through though he did try to dissuade them from making the journey.

The Littledales left Kashgar on the 29th March and their first significant destination was a village called Korla over a month away. They had three carts each pulled by four horses, their equipment was in two while they travelled in a third though often they had to walk many miles each day as the road proved so rough. The dust was terrible and they could not escape it, water was not easy to come by and this was the main route of the northern branch of the Silk Road, they feared what it would be like when they left the beaten track.

Each night they spent at official Chinese rest houses, basic mud built structures that looked as though a decent downpour would wash them away. They were lively but dirty places, with dust usually a couple of inches thick, and much used by traders on the Silk Road. Eventually they entered a dense Poplar forest said to be inhabited by deer, antelope and wolves though the Littledales saw nothing and while it became warmer the dust became even worse, often several inches thick and of a consistency of fine flour that just made its way into everything. Travelling became harder and they often travelled through the night, after several days of rough going they crossed the Kashgar River to reach the village of Aksu. The local Russian trade official gave them quiet and comfortable rooms and brought tea, bread, eggs and other luxuries. After resting for a few days they were off again though the night travel was taking its toll on both men and horse, one horse died and the men often fell asleep at their posts during the night. They passed through one small village, Bai, where they came across a man wearing a heavy iron collar around his neck attached to which was a 6ft long thick iron bar. The wearing of this was his punishment for stabbing a local Chinese man and he would have to wear it for the rest of his life.

Eventually they all arrived at the town of Kuchar where the local Russian agent provided them with good accommodation and apples, pears, radishes and a delightful pilau which they hungrily devoured. In 1890 a Captain Bower was sent to Kuchar to try to find an Afghan on the run, the murderer of Andrew Dalgleish, an agent of the British Central Asian Trading Company. Whilst looking for him Bower bought a book of a Turki which was later revealed as an ancient fifth century manuscript written in Sanskrit. The discovery of this book led to a stampede of scholars and archaeologists to the area to uncover buried civilisations. St George himself tried to buy some old manuscripts but the wily locals tried to con him with forgeries or modern books one of which had a picture of a frigate. St George however did visit the ancient site where the book was discovered and was the first westerner to do so in daylight, he saw many chambers and tombs hewn out of the soft sandstone and clay richly decorated with pictures and images of the Buddha. St George 'would have liked to have a few quiet days with a pick axe and a shovel to unearth some buried treasures'.

They left Kuchar that night and the weather turned cold again, a problem with the cart meant that St George and Tanny had to do long marches on foot. Thankfully on the 1st May 1893 they reached the city of Korla and a long rest would be needed as the next part of the journey would be much harder than what they had just come through. They would also need to replenish dwindling supplies for five months hard travel, source fresh animals and the men to care for them.

The Littledales spent ten days in Korla and St George took the time to practice his map making skills with the sextant and artificial horizon, initially they would be travelling on existing and known routes but once they reached a place called Lop Nor they would be on new and virtually unknown territory so map making would become an increasingly time consuming exercise for St George.

St George wrote to the Royal Geographical Society and his sister to advise of their plans, confidence to his patron but caution to the family proved to be the tone of the letters as this would prove to be a hazardous undertaking all the way to Peking. As always the horses proved a particular concern to the Littledales and it broke their hearts to realise that most of them would die in the course of the march, in this part of the world all caravans lost animals.

They left Korla on the 10th May accompanied by the local Russian agent as far as Lop Nor and who would prove invaluable to the Littledales in procuring extra supplies and local guides. They followed the river then took a two day shortcut across the desert when an incident took place that caused Teresa some concern, Tanny and the Russian agents dog got into a fight over a crust of bread and when Teresa tried to break them apart Tanny bit her finger and the other dog her arm, she nearly fainted a few times and had to lie down on the ground to rest. They soon reached the Tarim river, later called the Great Highway by the legendary Sven Hedin, and followed it through groves of trees, marshes and lakes – a green and blue lifeline through one of the most barren places on earth.

A dugout canoe passed the Littledales on its way to the village of Abdal some four days away in a canoe, but sixteen days on foot and horse. They had to cross the river twice and as they headed farther south the weather became increasingly hot. One night they were hit by a sand storm known locally as a Kara Buran, everything became black in the swirling sand hurricane which has been known to sweep people and sheep away never to be seen again.

They reached the small village of Abdal which consisted of just four houses and although the Littledales thought it an unhealthy place they had to spend five days there resting themselves and their animals, St George and Teresa took quinine as a precaution and imagined themselves somewhere else rather than this desolate place. The Russian agent returned to Korla after assisting with supplies, now they were on their own.

They left Abdal on the 3rd June and to avoid the worst of the swamps they retraced their steps a few miles back upriver to head south east along the edge of the marshy ground, the going underfoot proved so hard and dry that the horse's shoes quickly wore out. They were now on the Mongol pilgrim route to Tibet which had only once before been trod by a European and possibly Marco Polo, there was no water to be had for the next two days and the animals suffered greatly. Marching through the night made it slightly easier and they did finally reach some very muddy water caused by snow melt at Kurgan Bulak, here St George managed to shoot some sand grouse for the pot.

They spent a whole day at Kurgan Bulak to rest the animals as there was grazing to be had, they then marched south when they were overtaken by a sudden violent snowstorm. The deep dust of the trail was turned almost instantly into a sea of thick mud. The going became more treacherous as the animals were sliding everywhere and so in the teeth of the vicious storm they made camp.

When the storm abated St George continued with his map by taking observations of the stars, a lengthy and time consuming process but one that was essential for their Royal Geographical Society patronage. They were now in an unmapped and rarely frequented, by western peoples, area and St Georges map would be a useful addition to the geographical archives.

After several more days of tough going the mountainous terrain became impassable and so the Littledales descended to the desert, if anything it became even harder for them and their animals. It was ridiculously hot, water was very scarce and it had to be rationed as the guides were unsure as to where they could replenish supplies each day, there was no grazing for the animals and every afternoon a sandstorm would descend upon them forcing them to seek shelter in their tents.

On the 19th June their luck changed, St George had managed to shoot a few specimens of the wild camel which varied their diet but did not satisfy their taste buds with Teresa, on being told that the camel was thirty years old, saying that it tasted like it. St George kept the skins for the Natural History Museum as promised. They continued marching through the desert and their water supplies now became terribly low, there being enough only for the humans and it was somewhat distressing for St George to refuse the dogs their water. Thankfully the next day they reached a large clear stream with good grazing, at the stream was a Yurt occupied by a Chinese and two Lamas. St George offered them money for their services as a guide but they refused. The Chinese did say that a guide would be found at Dunhuang and he offered to take them there, even though it was out of their way a guide was essential and so St George accepted the offer.

At Dunhuang the first thing St George did was buy new horseshoes though it took three days of hard negotiation to find a guide who was prepared to take them to Koko Nor. The locals advised the Littledales that the surrounding mountains were full of outlaws, the Littledales own men even considered deserting them such was their fear of this unknown land. St George however was made of stronger stuff and reminded his men of how well they were being paid and he offered further inducements of presents at the end of their long journey. After a week at Dunhuang they set off into true Mongol country, stopping at a Yurt Teresa was offered some sour milk which she drank to avoid hurting the lamas feelings. He took the empty bowl off her, licked it clean and put it back on the shelf, clean again and ready for the next visitor. Teresa wished she had not been so polite.

They followed the river so there was no shortage of water and the grazing was good but wood was scarce forcing them to use horse dung for fuel. Another guide was found, a soldier called Lapkee, and he professed to know the way to Koko Nor. During the next couple of days St George managed to shoot a couple of yaks, these fine beasts of burden of the mountain varied the Littledales diet and provided another addition to the increasing number of specimens for the British Museums.

They now turned south and crossed the Humboldt mountains by the relatively easy Ping Dawan Pass, it was high though at over 16,000ft and both humans and animals suffered in the thin air. They descended the pass into a deep valley and were now in the country of the Tanguts, they are a Tibetan people to whom robbery was a way of life and the Littledales had been warned of their unpredictable nature. Caravans often grouped together for greater security in such territory though sometimes the bandit gangs of Tanguts outnumbered them – St George gave his men a lesson on how to fire a gun.

St George visited a nearby Tangut camp to see if another guide could be found as Lapkee was unsure of the way. The chief was surprised at this English visitor travelling with his wife and was not threatened by him though he did comment 'the Englishman has wonderful guns but very bad clothes'. The chief clearly thought that St George had his priorities right.

St George offered the usual inducements to the chief and secured the services of two guides who would take them across a pass three days away to Buhain Gol [River] which would eventually lead to Koko Nor. Three days later the Littledales crossed the Katin La and descended into a valley of rolling hills, they set up camp after the Tangut guides had left. It now rained almost every afternoon which improved the grazing and helped improve the condition of their horses who were getting stronger by the day.

A long and fast march brought the caravan within sight of the Koko Nor [Lake], they rode round to the north side of the lake and pitched their tents and yurts near a large Tangut encampment. During the night the last of the Littledales sheep disappeared, clearly stolen by the Tanguts. The Ladakhis were furious and wanted to return to the encampment to take fifty of their sheep, St George refused to allow them leave and his good judgment was proven as the following year a French explorer paid with his life for a similar occurrence.

Finally on the 9th August they reached Sining and while the main exploratory side of their journey was over, the adventure itself was not. A further march took then to Lanzhou where St George gave the twelve surviving horses and thirty four donkeys to their caravan men and guides and bid them a fond farewell, despite all the hardships they had remained largely loyal to the Littledales, such loyalty was appreciated by the Englishman and his wife.

St George and Teresa were now going on a journey down the Yellow River to Bautu, a short stage from Peking itself, their craft was to be a raft some 50ft x 18ft with a crew of twelve men to row and steer down the perilous waters, it was to be an exciting trip and one that no European had ever done before.

They left Lanzhou and entered the fast flowing waters of the Yellow River, descending a narrow gorge and speeding through a large rapid they made it to a sandy bank, secured the raft and spent the night out in the open. The next day the gorge narrowed to less than 20 yards and the river twisted and turned every few minutes during its descent. One hard bump broke some logs and the Littledales confidence was not increased when they noticed that each of the rafts-men had brought an inflated sheepskin life preserver in case they were tossed into the water, clearly no-one had thought of telling the Littledales of this simple life saver.

Finally after a few hours of furious paddling and steering the river widened and the pace slowed, this presented new difficulties as the raft frequently grounded on a sandy channel and it was a frightful struggle to release it. Often they had to dismantle the raft and rebuild it once an obstacle had been passed. One morning the men removed some logs from the raft saying they were going to make a smaller one to help tow the main raft off when it got stuck on an obstacle. After climbing onto the new raft the men then cut the rope and floated away leaving the Littledales and the three remaining men stranded, fortunately a small boat carrying wool soon passed and saved them and their baggage. They were headed to Ning-hsia and St George, while sat on the bales of wool, continued to take observations for his sketch map and each night he took a latitude bearing on his sextant. They drifted down the Yellow River passing portions of the Great Wall which Teresa noted as 'twisting and turning like a great snake' and on the 28th August they landed at Ning-hsia where the Littledales managed to secure another passage on a grain boat to Bautu some nine days away.

The Yellow River now flowed down the edge of a desert with few villages or inhabitants to be seen, the heat was intense so Teresa rigged up an awning to protect them-selves from the sun and each night they camped on the banks of the river. On the 12th September they arrived at Batu where they managed to hire a number of small carts to take them to Kweisui, a three day journey past ruined towns and villages, empty since the Tungan Rebellion of 1862 where 90% of the population was slain.

From Kweisui a journey of twelve days on improving roads and ever increasing prices for lodging told them they were near Peking and after again passing through the Great Wall only three days more travel saw them finally arrive at the Chinese capital. After settling into a small hotel

St George paid their faithful Turki interpreter in Rouble notes which he then sewed into the lining of his coat before setting off on his long and arduous four month return to Korla.

This had been a long and impressive journey for the Littledales and one that would put them to the fore of the world's leading explorers of Central Asia. They were glad to be heading home, however there was one more trip St George and Teresa desperately wanted to make and that would be to the forbidden country of Tibet and in particular its capital city, Lhasa. Many had been defeated in their efforts and yet St George felt that he had a chance and began to plan what would prove to be the most dangerous and difficult journey they would ever undertake.

They took a French steamer on the 14th October back to Europe and by late November the Littledales were back safely home in England.

Toward Tibet & Lhasa

On their arrival back in England they threw themselves back into their English way of life, St George delivered his specimens to the Natural History Museum and received a letter of thanks. He also delivered a lecture to the Royal Geographical Society which was well received, however time was pressing as they were getting no younger and they began to make real plans to visit Tibet which had closed its doors to foreigners at the beginning of the 19th Century. The mysterious forbidden city of Lhasa was the Littledales ultimate objective as it had not been visited by Europeans for nearly fifty years.

The journey would require another winter trip across the Tien Shan to Kashgar and so St George wrote to the Foreign Office to try and get the required permissions which once again were granted. St George wanted to leave England on the 1st November 1894 though the heavy items he required would need to be sent a month earlier. In addition he asked if it be possible to have an armed escort but the Indian Government refused them the Ghurkas needed and so Lord Roberts and Major Bower found some retired Pathan Sepoys (soldiers) instead.

St George describes their departure :-

We left England on November 10, 1894, the same party as usual:- Mrs. Littledale, myself and our dog, accompanied in addition by my nephew, Mr W.A.I. Fletcher of Oxford University boating renown, who proved himself in every respect an admirable travelling companion. My scheme was to strain every nerve to reach Tibet, and, if possible, Lhasa, with plenty of food and animals to carry it. Most of the other expeditions had failed owing to their arriving in a more or less destitute condition, and then of course, the Tibetans could dictate their own terms. We also relied upon bribery, and went well prepared with the sinews of war for wholesale corruption.

Teresa was still recovering from the Asia to Peking trip the previous year, that trip had pushed the Littledales far though this expedition would prove a much tougher proposition as they would have to spend many weeks, even months above 17,000ft on the cold dry Tibetan Plateau. St George was a fit and active man in his early forties, however when the trip began Teresa was fifty five and she was concerned as to how she would cope, hence it was decided to include a nephew of St George in the party. Willie Fletcher was a strong, fit young man with lots of stamina and determination and hailed from Allerton in Liverpool. He had attended Eton and Oxford though seemed more interested in the river and rowing than in his studies, he won the boat race with Oxford four times. A family story goes that one evening while at the dinner table their butler came in saying there was 'a whore' at the front door for Wille. His father replied 'give her a fiver and tell her to go away' the butler departed and came back a few minutes later with a large wooden oar.

They all left England on the now familiar route to Samarkand without any real incident apart from once when a Turkish Customs Official tried to remove Tanny from the train.

On the 4th December they arrived at Samarkand and on the 8th December, St George's forty third birthday, they celebrated the occasion by setting off on their fourth trip to Osh. The Littledales and Willie loaded up a tarantass by placing their tents on the bottom of the compartment and their beds on top though there proved to be no room for Willie who, wrapped in sheepskins slept outside next to the driver. They were travelling two months earlier in the year than the last time they had made the journey and consequently it was much colder but they had no choice, they simply had to reach the Tibetan Plateau by early spring to have any chance of reaching Lhasa. They met no other travellers, Teresa was starting to feel unwell and although she did not know it at the time she had developed dysentery which would plague her, on and off, for the rest of the trip.

The next day the road was slippery, the horses were struggling and it took over five hours to cover 21 miles, it started to snow and when they reached the village of Sarat they stopped for the night even though there was no fuel so they ate 'cold rations'. Four inches of snow fell during the night and when they reached Uratiube the horses were exhausted, a two day wait was endured while the party waited for fresh horses. It was so cold one of their drivers got frostbite in his hands and feet and their winter felt boots started to crack with the extreme cold. On the 13th December, despite an early start they had to wait for five hours as four of their drivers need treatment at a local hospital for frostbite. They rode on, at one point they crossed a partly frozen river which cracked under the weight of the tarantass and the water began to freeze around it, holding it fast. The best St George and Willie could do was hire a local Arba, move some of the baggage onto it and then ride to a local Sart's house to spend the night. Despite their best efforts the tarantass and some baggage had to be abandoned the next day and they arrived at the rest station at half past five in the morning after travelling a mere 33 miles.

Four days later they finally reached Osh where they had to spend three days drying out equipment, buying more supplies and hiring a cook. They were going to take the same route to Kashgar as they had the year previously, however now there was much more snow and the Tien Shan would prove to be a tough proposition under such demanding conditions. They left on the 22nd December and despite the rough road, they arrived at Langar in the early afternoon to crowd into the one roomed small mud house for a cold night. The next day they made their way to Gulcha where Teresa and St George took the only room available as Teresa was still poorly, Willie slept in the Yurt. Christmas Day was spent resting, mending the horse's harnesses and writing though by Boxing Day Teresa was feeling better and a little stronger so they could continue their march. The Arba driver refused to go any further without extra payment and so was promptly sacked by St George, from that point on they all rode horses, it was still so cold that icicles hung down from the animals. They started for the Terek Dawan and camped at 8,800ft in three Yurts in a biting cold wind. The following day they crossed the Terek Dawan, it was snowing lightly and Teresa put Tanny in a fur coat she had specially made for him, St George commented that Tanny was as warm as Lucifer while the rest of us just shivered.

Over the following two days the party crossed two high snowy passes in a snowstorm and Willie was thrown from his horse which landed on top of him though thankfully the deep snow prevented injury. They arrived at the Russian frontier post of Irkistan and the Littledales produced their passports, there proved to be a problem though the Littledales managed to sneak away while the border guards went to speak to their superiors.

It got colder and during the night, after they had crossed into Chinese Turkestan, Willie's moustache froze to the pillow. They soon reached Kashgar where they enjoyed the hospitality of George Macartney once again, the Littledales and Willie were mightily relieved to sleep in warm beds and eat at a table once more after two months hard travel. Teresa had by now lapsed back into poor health with both Willie & St George fearing for her and whether the trip could even go ahead. The hardest part was yet to come.

The Littledales spent two and a half weeks in Kashgar waiting for their fighting men, the sepoy's, who had been delayed by the cold and high snow covered passes. Their way was difficult crossing high passes over 16,000ft high, grazing was scarce and the path was littered with the corpses of those who had misjudged the conditions and been unlucky with the weather, in the late 19th century travel in the Himalaya was not easy. The Littledales gathered further supplies, including 400lb of silver, which gave them a headache as to how to pack it, paper money would have been easier for them but in the remote villages of Central Asia no-one would accept it.

The trip across the Karakoram passes in winter had taken its toll on the sepoy's feet which were badly frostbitten, as a consequence St George hired two more local men one of whom professed to know the route. The expedition finally left Kashgar on the 22nd January 1895 and all in the party were glad to be underway. Their destination was the city of Yarkand some 120 miles away which St George was to describe as 'very uninteresting' when they arrived after five days hard travel.

Teresa was horrified at the high incidence of goitre amongst the local population which was worse than any place she had ever been before. Yarkand was a similar walled city to Kashgar and was just as cold. The Littledales had to spend eight days in Yarkand due to difficulty in obtaining animals and Indian rupees, their frustration was eased slightly by the gifts of food, melons, raisins and sugar from the local traders, they told Teresa she was the first European woman to visit the city. They left on the 3rd February and after several hours they reached the Yarkand River and were ferried across in boats. They continued for another 15 miles through irrigated paddy fields until they came to a small village where they spent the night. The next day they reached Kargalik where they joined the southern branch of the old Silk Road which gradually became a rough dusty track which wound itself through the desert. It became windier thus exacerbating the cold which even the shining sun could do little to alleviate. They reached the town of Guma, a large oasis with good water which helped the animals but the next day the terrain worsened and the carts sank deeply into the sand forcing the horses to struggle. St George and Teresa continued to collect plants and insects for the British Museum despite the biting cold and wind.

For the next three days they struggled on through the desert experiencing many sand storms to finally arrive at the town of Khotan where they were met by Russian and Afghan officials. The Littledales had to spend two weeks in Khotan to buy more supplies and animals, they needed 4000lb of flour, rice and grain. Teresa made butter out of cream and put it into cans for the journey and she also made coats & hats out of Russian cloth for their men.

The caravan men enjoyed themselves in Khotan where it was possible to get married for a few days and then end the marriage by giving gifts to the, now dumped, bride. St George gave a big party for the men where the wine and Chinese brandy flowed freely, there was much dancing and joviality which lifted the men's spirits for the journey ahead. On the 25th February they left and camped for the first night on the edge of the Khotan oasis at a small village called Lob. For the next four days they travelled through a barren and rocky wasteland with much deep sand to arrive at another oasis, Keira. The sand was now so deep that it was impossible to take the carts any further and so further animals had to be found, the Littledales were anxious to keep the expedition animals unburdened to save their strength for the crossing of the high Tibetan plateau.

The local headman at Keira was reluctant to let the Littledales proceed any further but St George placated him by writing a letter absolving him and the Chinese government should anything go wrong. The headman responded by sending the Littledale caravan a sheep, rice and a good cook to create a feast for the tired travellers.

The caravan left Keira on the 5th March intending to travel to Cherchen, the grand parade now consisted of 14 horses, 10 mules and 65 donkeys. A further 66 horses were to be taken fully loaded to Cherchen where they would leave their loads and return back to Keira. Two days later they made it to Nia tired out after spending 12 hours on the saddle on a rough track where no water could be found for the horses, one of whom had collapsed five miles out of the village and the Littledales had to wait till late in the night for their luggage to arrive before they could bed down for the night.

One of the sepoy's had to return back to Kashgar as his feet, which were badly frostbitten, resulting in two toes being amputated it was just not possible for him to continue. He was most distraught at the prospect of having to return but St George paid his wages anyway together with sufficient monies to cover continuing medical expenses and other costs, this act of generosity made a favourable impression on the other men. They left Nia the next day for the long trip to Cherchen over rough desert and shifting sand dunes, they encountered frequent sand storms which blocked up the wells they so desperately needed to water the horses and themselves. They often had to be dug out which was time consuming and tiring.

For ten days they soldiered on, one day it would be hot and they staggered along under a blazing sun and the next it would be so cold Teresa would need her winter fur coat to keep out the biting wind. The wind remained constantly strong which made for much tougher going and eventually on the 19th March, after four months of tough travelling they reached the oasis of Cherchen where they took up a short residence in a large house with a garden. The easy part of their journey was over, the Tibetan plateau was beckoning.

The Littledales were hoping to spend only a week in Cherchen, to allow their animals to recover and make some repairs to equipment. However the snow on the passes was still too deep so they spent 24 days there waiting for the Akka Tagh, the range of mountains they would have to cross to reach the Tibetan Plateau, to clear. Their time in Cherchen was one of great activity, there were difficulties in keeping his sepoy's and men happy with frequent complaints over money and conditions. They had to purchase more supplies and the animals to transport them. The Littledales decided to rely on ponies and donkeys rather than camels which previous travellers to the area had used. They eventually were to have a caravan of 250 animals which they divided into two categories, one half for the trip across the Tibetan Plateau the other half to help get them to the start.

Grazing would be scarce and they had to start out with an enormous amount of corn for the animals, in fact they took 25,000lbs of the stuff. The long stay in Cherchen did have one benefit in that it allowed the animals they had brought with them the time to recover properly from their initial hard journey.

Willie and St George frequently went duck hunting in their spare time, they made a trip to dig for relics in the ruins of the old Cherchen city, long buried in the shifting sands. Teresa sewed and repaired constantly, she wrote many letters to family and friends as she knew it would be many months before she could write again.

On the 12th April the main party left Cherchen and made a path through soft sand to follow the course of the river till it wound its way through a narrow gorge forcing them to make a slight detour to the south east, after marching for hours under the blazing sun the party reached a camp site near the base of the impressive and snowy mountains.

The routine for each days march was similar. The expedition owned 85 donkeys and 30 mules and horses. In addition there were 135 hired animals to carry the supplies and these animals had their owners, led by Razak Akhun, with them to help with the loading and unloading each day, though St George and Willie helped with these tasks to ease their burden.

Every morning Razak Akhun and his men collected the animals, cleaned their saddles and fed them. While this was being done one man started a fire to boil water and cooked breakfast, Rassul Galwan, the Littledales faithful guide and servant, poured hot water into basins and filled Teresa's teapot. Then he laid out the breakfast table which consisted usually of bread, honey and meat. After breakfast Galwan cleaned up, packed the beds, took down the tents and packed all the loads onto the horses. Meanwhile all the other horses were also being loaded with the supplies.

The Littledales and Willie rode on horses, but when the going became more difficult they would dismount and walk for a while, often they would let one of their men ride the horse for a rest as they were more experienced horsemen and could handle them on the rough terrain. St George was always in front and the caravan followed him, when they reached camp everyone except Teresa helped unload the animals and pitched two tents for the Littledales and Willie. Galwan then laid out their beds and clothes. Only after all this was done did the men pitch their own tents.

Kalam would start a fire and prepare the evening meal, usually a meat stew with onions and rice, potatoes were cooked separately. Dessert was usually some fruit. At dinner time Galwan would set three places on the table. The Littledales and Willie would put some soup mixture into a cup and add hot water. Galwan then brought two hot plates, one with rice for Teresa and Willie and the other with potatoes for St George. Then he set out the stew followed by the fruit in a wooden bowl.

After dinner Kalam would wash up while Galwan brought hot water for baths, water was sometimes hard to find, however the Littledales and Willie washed every night whenever water supplies allowed. Finally Galwan filled a hot water bottle for Teresa to help warm her bed. Teresa and Willie wrote up their diaries while St George worked on his map. The men then cooked their own evening meal, smoked, told stories and sang songs.

There were additional chores, bread was often baked and Teresa insisted on Galwan doing the laundry twice a week. Everyone was constantly mending things, taking care of the humans was easy.....it was the animals that required the most care. Over 100 animals had to be fed and cleaned, sores on their backs treated and the saddles fixed. This entire routine was followed every day for months on end. It was this attention to detail that enabled the Littledales to go as far as they did on their journeys.

On the 14th April the caravan wound its way up a narrow valley to a campsite where an almighty row broke out amongst the Littledales men. The sepoys, always troublesome, had started eating the bread which was intended for camps where there would be no firewood and therefore no cooking. Galwan reported this to St George who diplomatically pointed out that they had already consumed three months supply of butter in just two weeks. At this rate they would run out of food before they could purchase any more supplies and they would starve like so many other travellers before them. St George knew that Galwan had the best sense of proportion as to the supplies and placed him in charge of all the food. St George told the sepoys that even he, Teresa and Willie would take Galwan's instruction now in relation to the food and therefore so must they.

The next day they climbed a steep narrow ravine up to the Chokur Pass which took a great amount of time and effort to get the animals over but on the other side was a good campsite with grazing and water. The party had now crossed their first barrier to the Tibetan Plateau.

A strong wind blew up in the night filling the tents with sand and it continued throughout the day negating the effect of the bright sun. The terrain became rougher and many animals lost their loads which had to be repacked. They reached the Cherchen river again and the only possible passage was a narrow ledge leading across a point of rock some 40ft above the swirling and fast flowing river. After crossing the river they had to avoid some alkali marshes and headed south over the mountains on rougher but safer ground. The animals were bearing well but the men began to suffer with the long arduous days, a day's rest at a good campsite helped both animals and men but they had to keep moving as supplies were rationed and they could ill afford too many delays.

The caravan crossed an easy river the next day and wound its way through the hills following a stream covered in 3ft of ice, sand and mud, it was rough going for both men and animals. They travelled through ice filled valleys between barren mountains to reach a gravel plain where they had to melt snow to get any water. One of their men had become ill and it was clear he would have to go back, however he was the only man who knew the way, St George thought it wise to give him a horse to ride. After enduring another cold night in camp they crossed the Musluk Tagh, an easy though snow covered pass, to descend to the Ulugh Su river, this they followed on a frozen marsh and at the ford they had to hack through an embankment of drifted snow to reach the water. The crossing had to be made quickly before the afternoon snowmelt raised the water level, it took many hours to get the animals across and they had to post a lookout upstream to warn of any large blocks of ice and stone that were heading their way. It is not uncommon for huge boulders to be carried downstream in a glacial river and the damage they can cause to an unwary person crossing is not hard to imagine, often with fatal consequences. The party then climbed a steep hill where Willie and St George encountered some antelope but given the terrain and altitude they were denied a decent shot, eventually after 15 miles hard going they pitched camp at a good site with some grazing. Teresa wrote *'the wind is bitterly cold and it looks like we shall have some snow soon. We are at 14,600ft and I suppose we shall not be much lower for many months. I dread the months of cold'*. After a day's rest they moved on and St George managed to shoot a Tibetan wild ass for the pot, an early camp was made as the next day a high pass was to be crossed.

This next pass was 17,450ft high, the altitude was affecting both men and animals and another early camp was needed though there was no grazing or water as the stream was frozen solid. They tried a short cut that would cost them dearly in time and effort, Willie's horse died as it entered camp and Teresa wrote *'I was so cold I took some brandy. We melted a little ice in a cup over a candle. There was no water. We breakfasted off cold tongue. It is a privation not getting hot tea on such a cold morning'.* Two more steep passes were crossed and St George soon realised they had come the wrong way, he feared they would have to return but soon they came to a broad plain with some grazing. The whole party was tired through and so they took a much needed four day rest. St George and Willie went hunting and shot four antelope though it remained continually windy and cold with frequent snowstorms throughout the day. The Littledales now agreed that most of the hired donkeys and men could return though 32 men and donkeys were to be hired for another week to carry the corn. On the last night the horses and donkeys were left to graze but by morning they had wandered far in search of good grass and consequently another day was to be lost in finding them. Teresa was still ill from the altitude and dysentery which she had had on and off for five months now though she kept her feelings and fears to herself, only occasionally venting her frustration in her diary.

It was clear to St George that they were now well and truly lost, he and a guide went on a reconnaissance while another guide tried to find a route elsewhere. Eventually St George found a way to get back on route that would only involve a two day march back down the way they had come. It would be hard as there was no grazing or firewood. On the 15th May they set out over terrain that was totally devoid of any living thing save for the caravan, they crossed the Kara Muran Dawan which took a great effort given that it lay at over 18,000ft high, though from the summit of the pass they could finally see the vast Tibetan Plateau. St George worked on his map constantly and was greatly impressed by the peak Ulugh Muztagh – 'Great Ice Mountain' whose waters fed the oasis of Cherchen and made the southern branch of the Silk Route possible.

They descended the pass and found a good site upon which to camp, they bought some more donkeys from their men and sent them back well paid to Cherchen. The caravan was now on its own in Tibet and though they had suffered in crossing the Akka Tagh range of mountains the real suffering was soon to begin as the Chang Tang was to prove more formidable than they could ever have believed.

Their caravan was now much reduced due to the deaths of so many animals already, and the situation was only partly relieved by the recently purchased animals from the men they sent back to Cherchen, and they were hardly in a perfect state for such an arduous journey. Galwan suggested to St George that they make shorter marches and take a long halt at least once a week to allow the animals time to recover, St George agreed that such a plan was necessary but feared over the extra time this would take to complete their journey, Galwan assured him that they had enough food to last them and their animals six whole months.

The Chang Tang beckoned before them and the landscape they would have to cross displayed a similar pattern each day, debilitating altitude, lack of water and grazing, a terrain that was hard to assess from one day to the next and uncertain and often extreme weather patterns.

One night the animals strayed and a heavy snowfall hid their tracks, all the men including St George and Willie spent an entire day looking for them. On the 30th May disaster struck when all of their sheep were killed by wolves as the men had neglected to tie them up at night. This was a hard thing to do as the grazing was often so poor that if they were tied up they would not have enough food to survive the journey, St George asked the men to keep watch each night, however the men often fell asleep due to the extreme tiredness and effort of the days march. The weather got worse and one night a big snow and hail storm came in and killed yet more of their animals as they strayed.

Teresa wrote *'22 donkeys missing this morning. The night was very windy and in stormy weather they always stray. All were found and we started at 10 o'clock..... 4 donkeys were left to die on the road. Our donkeys could not be worse managed. The nights are bitterly cold and they suffer from cold and only a few of them have sacks over them..... Rozahun is worse than useless.......... We have not given the animals a rest for 13 days which is too long, for even a short march is not the same as a rest......... St George thinks more of his map than anything else, and there is much else of even greater importance to be thought of. As for Lhasa, that is out of the reckoning altogether. We shall have much to be thankful for if we get through to civilisation at all'*

The altitude was adding to their woes, the extreme altitude of the Chang Tang, consistently above the height of Mont Blanc, the consequent lack of water and good grazing and the almost daily loss of animals made for really tough going. Over two days eight donkeys died and drastic measures were needed, the Littledales had to abandon everything they did not need to survive. They dispensed with clothes, camp furniture, museum specimens, extra horseshoes and most of the gifts they and the Ladakhis had bought on the way.

One day they crossed a stream with quicksand on the bottom, a horse sank in and it took seven men to pull him out of the icy water. The next day the caravan crossed a 19,300ft pass, St George observed that Tibet was one large mountain covered with lumps. After a short day of just 8 miles they descended a valley and reached a camp site with water and good grass, the party rested for five days. They had so far lost 39 donkeys, all their sheep, 4 horses and a mule. Despite her illness Teresa still managed to collect some small insects for the British Museum and a few plants for the Royal Botanic Gardens at Kew.

On the 26th June they reached a latitude that would mean two things, rain and humans – namely Tibetan nomads. They started to encounter abandoned nomad camps on their journey and one day they reached a good camp site in a deep valley (nullah) with water and excellent grazing. St George and Willie climbed a nearby hill to scout out the next day's route, in the plain below them they saw yaks and the first humans they had seen outside of their own party for two months. St George was anxious to remain undiscovered as if they were seen it would only be a matter of time before the officials in Lhasa would hear of them and try to stop them.

St George decided on a night march to avoid being discovered and after a full day's rest they left at 8 o'clock under a bright early moon. No-one spoke as they set off across the plain in a deathly silence, the horses and ponies shoes had been removed. They struggled through a swamp and it proved a great effort to keep the whole caravan together, as dawn broke they managed to get over a ridge and out of sight from the Tibetan's but Willie worried that their footprints may be seen by the nomads and might betray their presence.

The next night they managed to cross the pass that had eluded them the night before, the terrain became easier but now the 'human' difficulties would increase. That night they heard wolves howling around the camp, their animals were safe however and they resumed the daylight marches to make up for lost time, on the 29th June St George manage to shoot some wild bharal for fresh meat to supplement their meagre supplies. Willie commented in his diary how he spent most of the day looking for nomads so that they could avoid them at all costs.

The days were not hot and the caravan became more nervous as they headed deeper into Tibet, they chose camp sites that were well hidden and stopped frequently to allow the animals some good grazing. Occasionally night travel was still necessary to avoid detection though their rooster occasionally crowing left the caravan in constant fear of being found.

On one such night march, where they were aiming for a lake and had to pass a group of Tibetan's, the only way St George could see the compass was by using a luminous matchbox. The terrain was still difficult and while crossing a salt marsh it took them an hour to go just ¾ of a mile crossing a difficult deep nullah, an incident which caused them great concern was when a box of 800 candles fell off a horse and smashed everywhere, the Littledales and their men had to pick all the pieces up for fear of leaving any trace of their passing. At 2.00am they finally reached the lake and camped exhausted from the day's double march.

The next day more and more Tibetan's could be seen and St George knew their day of discovery was getting near. Once discovered St George knew they would have to march hard to avoid capture and confrontation with local officials, thankfully Galwan's assessment of the food supplies was proving correct and they could hope to make 50 or 60 miles over three days. On the 9th July they had to make a raft to cross a river which they could not ford, this was time consuming not just in construction but also in the effort and time involved in getting the baggage and animals across. Eventually they were all across and camped in a nearby nullah. Teresa's dysentery became worse due to some bad water and she felt her strength failing, she was dismayed when St George insisted on another night march to climb a high pass which once ascended would lead to better grass and water for the animals.

Willie was enjoying the great adventure. On the 12th July he wrote, *'We are about 69 miles from Tengri Nor. If we can get within......measured distance of Lhasa, we shall leave all our things, take about 4 men, leave the rest to look after camp, and make a rush, riding as hard as we can, but that is a big IF. Of course we shall bury all the silver etc.'*

The next day St George and Willie while on a reconnaissance espied Tibetan nomads everywhere and thousands of yak's, Willie really enjoyed the cat and mouse game, however it was clear they would be discovered anytime soon. The next day they left camp in a downpour, Willie rode half a mile ahead of the caravan when he came upon a Tibetan nomad camp, there was no choice but to pass it and camp, the donkeys arrived shortly after camp was established together with five of the Tibetan nomads. Willie noted in his diary, *'Done. We are discovered.'*

It was a false alarm as the Tibetans were unconcerned about the presence, however they became more wary, St George copied his map onto tracing muslin in case something happened to the original. Speed was now of the essence and St George gave the order to give the animals some of their precious corn to build up their strength.

Their day of real discovery came on the 16th July, a local herder shouted to them to come over as he thought they were merchants, they ignored him and carried on southwards though they could find nowhere to camp so they continued on their way. They came upon a tent with a woman sitting outside, they wished to buy a sheep and the woman said her husband would sell them one and she offered them fresh goats milk which Teresa enjoyed. Eventually the Herder returned to sell them a sheep for 2 rupees, moving on the caravan eventually happened upon a good camp site at 17, 800ft after a sixteen mile day. The next morning four mounted Tibetans armed with guns and swords arrived into camp as they were preparing to leave. The Tibetans followed them and St George tried to buy another sheep from them, they offered to sell them as many sheep as they wanted if they were to stop and re-camp. The caravan continued onwards and St George offered the men 5 rupees if they told him the best route. The Tibetans replied that if they did that they would lose their heads which was no exaggeration, the Tibetan people loathed violence against foreigners, however they were not so restrained when it came to dealing with their own people who assisted foreigners to penetrate into their country.

That night they pitched camp in a large nullah, St George and Willie reckoned Tengri Nor was only 21 days away, a number of rough looking armed Tibetans rode into camp though they were friendly enough even assisting Teresa's horse across the river. They learned from a Lama with the Tibetans that were not going to be stopped that day but a high official from Lhasa was on his way to meet them, though this would not be for a couple of days. More Tibetans descended upon them as they made their way over a small pass with Tibetans riding and marching on both sides of the caravan.

They made another camp and tried to buy more sheep but their 'escort' refused the transaction. The next morning they rose at 4.00am and the Lama asked them to stop packing and stay where they were but St George flatly refused saying he had a passport for the whole of China and no-one but the Amban from Lhasa could stop them. They crossed another small pass and finally saw the lake of Tengri Nor of which Teresa wrote *'It is a beautiful lake, the water is intensely blue............... and I am certainly the first European woman to ever see its waters'.* The party turned south and headed towards Tengri Nor and met another Lama on the way who directed them up a nullah on their right to as it would lead to a ford where they could cross the river, it was good advice but probably given so as to avoid a monastery directly ahead of them. As they crossed the nullah they looked down on a couple of white tents on the plain below and they feared the high official from Lhasa had arrived though their fears were assuaged when they were told it was just a local tax collector who had no power to stop them. Their hopes of reaching Lhasa rose and fell with every rumour, and if all else failed and they were to be expelled they hoped to make their way out of Tibet to India via Sikkim.

The Lhasa official arrived the next morning and asked the party to stop for the day though St George refused and ordered his party to start marching. They crossed an easy river which they had been warned would be difficult though the Tibetans were now becoming more agitated and when a second river proved more difficult to cross they searched for a ford while the Tibetan escort pleaded with them to stop and begged again that he not be made to lose his head if they continued. The river was crossed and eventually they reached a camp on marshy ground where everyone was worn out, the Tibetans were still quite friendly though anxious that the Littledale caravan stop marching. The following morning the Littledales caravan rose early and continued its march towards Lhasa, snow peaks rose all around them and glaciers topped all the nullahs, through his telescope Willie saw men ahead. The high official from Lhasa had clearly arrived.

The caravan marched forward entering a basin where St George and Willie noticed many armed Tibetans hiding behind rocks on three sides of them. St George was afraid that if they stopped it would be fatal to their hopes of reaching Lhasa and so he ordered his men to load their rifles. As a bluff those that did not have weapons he stuffed the telescope and camera legs into gun covers to create a greater impression of armed strength. Teresa was upset that she had to stay back with the baggage animals and that she was not armed.

Tibetan officials approached St George and his advance party and ordered him to stop, St George refused and continued onwards, the Tibetans threatened to fight but St George knew that this would be unlikely as neither side had the stomach for dealing with an international incident. As the Lama approached St George he ordered his men not to shoot but to allow time for the parties to talk, St George was winning the bluff game. St George showed the Lama his passport and reiterated that no-one could stop him other than the chief Amban at Lhasa. The Tibetans were somewhat frightened by the document which thankfully they could not read which is just as well as it precluded any excursion into Tibet.

The Lama asked who they were and St George replied that they were eminent and powerful Englishmen and personal friends of the Emperor of China. The Tibetans still refused them permission to go on and Galwan spoke up for St George saying that if they shot St George and or any of the English party they would incur the wrath of not just the English peoples but that of the Indian empire as well.

His words seemed to rattle the Tibetans a little and St George continued on his march forward with the Tibetans begging him to stop and promising to provide them with all the supplies they could need if they would stop for just three days. St George promised to stop when they reached good grass and wood at the other side of the Goring La and he promised a 'chit' to the Lama confirming he had used his best efforts to stop the caravan. St George promised to wait at the Goring La for the Amban from Lhasa and continued onwards through much more difficult terrain. The negotiations with the Lama were certainly cordial at times and the Tibetans took a great interest in the Littledales possessions, they appeared particularly enamoured with Teresa.

A steep narrow path led round a red sandstone hill by the side of a glacier, it started to snow and when they reached the summit of the Goring La at 19,587ft a snow storm was upon them. The descent from the pass was very difficult and night had fallen, St George led the way probing the glacier with his Alpenstock to avoid any crevasses. After 14 hours of continuously strenuous and stressful going they escaped from the glacier to make a rough camp in a harrowing storm. Willie wrote in his diary *'We are the first to cross the pass which is the highest and worst we have had anything to do with..... How Teresa has stood these long marches I don't know. It is hard work up at four and not getting to camp till 7.30'*

The next morning, after a very cold and wet night, they broke camp and continued marching in rotten weather, there was no wood and the yak dung they were hoping to use for fuel was soaked. They were enclosed in a narrow gorge and the rain fell continually, the Tibetans wanted them to camp but there was still no fuel and St George wanted some meat, the Tibetans promised a sheep for them that night. It had certainly been the toughest week for the Littledales and their men, St George promised them all an extra week's wages and an extra month's wages if they managed to make it all the way to Lhasa.

The Tibetan official finally arrived and St George, although he liked the man, said he was not happy with his rank and did not wish to discuss his plans with such a lowly official. He also said that they needed a better campsite and set off with the Tibetan officials following, matters were clearly coming to a head now and as the caravan passed through a narrow gorge the Tibetans blocked their path and threatened St George saying they may as well die from his bullets as by the sword of their own officials in Lhasa. St George knew they had gone as far as they could and he had no desire to hurt these wonderful people. They were about fifty miles away from Lhasa and had come as close as any European had done for over half a century.

The caravan had reached a nullah at 16,600ft with glacier covered mountains on both sides. They were still very cold and wet and the by now relieved Tibetans brought them firewood and two sheep. There were five high ranking officials in Lhasa debating what could be done with the Littledales, St George was advised by the local headman that Darjeeling was some 25 days away however the Goring La was now closed and where they were camped would be full of snow in a month.

All they could do was wait for the Lhasa officials, their animals were tired and in very poor shape. The Tibetans brought them milk and cream, in anticipation of a meeting with the officials, St George and Willie cut each other's hair so as not to appear as beggars.

Finally the proper Lhasa officials arrived and wanted to know who the Littledales where and why they wanted to visit Lhasa. St George replied that they were English and merely wanted to visit Lhasa to pay their respects to the Dalai Lama as they had heard he was a very important and good man. The officials replied that they could not visit Lhasa as they were not of the right religion and that they must return by the way they had come. St George advised that he had a Chinese passport, the Lama replied that the Chinese passport was nothing to do with Tibet. At this time the

Chinese wanted everyone to believe they controlled Tibet and the Tibetans went along with it but in reality they controlled and made all decisions in relation to their country.

The discussions lasted for many hours without getting anywhere. The Tibetans gave them some flour though they were insistent upon them going no further and so an impasse had been reached, St George wanted the Tibetans to come up with a solution as to how they could proceed. The quickest and easiest way back was by way of Darjeeling but the Tibetans were as insistent on denying them that route as they were of them going to Lhasa. There was no way they could go back the way they had come as it would mean almost certain death for Teresa if not for all of them, St George was hoping to use their 'golden key' of bribery.

Teresa's health continued to decline and her dysentery worsened, there was no medicine for her, she was not eating and could not sleep at night. The cold, damp and altitude were having a great effect on her morale and her strength was seeping away. Nearly three weeks passed and on the 12th August Teresa celebrated her 56th birthday but she could not and did not feel like celebrating it, she seemed to be ailing fast. The rain turned to snow and it soon became apparent to the Littledales that they would have to return to India by way of Ladakh and Kashmir, a journey of 1200 miles and one that involved a perilous crossing of the Zoji La.

The Littledales were becoming desperate and agreed to return over the Goring La and head south of the Garing Tso to Ladakh, a Palki (Sedan) chair was needed for Teresa and the Tibetans offered to make one for them. St George agreed to give them 400 rupees for the essential supplies they would need. The Tibetans then changed their mind and insisted that the, by now near exasperated, Littledales go north of the Garing Tso, a much harder journey. St George agreed as he was more than desperate and really feared for Teresa's health, he was anxious that the party be underway before the onset of winter as that would take all matters out of their hands.

They left for the Goring La on the 23rd August with twenty Tibetans assisting Teresa in her Palki to the foot of the glacier where she was put on a Yak for the journey across the ice. Once over the pass Teresa was put back in the Palki and the Tibetans resumed the difficult task of moving downhill over rough terrain, St George was anxious for Teresa's safety and promised the bearers an extra two rupees a day for bringing Teresa down safely which he did but noted with disgust that the Lama kept the money with the men who did the hard work receiving nothing.

Willie had been delayed a few days at the campsite procuring more supplies and hurried to catch the main caravan, he camped at the foot of the Goring La and sent a runner to St George advising that he was on his way with the essential supplies. Willie noted the magnificence of his surroundings, the snow peaks and glaciers inspired him and as he crossed the pass he would not have known that no other European would come this way till Heinrich Harrer and Peter Aufschnaiter made their way to Lhasa while escaping India for 'Seven years in Tibet'.

Teresa began to improve slightly though she was still very frail, over the next few days they covered a good distance and eventually re-crossed the Sachu Chu but this time, thankfully, without the need for a raft as the water was much lower. Their original Tibetan escorts left to be replaced by some local Tibetans who promised to take them west where the grass and water was good and they were to be given whatever supplies they needed. The next day the party was hit by severe thunderstorm and they were pelted with huge hailstones, the wind proved to be so strong that they had to sit out a cold night as no dry fuel was available.

On the 10th September they passed the Garing Tso and turned west toward Ladakh. They were now in new country and only needed to go parallel to the ridges and not over them though they were still some 600 miles from Ladakh itself. To ease the difficulties for Teresa they made longer marches through rolling hills with snow covered mountains to the north and south. Come the 19th September they were only 464 miles from Ladakh, though two days later they had to call a rest day for the animals and they needed to replace the yaks which had not yet arrived. Teresa had a slight relapse and had such little sleep that only a short stage was possible the next day, St George observed that her dysentery was as up and down as the Tibetan landscape and a further two days rest was needed for her to settle down again. The days and nights were getting colder, their clothes were falling apart and Willie observed that his knickerbockers were becoming quite 'artistic but chilly'.

Now it was St George's turn to feel unwell and as Teresa was 'completely helpless', it was time for Willie to take charge for a while. He proved quite imaginative and with Galwan's help he managed to convince some local yak herders that Teresa was a sister of Queen Victoria so the yaks were provided without charge. They pushed their luck and eventually the local herders were supplying them with firewood and watching their animals overnight, their luck held out for several days till they reached the district of Rudok where the inhabitants proved not so gullible. On the 4th October Willie estimated that they were only 340 miles from Leh and safety. They pushed hard and fast but the pace was taking its toll on the animals, the Ravens would land on their bloodied backs and pick at the raw flesh. One day they had to cross a high pass of 17,000ft but it was to prove too steep for the Palki and Teresa had to ride a horse for a while despite the intense cold.

Teresa's health was now improving properly and she could eat a little solid food which raised the party's spirits as there were still many hard days ahead. A day was spent re-shoeing the horses and collecting ice as there would be no water for the next two marches. A problem arose at one stage when they were changing yaks when the local headman tried to order the caravan back all the way to Cherchen. Understandably St George refused and ordered his sepoy's to load their rifles, needless to say the caravan marched onward towards the border with Ladakh which was now only three days away. It was still terribly cold and St George noted ....

'If we.......forgot to take the bread to bed, we found a frozen loaf made a poor breakfast. The difficulty of dressing in the morning, with the thermometer 6,8, & 10 degrees below zero in the tent, was overcome by not undressing overnight. Wherever our breath touched the sheet was ice in the morning; and on one occasions Willie found that before he could lift his head he had to loosen his hair from the pillow, to which it was frozen fast.'

St George had to give a letter to the Munshi from Rudok saying that he had tried to stop them and the caravan then made its way to the town of Rudok which they passed two miles to the south. After crossing the plain they ascended a nullah which led to a small village where they came across the first trees and cultivation they'd seen in six hard months.

Galwan now came into his own and wrote to all his Ladakhi friends asking that when the caravan passes through their village that everything be ready and available for the Littledales assistance. The horses and donkeys were now in a really pitiful condition, thankfully the local Munshi provided yaks and the party made a fast march down the valley past a freshwater lake to camp by a fast flowing stream after an 18 mile day. They were now at 15,100ft and as they neared the border the Ladakhis put on their finest clothes, making an impressive sight.

Although they were now in British territory the weather recognised no borders and it continued to be bitterly cold. On the 27th October they reached the village of Shusall and as they were now losing height Teresa's health began to improve. They dropped below 14,000ft for the first time in six months and celebrated with a Tamasha however someone had neglected to secure the animals and the fodder was stolen with what proved to be disastrous results as ten horses would have to be left behind as they crossed the 18,400ft Chang La the next day.

The following day they reached a village where extra horses awaited them and with these they made their way to the Indus river to travel through cultivated land alongside its banks. They passed under trees and through fields of grain in a large valet with high mountains on all sides and after 17 long miles they pitched a delightfully situated camp. The next day they reached the village of Leh, the Ladakhis celebrated with their friends and families, they had been gone for over a year on one of the greatest expeditions through Central Asia ever undertaken by such a small non military party – the Littledales and Willie just slept. Galwan still had one more duty to perform for the Littledales and that was to accompany them over the Zoji La to Srinigar, his wife was most unhappy about this though he did his best to placate her. Teresa though while improving was far from being in good health and this last stage would prove a very tough undertaking. The Littledales threw a final party for their men though they could not last the entire night as the thought of reaching Kashmir as soon as possible before the winter set in was at the front of their minds.

They left at noon after packing the animals and paying their men, they made double stages on the route to make up time and were clearly anxious to beat the winter snows. The now much smaller caravan followed the same route they had taken in 1877, three days later they finally crossed into Kashmir where they met a man who had recently crossed the Zoji La, he reported snow up to 8ft deep on the summit of this perilous pass. This increased the Littledales desire to press on lest all hope be lost and they had to spend an entire winter in Ladakh which could prove disastrous for Teresa's health. On the 10th November, exactly one year after they had left Charing Cross in London they left the village of Kargil heading for the village of Dras on the north side of the Zoji La, gratefully they reached the village and collapsed in a state of complete exhaustion.

Two days later they were blessed with good weather and crossed the Zoji La though conditions underfoot were far from ideal. Willie lost his horse when it slipped and fell but thankfully he was not riding at the time, he was merely leading it and managed to get out of its way as it fell. The Littledales were relieved to reach the little guesthouse at the village of Baltal and the next day on the 16th November they finally reached Srinigar where it was raining heavily.

It was with great sadness that St George, Teresa and Willie bade goodbye to their faithful men, especially Galwan who had proved a staunch ally. Teresa was seen by a doctor who forbid any visitors such was her frailty, she herself could not say goodbye to Galwan whom she looked upon almost like a son. It had proved an incredible journey of over one year and they had come closer to Lhasa than any other westerner in nearly fifty years. Out of 170 animals taken with them only 8 had made it to Srinigar and while recognition and honours would come later as they lay in their rooms the real accomplishment from the expedition dawned upon them and that was that they had come back alive.

On the 22nd December 1895 they arrived back in England and with the last of her strength Teresa made it back to the hotel in London where they were both to stay for the next couple of months while she recovered her strength.

Their expedition proved to be highly successful and they were rightly praised from all quarters, a new grass had been discovered on the Tibetan Plateau which was named after St George. When he read his paper to the Royal Geographical Society it was so well received that it helped earn St George the prestigious Patron's Medal. St George was offered an advance of £300 for a book about their travels, which the well known publisher Edward Arnold assured him would be a classic, though as St George did not need the money nor the fame he turned the offer down.

St George received an invitation from the Russian Prince Demidoff to go hunting with him in the Caucasus which he gratefully accepted though he had to travel on his own this time as Teresa was still recovering. In December 1896 the Littledales faithful dog Tanny received a silver collar from the Royal Geographical Society for his 'pluck and fidelity' in accompanying the Littledales on their Asian travels. Teresa was delighted with the award.

Another trip to the Altai and Mongolia took place in 1897 with St George, Teresa and the Prince Demidoff entourage making their way to the Siberian – Mongolian frontier where they hunted and explored for five months and St George had managed to shoot the largest Ovis Ammon ever recorded.

For the next three years St George continued to travel and hunt though his health slowly declined as he simply refused to slow down. After returning home from a four month trip in late September 1900 he decided to sell the Oak Hill estate in Liverpool, this lay adjacent to Highfield House and was perhaps done to simplify his life at home. In 1901 another trip to the Tien Shan took place but this time St George went on his own, he was only away for four months, collecting botanical specimens for Kew and hunting Ibex.

On the 22nd January 1902 the Littledales had King Edward VII for lunch at their Wick Hill home, he took a great interest in the Littledales residence and in particular their many trophies and souvenirs from their Asian travels. They entertained the king well for he said 'I see Mr. Littledale you are not only my greatest traveller and sportsman, but you are also a connoisseur'. St George presented the king with a set of horns which were to be hung in Windsor Castle.

In 1903, St George & Teresa visited New Zealand for the hunting and then they re-visited Japan and Java before returning back to the United States stopping over to visit the President. Every year they went away for at least a few months visiting China, Alaska and in 1907 St George's last big hunting trip was to Newfoundland where he shot Caribou and little else.

Life slowed considerably now for both Teresa and St George, they entertained many guests at their Wick Hill House though still managing short trips abroad and certainly without the drama of their previous expeditions. On the 27th February 1925 Teresa and St George celebrated their golden wedding anniversary. Sadly on the 1st November 1928 Teresa died suddenly at the grand old age of 89. There can have been few women, if any, alive at that time who had travelled so much and seen so much of the Asian continent.

St George went into a deep depression for a time as he had lost his soul mate and one true companion, one who had shared so many of his adventures and exploits. St George still took the occasional trip abroad after the death of his beloved wife, in 1929 he visited the French Pyrenees and his old friends the Demidoff's tried to persuade him to go hunting in Greece. St George developed gout which afflicted him terribly leaving him fearful that he would not be able to pursue his love of salmon fishing.

In late March 1931 St George returned home after six weeks salmon fishing in Scotland in very poor health, so poorly was he that he went straight to bed. He managed to get well enough to attend a friend's funeral but the next day he had a severe attack of angina and on the 16th April 1931 while sitting up in bed talking to his nephew he suddenly keeled over and died.

The funeral took place on the 20th April and he was laid to rest next to his beloved Teresa in the cemetery of Easthampstead Parish Church.

So ended the life of one this country's greatest and most humble of explorers of the Asian continent and it is worth quoting, what should become, a classic book about the Littledales by Eilzabeth and Nicholas Clinch 'Through a Land of Extremes' ....They never wrote a book and vanished into the footnotes of history. They appeared to be just a husband and wife travelling with a little dog, but inside them was a hard core of skill and will. They pushed to their limits but could judge the line they should not cross. They barely made it out of Tibet alive, but they made it. Throughout their many expeditions, they contributed to science, geography, and to their country. The Littledales did it right.

H. W. (Bill) Tilman

There has rarely been an individual who has achieved so much in a single lifespan as Major Harold William Tilman and yet his name barely raises a murmur of recognition amongst the citizens of Merseyside. A decorated war hero in both world wars, a man who climbed the highest peak achieved by anyone else at the time in 1936 with his ascent of Nanda Devi, a man who became one of the first westerner's to be allowed into Nepal and inspect the Khumbu Icefall, which was to prove the key to the successful ascent of Everest a few years later. A man who when he became, in his words, 'too old' for high altitude mountaineering took up sailing in a small boat to the southern oceans and northern seas to frequent uninhabited islands to climb their mountains for the first time. H. W. Tilman wrote a total of fifteen books, all of which are considered classics of their genre, and yet he did it all with a minimum of fuss and a distinct lack of pomp and ceremony.

Harold William Tilman (known as Bill) was born on Valentine's Day 1898 to the family of a wealthy Liverpool sugar merchant. Bill was the youngest child of John and Adeline Tilman, they had two other children, Gertrude Adeline aged seven and Kenneth aged two. Even for the late Victorian era, theirs was a small and modest family.

Bill's father, John Hinkes Tilman left school at fourteen to become an office boy for a firm of Liverpool sugar merchants, by 1895 he had left and set up in business as a sugar broker, a trade from which he was to derive his own, not inconsiderable, fortune. The family lived for a while in Birkenhead before moving to a large house, Seacroft, on Grove Road in Wallasey resplendent with cook, maids and all the domestic baggage of the well to do. It was this world that Bill was born into and was to remain a constant for most of his life. John Tilman was a proud, dominating and forceful man who sat on the committee of the Mersey Docks and Harbour Board and he liked to have things his own way. He was as sure of himself and his place in the world as he was of the British Empire itself, however he did have insecurities and often feared the many and varied world economic pitfalls that could cause him to lose his wealth and status. He was often careful with money and this is one attribute that he clearly passed onto Bill.

Bill Tilman attended the fee paying Wallasey Grammar School and in

1909 went to Berkhampstead School in Hertfordshire. His headmaster was Charles Greene, the father of Graham Greene the novelist and Raymond Greene who was himself to become a famous mountaineer. Bill was a likeable pupil but often remote from his peers, he was quiet, thoughtful and a middling all rounder in sports. He enjoyed his time at Berkampstead though frequently returned home whenever possible, he became very close to his sister Adeline who in time would become his main link to the family home and doings when he was away.

We can never know how Bill's life would have turned out, he was certainly well read and could have gone onto university for a life of academia, however an event took place that was to change his world and perhaps changed the man he was to become forever. The First World War began when he was in his seventeenth year and it would end when he was just twenty, the events of his wartime experience between 1916 and 1918 make for fascinating reading.

Like many young men he was excited by the war, anxious to 'do his bit' he willingly joined the Royal Military Academy at Woolwich after he left Berkhampstead in December 1914. He trained as a regular army officer becoming a second lieutenant in the Royal Field Artillery on the 28th July 1915, though as he was not yet 18 he could not be sent to the front and so was posted to 2A Reserve Brigade in Preston.

Bill was fretting in Preston waiting for his call up, in letters home he wrote with a 'boy's own' enthusiasm for the thrills to come. He came home to Wallasey on January 15th 1916 and while there he received his much longed for call up papers, by the 18th January he was at Le Havre and posted to B Battery, 161st Brigade of the Royal Field Artillery. This brigade was made up of the Yorkshire 'Pals' and Bill fought with the Scarborough lads to occupy a position near the River Ancre on a relatively quiet part of the front.

Bill's initial letters home were peppered with enthusiasm for the great goings on and there is a certain naivety in his writings which would change as the war and his experiences developed. There were frequent gas alarms and they were often shot and shelled at, Bill chose to volunteer for one of the more difficult tasks of setting up an OP (observation post) which involved crawling out into no-man's land and using a telephone to communicate to his battery in the trenches behind. In March 1916 Bill was wounded slightly by a rifle grenade though he was back in the thick of it come the beginning of April. He took part in the Battle of the Somme with his battery firing over 16,000 shells in three weeks, he described the wire cutting as a total failure and the gloss of war was certainly wearing thin given the wholesale slaughter he was witnessing every day.

In January 1917 Bill received a serious injury while the British were taking the 'Munich Trench' which was part of the German line at Auchonvillers. Bill was picked to select OP's in the trench after it had been captured and was wounded as he was moving to the trench. Even so he continued to bravely work until the telephone line was established and for this he was awarded the Military Cross. He recorded his pleasure at the award in a letter home *'...I suppose it's for the FOO stunt on the 11th , though I don't quite see why. What pleases me is that it is an immediate award by the Corps Commander, and not given out as a divisional allotment like a good many are.'*

The injuries Bill received were serious and despite his initial optimism about being up and about in no time he was in hospital in France and then England for three months. He had developed a black wit while in the trenches and joked about being a 'wangler' and avoiding a return to the front, however by mid May he was back in France and ready to do what had to be done.

Bill's unit had been moved to the far west of the front line close to the Belgian coast, Bill loved to swim at the best of times and the proximity to the sea made a dip seem irresistible, unfortunately he was stung by a Jellyfish though he laughed the incident off and said the Jellyfish was clearly a German secret weapon or spy. He was now a full lieutenant and after a particularly fierce battle he wrote home-

'On the 10th I fear we met our Waterloo. What a party! It beat everything in the way of Boche bomboes we have struck, it brightened our ideas considerably. I was OC battery at the time. The Boche could not have known it (perhaps he did, though!), I was also unfortunately at the OP which was blown in as a preliminary. As you see, I did not follow the O Pippers example, although an officer of the heavies who was also there did.'

Bill was referring to the particularly high casualty rate of the observation post men, other casualties occurred and he lost his 'batman' to a bad wound, he was to feel quite lost without him. At this time he received a bar to his Military Cross though he never knew why, it is supposed to have been awarded for his stalwart efforts as temporary OC in July while under constant bombardment by the Germans.

His letters home became shorter and less frequent as they moved to Ypres, to a scene 'out of hell'. At a point only 500 yards from the German lines, Bill's unit had to move shells up by night through a landscape of shell-holes full of the dead and decaying men and horses.

In November 1917 Bill got a transfer to join 1 Battery, RHA and because of this and the extra work involved he would miss Adeline's marriage. It was becoming clear the German's were getting ready for one big final push as they had been withdrawing numbers from the Eastern Front for months and in March they finally attacked.

Bill's battery, as part of the mobile reserve the cavalry and the RHA constituted, entered a period of rapid deployment from one battlefield to another. They crossed the Somme with Bill and one gun being the last to withdraw when the Germans' attack was successful, Bill was clearly enjoying himself in a way that he would not again – in wartime – until the Second World War when he was posted to Special Operations in Albania and Northern Italy.

The Allied forces held their line and eventually counter attacked, by July the Germans had lost half a million men, the Allies even more though American reinforcements were arriving fast, the Germans knew the game was up. Bill was enjoying the last few months of the war and on the 14th November wrote home *'Hope you've all recovered from celebrating, did the Guv [his father] get blotto? We're all getting ready for the march into Germany, posh clothes, standards, pennons, bands etc.'*

They crossed the German border on the 1st December 1918 and on the 8th December he wrote 'Our dreams have been realised, a castle on the Rhine........ priceless bedrooms and a topping big dining room all done in oak and lit by about fifty electric lights all cunningly placed' He added that there was no hope of getting Christmas leave.

The war had made a lasting impression on Bill Tilman, he had seen things that a young man should never see. He was fresh out of school and found himself immersed in the horrors of the bloodiest war mankind had ever raged. Attendant to all this was the feeling of guilt, many men survived the horror of the trenches only to suffer terrible dreams and extreme guilt that they had survived while other equally good men died.

Africa

Bill was unsure as to how quickly he could resign his commission however he soon found that he could resign it much quicker than he thought, a new phase in his life was about to begin in the shape of that of a Coffee Plantation owner in Africa.

He returned to England in April 1919 but by the August he was on a ship bound for East Africa. His father had wanted Bill to follow him into the sugar trade though he resisted and relations between the two of them cooled somewhat for a time. It seemed that Bill wanted to choose his own path in life and the move to Kenya suited him for he had always been somewhat distant. The time in Africa would prove to be a period of great struggle and these were the years in which Bills solitary character would come to the fore.

Bill paid £35 for a one way passage to East Africa from Liverpool and by October he had arrived at the site of his new home, one square mile of overgrown bush land which needed to be cleared by hand. He planned to grow Flax initially then coffee, sadly he nor any of the other plantation owners realised that tea, which grew wild, was the one crop that would make them rich. The first thing Bill and a nearby plantation owner had to do was build a bridge across the river to facilitate the delivery of supplies. There was no road and only an ox cart could take them to the rail head at Lumbwa.

Initially Bill lived in a tent before building a mud and wattle hut, life was hard and surprisingly for Bill somewhat lonely. He worked away at his plot of land and took pride in the rows of coffee bushes as he sat on the porch of his house. He became an even greater reader than previously, it became something of a family legend that he would read the entire 'Everyman's Library' while in Africa, no mean feat considering there were over 500 volumes in print at that time. He did socialise with his neighbouring farmers but not too much, often preferring his own company and the sound of the bush to the mindless chatter of others.

In 1924 the terrible news of his brother's death arrived, he had been killed in a flying accident while landing his plane on the Royal Navy's first purpose built aircraft carrier. Bill returned to England for the funeral and chatted long with his sister whose marriage was failing, he felt so strongly for Adeline, who had married his close friend Alec that he went to the United States to try and resolve matters between them. However Adeline packed her bags and she and her daughters returned back to Wallasey to stay. Adeline also helped assuage the coolness between Bill and their father to the extent that in 1926 John Tilman visited Bill and chose to invest in his youngest son's enterprise, with his backing Bill bought nearly 2000 acres of land for coffee growing. He also took on a partner who was more adept at the daily farming routine, as a consequence Bill found himself with more time on his hands.

Things were going well in Africa on a financial and business level, he'd been there ten years and was slowly getting tired of attending to the plantation every day, he decided that he needed some excitement back in his life. He took to hunting game for a while, though not for the thrill of the kill but for the thrill of adventure. Bill was not a particularly great shot, though he bought a licence to shoot elephant which was expensive but could be offset against the value of the ivory in the tusks. He shot one large bull, however the whole thing, while exciting at times, did not satisfy him. There followed a short period of prospecting for gold and while it proved hard work it was not profitable and he lost money on the venture. So in 1930 he substituted his rifle for an ice-axe and although he was surely not aware of it at the time the next few months would change his life forever.

Bill wrote to a fellow coffee planter about 160 miles away from his farm as he was told by a friend that the fellow farmer was something of a climber and Bill was keen to give it a go. It was one of the most fortunate meetings in the history of mountaineering, the farmer was none other than Eric Shipton. On the last day in February 1930 the pair met in Nairobi and drove by car to Kilimanjaro (19,710ft), the highest mountain on the continent and actually an extinct volcano.

The climb was not a difficult one though Bill did suffer from the altitude and they nearly reached the highest summit on the crater rim, Kibo, after a hard struggle through soft, deep snow. Bill describes the summit of the mountain:

'On top of Kilimanjaro is a great flat-bottomed crater, possibly a mile across at its longest diameter, filled with ice and snow. The rim is gained by a notch at its lowest point, which is close on 19,000ft, and then the climber turns left-handed to follow the crater wall round to the south and west. I was not feeling very well myself; in fact I was being sick at regular intervals; but we ploughed slowly on through waist deep snow.'

Bill's appetite was whetted and six months later with Eric Shipton they attempted a much harder climb on Mount Kenya, Eric had been there the year before though it was Bill's first time on the mountain. Eric suggested to Bill that they attempt to traverse the two main peaks which had not been done before and clearly Eric thought that Bill was capable. The equipment they were using was not much different from their Victorian ancestors, nailed boots and a hemp rope – little else was available or required.

They reckoned that two weeks would be enough time to climb the peak and explore the area, on the first night they camped in a grassy glade with a roaring fire and soft grass to make a delightful open air bedroom. They marched through the forest and as altitude was gained they hit dense bamboo and then onto open moorland studded with giant Groundsel and Lobelia, at 14,000ft they reached a cave which was to be their base camp for the climb.

The next day they made a reconnaissance of the main peak and the following morning they rose at 3.00am to attempt the climb proper. First they had to traverse the Petit Gendarme, a huge monolith of rock, to get to the Grand Gendarme and so they climbed over rocks that were steep, exposed and often icy to find that thankfully the rocks of the Grand Gendarme were free of snow and ice and thus easier to climb.

The climbing was easy and they could often move together though in places the ridge was so narrow that it had to be tackled head on which made for much harder climbing, this was a concern for Eric given Bill's inexperience of mountaineering. However Bill was a quick learner and thirteen hours after setting out they reached the summit of Batian, the highest peak of Mount Kenya, Eric wrote:

At last, in place of the sharp pinnacle we had come to expect, a huge dark-grey mass loomed ahead of us. A few steps cut in the icy floor of a gully, a breathless scramble up easy rocks, and we were there beside our little cairn on the summit of Batian. There was no chance of getting down before nightfall, but no consideration of that sort could stem the flood of my joy and, let it be admitted, relief. I do not know what Tilman thought about it. He did not know the way down the south-east face. If He imagined it to involve climbing of a similar standard to that which we had just done he must have had some misgivings, though characteristically he expressed none.

They descended to a gap between the two summits and quickly climbed Nelion the lower of the two before climbing down the south-east face where Bill later wrote *'Things now began to happen'*. Eric developed a sickness caused by some meat paste he had eaten earlier and that had gone off, Bill broke then dropped his ice axe and despite the temptation to bivouac they continued down to Point Lehana where a five hour walk brought them to a hut at 2.00am. They 'holed up' for the night and at dawn they continued downwards finally reaching their camp at 8.00am totally exhausted but well pleased with their climb.

They still had a week of their holiday left and decided to attempt another peak in the vicinity called Point Piggot which was easily dispatched and afforded them fine views of Batian. On their final climb however there was an accident which nearly ended Bill's climbing career if not his life.

The two of them attempted to make one more summit, that of Midget Peak which they arrived on about midday. It began to get misty and started to snow, hurriedly they started to descend reaching a very narrow gully which Bill began to climb down while Eric belayed him to a large rock bollard. Suddenly there was a sickening jerk and the rope went taut 'as a wire hawser from a dragging ship'. There was little Eric could do as Bill had clearly taken a fall, eventually Eric decided to lower Bill as far as he could in the hope that he would land on a ledge and relieve the strain on the rope. After a few feet the rope did slacken off and Eric could climb down to where he could at least see Bill, he could see that Bill was concussed though was thankfully lucid and rational. Eric needed Bill to climb up to him as it was not possible to descend the way Bill had gone and with some effort Bill was able to do this.

They had to find a way down by abseiling and this involved cutting their 120ft rope to make slings, without a knife they had to use a sharp stone and when they finally reached the glacier their rope was a mere 43ft. Despite this accident they both had a fantastic time on Mount Kenya so much so that another trip was planned for eighteen months time in the Ruwenzori 'mountains of the Moon' range. They would have gone sooner but Eric Shipton was in the Himalaya climbing Kamet, at that time the highest mountain ever climbed by man, to keep himself fit Bill climbed the outside walls of the local farmers club.

In January 1932 Eric and Bill drove the 500 miles to the Ruwenzori and collected 14 porters to carry their supplies for this trip which was to be their biggest yet. They were now developing the idea of travelling light in the mountains with minimal equipment and, where possible, living off the land. This mode of travel had many advantages, a trip was cheaper and easier to organise and they could move much quicker in the mountains thus covering more terrain.

They followed the valley of the Bujuku River where the vegetation was everywhere dense and perpetually wet, sometimes they would walk for half an hour without touching the ground merely stepping from tree root to tree root. At just under 10,000ft they left the forest and came to an area of dense bamboo and then a forest of tree heaths, some thirty feet high and covered in fronds of lichen. After the tree heaths they entered an area of rotting Giant Grounsel which made for very tough going before they arrived at a *'damp but welcoming cave'* at 13,000ft.

On the 17th January they began their first attempt to climb in this eerie landscape where the mountains are shrouded in mist for most of the year. They established a bivouac camp at 15,000ft before pushing on to the Mount Stanley plateau, when they arrived the mist was so dense and disorientating that they decided to pitch camp and see what happened with the weather. It cleared briefly that evening giving them an opportunity to see where their route layup Alexandra Peak (16,740ft) however the mists soon closed in again and they were tent bound for three more days before it cleared slightly and they could climb the peak which they had come to climb, theirs was only the third ascent of this graceful and elusive mountain.

Next on their agenda was Margherita Peak (16,815ft) the highest peak in the Ruwenzori range. The mist was still ever present though they still set out and after a few hours wandering around on the snows they came across another set of footprints in the snow, they were somewhat bewildered that someone else was in this range of mountains as them before realising it was their own footprints they were looking at from the previous day and they were in fact ascending Alexandra Peak again. They retreated to their tent somewhat chastened but equally determined to climb the highest peak which they eventually did on the 21st January 1932.

Another climb was made on the 23rd January to Mount Stanley (16,080ft) which they climbed in a very long and tiring day. The Ruwenzori trip was a complete success as they climbed the three major summits in the range, each ascent being only the third time the mountains had been climbed and Bill noted that he and Eric had spent less time in the mountains than the Duke of Abruzzi had spent getting to the mountains from Kampala and yet they had achieved the same objectives as he at a fraction of the cost.

Later in the year Bill returned to England and went to the Lake District with his sister Adeline, they were staying in Coniston and Bill took the opportunity to go climbing on Dow Crag. There was an accident, Bill was pulled from the rock by his two companions and fell to the bottom of the crag, he was badly injured but summoned up the strength to crawl the four miles to Coniston village where he could summon help. The leader of the party died and Bill was told that as a result of his injuries he would never climb again. Not to be deterred Bill did climb again later that summer when he went to the French Alps and climbed many of the great peaks such as the Meije and Mont Blanc. He did throughout his life suffer back problems as a result of this accident however he rarely complained and stoically carried on as before.

In 1933 he made another attempt to climb Kilimanjaro, this time alone and he successfully summitted, this helped to assuage his very real fears over the problem of his seeming inability to acclimatise properly.

Later that year Bill decided to leave Africa for good and return to England, however it was not to be a conventional trip back as Bill decided he would like to leave Africa his way, no boat or car journey for him, he decided to ride back on a bicycle – a trip of some 3000 miles.

Bill bought a bike for £6.00, took no tent just a sleeping bag as he preferred to sleep out, some clothes and about twenty pounds of food though he hoped to be able to live off the land as he went.

On his first day he covered sixty miles and camped by Lake Victoria, he said:

The natives were always horrified at my sleeping out, and it was not easy to make them understand my reasons for it. On two occasions in Uganda, I heard lions grunting at night, but there was little to fear from them, while there was good deal to fear from the tick-infested huts'.

As much as anything else the locals were amazed at a white man cycling alone and many of the local headmen clearly worried in case any harm came to him while he was in their vicinity. After a week Bill crossed into the Belgian Congo (now Zaire) and had to accept his only lift from an Indian driver as the road was so rough crossing broken lava. From Lake Kivu he headed towards Stanleyville until finally he came to the great Congo rainforest, Bill wrote:

I beheld, far below me, a smooth expanse of dark olive green stretching away into the distance, flat and unbroken, like the sea. It was the Congo forest, reaching westwards to the sea and extending to four degrees north and south of the equatorial line. That afternoon I entered what was to be my environment for the next fortnight. Within this tract of low-lying virgin forest, terrifying for its silent immensity, the atmosphere is that of a hothouse, sapping the energy of both mind and body. The only road crossing this sea of vegetation in which I was now submerged stretches endlessly before one like a thin red band at the bottom of a canyon of living greenery. The dark wall of foliage towers up on either hand for nearly two hundred feet, to arch and almost meet overhead, as if to reclaim for the forest this pitiful strip that man has wrested from it.'

He had his first puncture just 200 miles short of Stanleyville and in a local village he was shown how to re-inflate the tyre using a pump and a piece of wet rag – it was hard work but apparently effective. Fifty six days out from Kampala Bill finally made out the Atlantic Ocean on the far horizon and ended his journey by train from Edea to Duala before catching a ship back to England. Bill was not overly impressed with his bicycle ride across Africa and was disappointed with the sameness and tameness of the terrain and landscape.

The bicycle still survives in a museum in Coventry and upon his return Bill wrote to the manufacturers hoping that they would send him a new one as a reward though he only received a polite letter thanking him for his interest. What Africa had given Bill, if not his fortune was mountains and friends and above all the peace of mind that he could live with himself after enduring the horrors of the First World War.

Nanda Devi

Bill's great friend Eric Shipton had been included on the unsuccessful British Everest expedition of 1933 and Eric was becoming increasingly unhappy with the large, grand and often lavishly equipped expeditions that were deemed necessary to 'conquer' the Himalayan giants. He and Bill believed that small is beautiful when it comes to travelling and they wished to explore the mountains and valleys of the Himalaya with a small select number of companions and porters, being able to move quicker and living off locally acquired supplies. Bill was later to write that if an expedition could not be planned on the back of an envelope then it is too big.

Eric wanted to organise a small expedition to the Himalaya but one that would last five months or so, by living off the land where possible and using only a few local porters he calculated that such a trip would only cost £150. Bill was keen and in fact their first expedition would prove to cost only £286 between them, they chose the Garwhal Himalaya as there would be no difficulties with permits given that the area lay largely within the Indian borders of the British Empire.

Nanda Devi (25,660ft) was an obvious choice as it was surrounded by a high mountain barrier that had never been penetrated by man, the only breach in this barrier was on its western side where the Rishi Ganga gorge cut a deep, twenty mile canyon through to the much longed for high sanctuary of Nanda Devi. This elusive sanctuary had been looked upon from the surrounding high mountains but never penetrated and it was not even known whether it could be accessed from the valleys below.

Bill and Eric engaged three porters, however they were taken on as equals to Bill and Eric unlike the previous British expeditions who looked upon them as mere employees. The Nanda Devi sanctuary was 'shut off' from the surrounding valleys by a mountain wall of some seventy miles circumference with the encircling peaks rising to over 21,000ft in places. If one were to imagine a ring donut the dough would be the mountains encircling the empty ring however in our 'donut' the ring would not be empty but would have a single peak rising to nearly 26,000ft in its centre, there was but one breach – the formidable Rishi Ganga gorge, a thin and very steep slice cutting through the metaphorical donut.

They met their porters in Calcutta and took the train to the village of Ranikhet where they rested in a government rest house and spent a day and a half procuring further supplies for the arduous journey ahead. They had brought from England some cheese and pemmican (beef jerky) to supplement their local diet of chupattis (unleavened bread) and tsampa (roasted barley), it proved to be a spartan diet to which Eric had some difficulty in getting used to, however Bill thought it was more than adequate.

They intended to place a base camp in the Rishi Gorge itself, however many of their locally engaged porters from the nearby villages deserted them as the difficulties in negotiating the lower reaches of the gorge were intimidating. The small party struggled for two days through deep snow, at times up to their armpits, till they eventually found a way into the gorge proper though route finding was a nightmare and they often had to retreat after following a 'blind alley'.

The gorge was becoming increasingly oppressive and intimidating, the steep walls seemed to overhang and almost touch overhead. The noise of the river was deafening and each day the atmosphere became more threatening, no wonder the locals became more and more fearful of the outcome. Eventually they reached a site suitable for a good base camp which would allow them a chance to explore the upper reaches of the gorge and possibly attain the sanctuary itself, Eric and Bill discharged the local Dhotial porters. They had enough food for five weeks with plenty of fuel available from the surrounding birch trees and the steepness of the gorge walls ensured they would be dry whatever the weather.

The gorge steepened dramatically above them, the walls enclosed and were formidably smooth though a series of terrifying ledges led westwards for four miles and offered a way up though it would take a total of nine days to overcome this short distance. The last mile was the worst and the river below was now rising due to the ever increasing snow melt from the glaciers within the sanctuary, retreat back down the gorge would now not be easy if not impossible. After two weeks hard struggle they finally entered the Nanda Devi sanctuary and were the first known people ever to do so, they had food for three weeks and the time was ripe to explore to their hearts content though given the lateness of the season they would not have enough time to explore the whole of the sanctuary, they decided they would have to come back again in September.

Eric wrote in his wonderful book 'Nanda Devi' '...'*it was a glorious place, and, of course, the fact that we were the first to reach it lent a special enchantment to our surroundings'*. They slept in the open on pastures strewn with wild flowers and climbed three cols on the eastern and northern rim of the sanctuary to give them a better idea of the scale of this vast mountain stronghold. They attempted the occasional new peak, climbing one of 21,000ft and failing on another at over 23,000ft, by June the monsoon had arrived and a retreat down the gorge in torrential rain led back to the Dhaoli Valley and safety.

For the following two months Eric and Bill explored the mountains and passes of the nearby Badrinath range and among other things made the first direct connection between the three sources of the River Ganges, that most famous of rivers connected to the Hindu faith. On their second crossing they nearly suffered a disaster after descending into what appeared to be a lush valley but on closer inspection proved to be a fearful gorge from which there was to be no escape after they had abseiled into it. The weather was continually wet with the terrain frightful to negotiate, at one point it took them over an hour to negotiate just 25 yards. Their food ran out and they only survived by eating tree fungus and bamboo shoots for nearly a week until they happened upon a tiny hamlet where they were able to procure some flour, cucumber and a handful of dried apricots which allowed them to make their way back to the start of Rishi Ganga gorge at the beginning of September.

Knowing the way they made it back into the Nanda Devi sanctuary in a mere eight days where they were able to survey the southern part of the range and, more importantly, discovering a viable way up the mighty Nanda Devi itself by the southern ridge.

They attempted the line but had clearly not brought enough equipment for such a major ascent and after their labours of the past few months whatever equipment they had left proved rather threadbare and worn to say the least. They did have enough equipment though to find another way out of the basin and focussed their efforts at the lowest point of the encircling ridge. They climbed a 23,360ft peak to look down upon a col some 5000ft beneath them, they managed to descend with no mean difficulty and on the way the climbing they encountered was to prove the hardest of the whole expedition.

The expedition was now over and both Eric and Bill were very pleased to discover that they had both spent £7 less than their planned budget.

Plans were made to re-visit Nanda Devi in 1935 however the Tibetan government had decided to allow the British access to Everest again and so Bill and Eric went to the Everest region, of which more later.

Another British expedition was organised for 1936, the 1935 expedition was merely considered a reconnaissance, and Bill was surprised not to be invited as the Mount Everest committee considered he was too much of a liability at altitude – how wrong he was to prove them in 1936. Eric went to Everest with reluctance as he despised the 'siege' mentality of such big trips preferring smaller teams that were more cohesive and faster than an unwieldy slow train of climbers and porters following a line of fixed ropes. A group of young Americans were toying with the idea of attempting Kanchenjunga (28,160ft), the third highest mountain in the world, however access and permission were difficult to obtain and so Bill suggested that they might like to consider Nanda Devi instead.

Once permission had definitely been refused by the authorities for

Kanchenjunga the party wholeheartedly put their efforts into Nanda Devi. In April 1936 Bill made his way to India ahead of the main party in order to make the necessary preparations. He had difficulty in recruiting sherpa's as many had been seconded to the big Everest expedition that Eric was on. Although Kanchenjunga was denied them Bill did visit Sikkim and tried to cross the Zemu Gap, a high pass on the Kanchenjunga massif, they made their high camp at 18,000ft at the top of an icefall, Bill wrote:

Pasang Kikuli joined in the assault next morning, and together we hacked a big staircase up the 30 foot of steep ice, a job which took two hours. Above that we were able to kick steps, but there were only a few inches of snow overlying the ice, and we realised that when the sun had risen and done its work the snow covering would not hold. A little higher we came to a horribly frail bridge over a deep crevasse.

They crawled over this and so frail did the bridge look that Bill seriously doubted it would hold the weight of a man with a rucksack, the final ice wall loomed steeply overhead and they decided to beat a retreat while they still could. They had to make some frightening abseils over the ice cliffs back to their base camp and Bill, keen as ever to be going, made his way back to Darjeeling to meet the first of the Americans who had just arrived in India.

From Darjeeling Bill made his way to Bombay and then Ranikhet intending to start ferrying supplies up the Rishi Ganga to save time before the rest of the Americans arrived. Bill was not happy man at this point as he had lost his pipes and was suffering from a bad bout of diarrhoea. As they struggled up the gorge, they relied mainly on tree roots and tufts of grasses to aid their ascent. They came to a smooth slab of rock which they ascended and began hauling the porter loads up the smooth rock when Bill descended the rope to a small ledge in an effort to hurry things along, his words alone are best presented to create the picture:

To superintend this I was standing on a narrow ledge about twenty feet above the floor of the gully and, thick-headedly enough, almost under the rope. Things then happened quickly. Gazing at an ascending load I was petrified to see a large flake of rock, probably loosened by the rope, sliding down the wall straight for me. Whether it hit me, or whether I stepped back to avoid it, is only of academic interest because the result was the same, and next instant I was falling twenty feet onto the slabs, head first and face to the wall, for I distinctly remember seeing it go past. Hitting the slabs I rolled for a bit and then luckily came to a rest before completing the

1400-odd feet into the river.

Bill wrote in his diary '*I thought I was finished but stopped rolling before the slabs. Left thigh and knee bruised. Left shoulder wrenched, ditto neck and hands badly cut. Altogether a pretty mess but might have been worse'.* He also realised later that he had cracked a rib.

He eventually managed to make his way back with the others to Ranikhet, he walked slowly and, in his own words, feeling very sorry for himself. In truth he could barely walk and in places had to be lowered down the steep bits. When they reached Ranikhet on the 25th June Bill was feeling much better which he attributed to the walk out and there he met the rest of the party and their supplies from Delhi. Originally they had planned to climb Kanchenjunga with a party of twelve, now they were attempting a lower peak with less climbers, basically they had too many supplies and so Bill decided what was needed and what they could afford to leave behind. A culling of the equipment took place which would have left his British friends, apart from Eric, aghast but the Americans were in complete agreement with his choices. The Americans were used to a greater degree of self reliance in their own mountains and the combing out of all but the essentials was carried out in a spirit of complete harmony.

On the 10th July they left Ranikhet and made their way to the small village of Garul where they engaged some local Dotial porters, the same people who had helped them so valiantly back in 1934. They then made their way to Mana and engaged ten more men. It continued to rain as they made their way back up the Risha Ganga over terrain that Bill now knew well enough though extra difficulties presented themselves to Bill and his party as the river had swollen badly due to the near constant rainfall and thus the numerous crossings that had be made were much more difficult. Due to the difficulties many porters left before they reached the sanctuary and the logistical problems increased as they needed to get as many supplies to base camp as humanly possible otherwise the mountain would not be climbed. They re-packaged many loads and even the climbers themselves had to carry full packs, normally the climbers go largely un-laden to save their energies for later on but in this instance they had no choice.

Thankfully on the 7th August they reached the site for their base camp in the Nanda Devi sanctuary itself though supplies were spartan Bill calculated that they had enough for an assault on this most beautiful and isolated of mountains.

They established camp one at 19,000ft with the climbers carrying forty pounds each, a previously unheard of feat for a sahib! The sherpa's carried sixty pounds though they were not expected to summit the mountain. Once at camp one they were engulfed in a blizzard and lost a day's climbing, they set out again on the 11th August hoping to establish camp two at over 20,400ft which was situated on the ridge proper, the rock was loose and the snow conditions were less than ideal. An American, Charles Houston and the English climber T. Graham Brown climbed up to 21,400ft to establish camp three while the other climbers and sherpa's ensured that enough supplies could be brought up to camp two to aid a continuing ascent. Thankfully the weather held good while all this was going on and by the 21st August all the climbers had been to this camp to acclimatise and ensure that there was enough food and other supplies.

Most of the climbers were now suffering to some degree with the altitude and some of the sherpa's had dysentery. One Sherpa died at base camp which broke the spirit of the rest who largely deserted and so the climbers were all on their own, they elected Bill as the leader, prior to this all decisions were arrived at by a sort of democratic consensus. The first thing he had to deal with however was the drastic loss of the expedition tea over a precipice at camp two, tea being a valuable aid to avoiding dehydration at altitude.

Camp four was established but only 500ft above camp three and Bill knew that if they could establish a bivouac camp a couple of thousand feet higher then the summit would be in reach. A blizzard held them up again though when it cleared they managed to stock camp four with enough supplies for two weeks, Bill decided that Noel Odell and Charles Houston were the strongest climbers and that they would form the first summit team.

On the 25th August five climbers, including Bill, set out from camp four carrying light sacks of only 15lbs each and as a consequence they managed to gain an extra 1500ft which enabled Odell and Houston to pitch the highest camp at somewhere around 23,500ft. The next day was quiet and Bill fretted in camp four about who should form the second summit pair, the American Loomis complained with frostbite so he was out of the reckoning and as Bill pondered about their prospects he heard a shout from above that startled him and the others.

Two ascending climbers had also heard the yell from the top camp where they heard Odell shout *'Charlie is killed'* they gathered some belongings and made their way up to the top camp by a difficult climb made no easier by their anxiety at what they would find at the top camp.

They found to their relief that Noel Odell had actually shouted that *'Charlie is ill'* as a result of a bad tin of corned beef. The climbers, including Charlie Houston, began to descend though Bill noted in his diary that he 'fortunately had some extra clothes with me'. He would get the first crack at the summit after all with Noel Odell. The next day the weather was still good and so they climbed back up making a higher bivouac at about 24,000ft

On the 29th August they rose early and began climbing the steep snow and rocky ridge ever upwards towards the summit. At 1.00pm they reached the final rocks where Noel Odell took over the lead and, avoiding a small avalanche, they reached the summit of Nanda Devi at 3.00pm, Bill wrote:

It was difficult to realise that we were actually standing on top of the same peak which we had viewed two months ago from Ranikhet, and which had then appeared incredibly remote and inaccessible, and it gave a curious feeling of exaltation to know we were above every other peak within hundreds of miles on either hand. I believe we so far forgot ourselves as to shake hands on it.

Although man had climbed higher on Everest this was the highest mountain ever ascended by man at that time and it made Bill quite famous back in England , he was to find himself on the front pages on many newspapers. His natural reserve had dropped on the summit when he allowed Odell to shake his hand and for the rest of his life Bill recalled this expedition as his most successful and rewarding mountaineering trip. On the way out of the sanctuary he and Charles Houston, who had now recovered from his illness, made the first crossing of Longstaff's Col as an alternative way of escaping the sanctuary.

Bill wrote later about the expedition *'The game is more than the players of the game, and the ship is more than the crew'*. He made a lifelong friendship with Charles Houston and Peter Lloyd and, though he was not to know it at the time as he made his way over Longstaff's Col, his father had passed away and his life would take yet another twist as the financial independence he would inherit would leave him free to pursue a life of adventure and exploration, he would certainly make the most of it.

The 1935 Everest Reconnaissance Expedition

Upon Eric and Bill's return from Nanda Devi in 1934 they had hoped to return the following year but with the Tibetan Governments approval, an attempt could be made on Everest from the North Side and Eric proposed to the Mount Everest Committee in London to lead a small reconnaissance trip in 1935 with the view of making a full attempt in 1936.

What followed has gone down in the annals of mountaineering as one of the most productive, successful and impressive Himalayan expeditions of all time.

Eric persuaded The Mount Everest Committee to part with a sum of £200 per head for six climbers to visit the Everest region and he was confident of putting a party on the north col of Everest at a fraction of the costs incurred by the previous Everest expeditions. He and Bill were determined to prove that the best way to climb the higher mountains of the Himalaya was with a small party that could move quicker and with less demand on the local population and resources.

Eric and Bill were already dubbed 'the terrible twins' due to their frugal approach though they were also known to care as much for exploration than summit-bagging. Bill was not overly pleased to receive an invitation from Eric to join the expedition as although he wanted to climb Everest, he thought six was too great a number of climbers!

To keep the costs of the expedition down Eric took advice on diet and nutrition and worked out a menu of what some described as extreme monotony even if it was practical and sufficient for their needs. There were six British climbers augmented by local sherpa's including a young Tenzing Norgay, at only twenty years of age and on his first expedition, who could have foretold what lay in store for this young man.

The team left Darjeeling at the end of May 1935 and crossed a pass travelling west across the Tibetan border until they reached the town of Sar. They rested at this altitude for two weeks exploring the local mountain ranges, under the guise of an acclimatisation process, when really Eric and Bill were indulging their new found passion for exploring rather than climbing mountains. From where they were they could see Everest in the far distance and many people believed that if Bill and Eric had thrown 'caution to the wind' and headed straight for Everest they could have possibly climbed it and proven their critics wrong, as some say they could have ' pulled of the greatest mountaineering coup of all time'.

They reached the Rongbuk monastery in early July, the monsoon had broken and none of the climbers were in good health. The Tibetan plateau is very high and the air is dry, it is all too easy to develop a cough which can last for weeks and seriously impede your chances on the mountain. They left base camp at the monastery on the 6th July and made camp three at 21,000ft on the 9th July, 500ft higher they fell upon a food dump from the 1933 expedition which augmented their supplies.

All the climbers were now ill, they traversed out on the steep snow slopes leading to the north col where they hoped to establish camp four and which was duly accomplished on the 12th July. Bill was too ill to be in this party so he with a colleague climbed the Lhakpa La and from there managed to climb a couple of previously unclimbed summits. The north col team had to beat a hasty retreat in the face of deadly snow conditions that frequently avalanched and threatened to overwhelm the whole party. Eric had achieved what he had set out to do though in that he put a party of climbers on the north col of Everest at a fraction of the previous cost.

When the parties came together again they went on what has been described as 'an orgy of peak bagging' climbing a total of twenty six peaks over 20,000ft and furthermore they managed to keep within their tight budget, the expedition was rightly heralded as one of the most successful Himalayan expeditions of all time.

Eric returned to Everest in 1936 where the expedition as a whole achieved little due to the early onset of the monsoon and some truly horrible snow conditions on the mountain. However, rather surprisingly, Bill was given his chance at Everest in 1938 when he was appointed leader of a small group of experienced climbers. Though before we refer to that in any detail there is the small matter of another expedition to deal with which took place in 1937.

Blank on the Map

The Karakoram range of mountains, now in modern day Pakistan, has the greatest concentration of high mountains anywhere in the world. When on Everest in 1936 Eric planned a trip to explore the basin of the Shaksgam River, an unknown region of several thousand square miles and on the available maps to the area they were marked simply blank and unexplored, an enticing prospect.

Bill and Eric planned to go with only two other westerners, Michael Spender and John Auden. They managed to easily secure funding for the entire four months from the Royal Geographical Society, easily as the total amount required was only £855 for the four of them plus seven sherpa's and four local baltis.

The party arrived in India in late April and made their way to Rawalpindi where they met their sherpa's on the 27th April. The sherpa's were good strong men, reliable and devoted as well as good friends to the westerners. They marched up the Sind Valley to Skardu where they bought further supplies and shortly after the party crossed the Indus which marked the divide between the Himalaya and the Karakoram. They made their way up a difficult valley to Askole finally reaching this last outpost of civilisation on the 24th May after a month of hard travel.

The expedition now began properly and the logistical problems soon became apparent in that they had over two tons of supplies to keep the fifteen of them alive for the next two months at high altitude. Clearly porters were required and Eric calculated that 104 would be needed in total, including porters to carry food for the other porters etc. Another two tons of flour were needed for their food and a complex plan was set in motion where supplies could be dropped along the route for the return journey thus allowing porters to be dispensed with at each stage.

The local tribesmen were initially reluctant to have anything to do with this small party of seemingly poor Englishmen, previous expeditions to the area had been lavishly equipped and money was not a problem and yet here were a group of apparently wealthy westerners living as frugally as themselves. Eventually they realised that a bird in the hand, so to speak, was better than nothing at all so that they agreed to work for them as porters.

The party left Askole on the 26th May under a heavy sky and near constant rain to make their way up the impressive Biafo Glacier a few hours away where they made their first camp. Bill seemed to come down with a fever as did Sen Tenzing, one of their sherpa's, and Eric decided to leave Auden behind with them till they recovered while he and Spender would push on. The terrain became harsher and the Balti porters were increasingly unhappy in having to spend cold nights sleeping on the bare glacier, they feared that the Englishmen would take them to a place where they would not be able to return without assistance. Morale was low and a few days later Eric paid off the remaining balti porters so there were only the sherpa's and some tougher Skardu men left to carry the supplies.

A week later Bill and Sen Tenzing had recovered enough to catch the main party up and they all established a base camp nine miles from the Shaksgam River, Eric discharged all but four of the Skardu men, the exploratory side of the expedition could now began in earnest. They had enough food for three and a half months and had an area of some 18,000 square miles, amongst some of the highest mountains in the world, to survey, map and explore.

For the next nine weeks they wandered to their hearts content, climbing many unclimbed peaks and passes. Their first objective was to survey the pass across the Aghil mountains which had once been crossed by the legendary Sir Francis Younghusband in 1887, Bill, Eric and their party were the first westerners to see it since that time and they accurately located and surveyed it. Bill and Eric then went to look for the Zug (false) Shaksgam and to do so they had to climb a 20,000ft peak to get a good view. They managed to find and follow the river where it joined the Yarkand and were able to re-cross the Shaksgam River just before the water levels became too high due to the summer ice melt.

The next ten days they spent on the glaciers surrounding K2, the second highest mountain in the world, where they watched avalanches falling in one 12,000ft swoop from the summit dome. They also solved the riddle of the 'snow lake' which had been discovered by Sir William Martin Conway in 1892 who named it, he believed it to be a snow basin of some 300 square miles. The well known Himalayan wanderers 'the Workmans' believed it to be an ice-cap which was unknown outside of the Polar regions, Bill and Eric wanted to find out exactly what it was.

The party of westerners divided into three teams, a necessary decision given the size of the area to be surveyed and it was Bill, travelling west with two sherpa's, who crossed the Snow Lake and ascertained it to be not an ice-cap but one of seven contiguous glaciers.

Eventually Bill, with his faithful sherpa's, broke through the great rock wall to the south of the Hispar Pass and on their journey they came across some footprints in the snow of an animal, they followed the tracks for over a mile and measured them. The tracks were sixteen inches apart and the footprints themselves were 6-8 inches in diameter. This was Bill's first sighting of a Yeti track and while it is not known whether Bill believed in the existence of this fabled creature, his love of adventure, mischief and mystery suggests that he would surely want to believe.

The three teams re-united in Kashmir in September 1937 looking more like tramps in their tattered and worn clothes than hardy mountaineers and explorers. What they had achieved in such a short time though was remarkable and they were highly praised by such august bodies as the Royal Geographical Society in London.

Eric and Bill were seriously enamoured with the Karakoram and considered returning the following year, however the Mount Everest Committee had secured funding for another small expedition to the mountain. Bill was invited to the committee to discuss such a trip along with Eric, Frank Smythe and Charles Warren, the committee were clearly coming round to Bill and Eric's approach of small lightweight expeditions as a way of climbing the Himalayan giants.

Everest 1938

The failure of the 1936 Everest expedition had used up all available funds held by the committee and it was only a £2000 advance from the publishers of the subsequent book that enabled the committee to clear its debts. They were reluctant to ask an increasingly sceptical public for more funds given that there had been so many failures and it was only through the generosity of Tom Longstaff, the doctor from the 1922 expedition, that the committee could consider another expedition. Longstaff made a gift of £3000 to the committee on the proviso that either Bill or Eric were confirmed as leader, and that there would be no advance publicity. The committee decided on Bill as leader of the 1938 Everest expedition and he set about gathering his team and with Eric they worked out a budget of £2360 for seven climbers.

Bill was persuaded to take bottled oxygen which went against all his principles though perhaps at the back of his mind was his previous struggles at extreme altitude. The team of climbers were subjected to the Tilman / Shipton diet of two pounds per man per day and plain food at that though high in carbohydrates which help at altitude as it is easier to turn such food into energy. Notably Bill refused a free crate of champagne though he did accept a case of tinned tongue, Noel Odell despised the rations and criticised Bill for his choices, Bill looked upon porridge and soup as a luxury food.

Bill was a born leader, and was very hard on those who were on expeditions with him however he was equally as hard on himself. One can attribute this to the horrors of the First World War where he encountered true suffering and hardship and in part perhaps to the attitude of his stern Victorian father. Bill kept up a wall of seeming toughness and indifference to suffering, incompetence he could accept to a degree but complaining was an absolute anathema to him.

The party arrived at Sikkim on 3rd March 1938 and they marched up the Tista valley into Tibet, their aim was to reach the Rongbuk glacier earlier than previous expeditions in the hope of reaching the mountain before the monsoon broke which deposited large amounts of snow on the route making it more dangerous, difficult and nearly impossible to climb.

They reached Rongbuk on the 6th April and saw that the summit of Everest was clear though it was being battered by strong winds, they had acquired a fine bunch of sherpa's, including the young Tenzing Norgay, and quickly they set up base camp. Come the end of April camp three was established under the north col though Bill was suffering from a bout of flu. They had a month's supply of food at this camp but could go no higher as many of the team were weak with cold and flu, probably caused by their poor and sparse diet. Bill decided that everyone should beat a retreat to a lower altitude in the Kharta Valley where the team could recuperate.

At the beginning of May they made their way back to base camp only to be greeted by the horrifying sight of Everest's summit covered in snow, the monsoon had clearly broken early and it was a bitter blow to their hopes of climbing the mountain. They returned back up to camp three and tried to force the route even higher, Eric and Frank Smythe were Bill's favoured summit pair and he had deliberately held them back from the more strenuous duties in an effort to keep them as fresh as possible. On the 24th May Eric and Smythe made it up to the north col together with twenty six heavily laden porters, they deposited their loads and beat a retreat to camp three. The next day Bill and Smythe made it up to the north col but saw the peak covered in soft snow and so they too returned to the lower camp.

On the 28th May Bill with Odell, Warren and Oliver occupied camp four again and the next day they made their way up on to the north ridge of Everest eventually coming to a halt at 24,500ft at 1.00pm. At 2.00pm they were back at camp four and by 3.30pm the snow started to fall eventually depositing an accumulation of over a foot deep.

On the 6th June they started up the ridge again and were surprised to find the snow had hardened, they made it to camp five and deposited their loads while Eric and Smythe set up a camp. The sherpa's were exhausted as they descended with Bill to camp four however they still managed to make another carry the next day while Eric and Smythe tried and succeeded in establishing camp six at 27,200ft on a gentle scree slope below a feature known as the 'yellow band'.

The next day more snow fell and above camp six it was deep and powdery, Eric decided it would be foolish to go any further under such treacherous conditions and so they beat a retreat to camp five where they met Bill and Peter Lloyd who decided to carry on up past camp six eventually stopping at 27,400ft just 1800ft below the summit of the highest mountain on earth. This was as high as any of them would get and the expedition had failed. However given the size of the team and expense incurred it was a remarkable achievement and Bill later wrote:

There can be no doubt that one day someone will reach the top of Everest, and probably he will reach it quite easily, but to do so he must have good conditions and fine weather, a combination which we now realise is much more rare than it had been supposed by the pioneers on the mountain. It is difficult to give the layman much idea of the actual physical difficulties of the last 2000ft of Everest. The Alpine mountaineer can visualise them when he is told the slabs which we are trying to climb are very similar to those on the Tiefenmatten face of the Matterhorn, and he will know that though these slabs are easy enough when clear of ice and snow they can be desperately difficult when covered in deep powder snow. He should also remember that a climber on the upper slopes of Everest is like a sick man climbing in a dream.

This was the last time Everest would be attempted from the northern Tibetan side for many decades, war was soon to engulf Europe, after the war China would invade Tibet and access would not be granted to westerners for many years.

Bill decided not to return straight to England but chose to renew his battle with the Zemu Gap on the slopes of Kanchenjunga. This time he managed to get to the top without too much difficulty as he had decided to cross the gap from the other side, Bill also found more Yeti tracks. The problem was now on how to get down the other side which they had failed to climb in 1936. Bill wrote:

From our visit in 1936 I knew of the steep ice-wall on the south side, and had taken the precaution of bringing 240ft of Alpine line. Even so on first looking over the top I got a shock. There was a wall, over 200ft of it, and overhanging sufficiently to prevent one from seeing where one would land. We could not use the rope down this. However, search revealed a very steep and narrow gully descending from the junction of the crest of the pass and the precipitous shoulder of Simvu. Between two runnels of ice was a thin ribbon of snow.

The snow was loose and wet as they made their way down the near vertical wall, Bill went first and hacked out a ledge as he reached the end of the rope so that the others may descend and in this manner they reached the bottom. The ice-wall now facing them, which had defeated them last time, had changed out of all recognition and a great chasm had opened up before them. In Bill's words they had 'burned their boats' and they had to go on. They had to descend into the chasm and find a way out the other side a feat easier to say than to do, however it was accomplished with greater ease than expected, Bill had now made the first recorded crossing of this precipitous pass. He wrote,

:..One more Himalayan season was over. It was time to begin thinking of the next. 'Strenuousness is the immortal path, sloth is the way of death.'

In early 1939 many people realised that another war was becoming inevitable and Bill was among them. That is why he declined Eric's offer of another trip to the Karakoram mountains as he wanted to stay in closer touch with events. That did not mean Bill did not wish to visit the mountains he just chose to visit those that were easier of access. He went to the Assam Himalaya to attempt an ascent of Gori Chen (21,450ft). In March Germany invaded Czechoslovakia and the path to war had begun, the trip was not a good one as Bill contracted cerebral malaria as did one of his porters who was sadly to die as a result, he abandoned the expedition which he later described as an 'unqualified failure'.

Bill returned to England and to life in the army where he had re-enlisted as a gunnery officer, for the next six years his path in life was settled for him. That he managed any climbing during the war is testament to his determination to salvage something of worth from the futility of this the second global conflict taking place in his lifetime.

The Second World War

His regiment, 32nd Field Regiment of the Royal Artillery, was sent to France in the autumn of 1939 as part of the British Expeditionary Force. Come April 1940 the German's started to attack the west by invading Norway before then turning their attention to the Netherlands and Belgium, as in the First World War France was surely to follow. Sure enough the British forces were overwhelmed and they bid a hasty retreat to Dunkirk, once back in Britain Bill was promoted to the rank of Major, the highest rank he would hold, and put in charge of 120 Battery in Suffolk.

Not one to want to miss out on any action Bill sought a transfer to where he could be of some use and despite a near miss in being sent to Singapore of which he knew nothing, he managed to extricate himself at the last minute and found himself bound for North Africa and the Gulf where he knew at least something of the country and the people.

At first he found himself in Iraq after a trip up the Persian Gulf, after a week in Basra they drove up the valley of the Tigris to Mosul. Despite the thinness of their numbers and poor equipment, some of which was left over from the First World War, they were to pursue a policy of containment which proved nigh on impossible given the enemies strength though for now it was quiet and Bill's unit settled down. So quiet did it prove that Bill even managed to plant a small vegetable garden around his tent in Mosul.

The daily work was routine, the type that Bill detested the most and he began to ruffle the feathers of his superiors, when he got the chance of disappearing into the mountains for a week he relished the prospect even if it was under the guise of checking charcoal prices. He and two other soldiers headed for Amadia in February 1942 where they climbed a peak 'almost of Alpine standard'. On another occasion he took up the offer of a brigadier to inspect the defences in Iran and managed to climb another peak, Bisitun, at over 10,000ft, on the descent he partook of one of his 'memorable bathes' for which Bill would become a true aficionado, Bill wrote:

To qualify, the first essential is for the bather to be really hot and tired. Then, if not sea-water, the water must be clear, deep and cool (or otherwise have some unusual compensating feature), so that as it closes over one's head the whole body seems to absorb its clean , refreshing goodness. *To make this clear, a bathe in the Dead Sea, for example, would not be refreshing but might qualify as unusual. Lastly, and this is important, one must be stark naked, with no clinging costume to impair the unity of body and water.*

By May Bill had been moved with his regiment to Habbaniya, west of Baghdad. The North African campaign was not going well for the British and it was only to be a matter of time before Bill and his regiment were to be called for their stint at the front and so after only seven days at Habbaniya the orders came through. Bill with his regiment began to move south and west towards Syria, for the next few months, until the defeat of the Germans at El Alamein, it was to be all fighting.

They wandered the North African desert picking fights with the enemy and often having to use their own initiative as contact with the 'interfering HQ' was difficult. It was warfare that suited Bill and his temperament, the kind of getting out of tight spots he had long known and understood in his mountaineering exploits. He worked closely with his men and they respected him equally however all good things must come to an end and eventually they had to dig themselves in on the Ruweisat ridge where they 'connected themselves by telephone to inquisitive and interfering headquarters from division downwards'.

This was to be the start of the first phase of El Alamein, the defensive positions the British held and Rommel failed to break through, the British then counter attacked with Bill's unit being one of the many that would eventually sweep the Germans out of North Africa and by the end of the year the British were triumphant. They moved westwards until they reached Tunisia where Bill saw something that he had longed to see for the past few months, a mountain.

We dropped our trails more or less where we stood. My choice of site for Regimental HQ was possibly influenced by the presence of two German field kitchens, one with a copper full of stew ready for dishing up, the other containing a slightly overdone rice pudding. .... Naturally, since coming into those parts from the 8th Army front I'd had my eye on Zaghoua, the only mountain I had seen since Bisitun. Many long broken limestone ridges help to form a striking mass which on the north and west ridges, rises abruptly from the Tunis plain.

He set off with one of his battery commanders after promising his CO he would be back before dawn, they reached the summit just before dawn and polished of some German rations which proved much tastier than the

British ones they were used to.

The North African campaign was now over and the invasion of Italy was being planned, Bill was now forty five years of age and not ready to sit back and relax. He did not want promotion and signified his intention to remain as a Major for the duration of the war, he was thus passed over for promotion, a signal was received at HQ asking for volunteer officers who wished to be put forward for special training, involving their being dropped behind enemy lines. Bill thought it better to 'Rein in Hell than serve in Heaven' and wrote out his application.

One may have thought that at forty five Bill would be too old for these 'special operations' however the opposite proved to be the case. The attributes required were resourcefulness, great fitness and the ability to work on one's own for long periods, Bill was highly qualified and capable on all counts, he had no trouble being selected.

Bill's special training took place in Haifa and though he enjoyed it he was by far the oldest member on the team, by August 1943 he had passed the course and was sent to Libya from where the Halifax aircraft would drop him off in occupied Europe on a mission codenamed Sculptor. There was Bill and two NCO's on the drop, one was an expert at bridge-blowing the other a wireless operator. On the 9th August after a four hour flight from Derna they reached the drop zone above Albania, Italy had invaded Albania but now she was on her knees and ready to throw the towel in at any moment (or so they thought) and Bill believed that their job would be one of stopping the Albanians from massacring the Italians, how wrong he was proved to be.

Albania was a harsh and Bill decided an unhappy country:

If it is true that 'happy is the nation that has no history', then Albania must be one of the unhappiest. Her history is an unbroken record of invasion, oppression, and wrong by the Turk, Greek, Austrian, Serbian, Bulgarian and German. Few countries can have been so ravaged and so subjected to oppression at the hands of its stronger neighbours, and yet have retained its will for independence unbroken as the Albanians for 500 years.

Bill and his companions were dropped in southern Albania and what followed was twelve months of cat and mouse mayhem with the Albanian partisans fighting against initially the Italian and then the German armies. They helped equip and train the Albanian partisans, when they felt they could trust them and took part in raids, blew up bridges etc. Bill surprisingly seemed to get on better with the communist Albanians rather than any of the other tribal / political factions. Surprisingly as although usually coy about his political persuasions Bill was a natural conservative.

Bill liked the Albanians a lot, for what they lacked in weapons they made up for in spirit and he was determined to help them. On the 8th September the Italians collapsed and Bill with his fellow men had only a short time in which to get as many arms off the Italians as possible before the Germans arrived as they surely would. Bill wrote a cheeky letter to one Italian General asking him to meet with him to discuss surrender terms, unbeknown to Bill another rival Albanian partisan with a different political / cultural outlook from his own group also wrote a letter asking the Italians to surrender their arms to them. This was a continuing problem for Bill in that there were many Albanian factions and it was impossible to unite them all which in many ways helped their invaders, on some occasions the Balli's preferred to aid the German invaders rather than help their own Albanian communists!

Bill decided, after fruitless negotiations, to cut off the water supplies to the Italian Garrison but the Italians deserted the Garrison and burned all they could before making for the coast and a return to Italy. Bill chased after them but with a slight diversion to the Greek frontier to blow a bridge which would prove useful to the Germans when they came, he hoped to delay their arrival as long as possible. He caught up with the Italian General and his troops and they agreed to surrender their weapons apart from their small arms, the Albanians and Bill would need them as the Germans advanced and Bill wrote:

On the morning of 1 October, I watched the long-expected German column drive past. From the monastery spur several miles of white ribbon of road were in sight before it disappeared round a corner just short of the bridge about to be blown. Headed by motor-cyclists and staff cars, sixty troop carrying vehicles and two 115mm guns crossed the bridge at the bottom of the valley.

The bridge was blown and a battle ensued where the German's exacted a cruel revenge by burning to the ground a local village that had been captured. Their supplies by Halifax bomber aircraft were still getting through however, so they were well provided for and were able to continue to train the Albanian partisans though they were becoming increasingly agitated at the lack of a British invasion to help them.

Eventually the allies managed to get five mobile brigades established in Albania and they located a small sea bay where arms and supplies could be delivered without being discovered by the Balli's or the German's.

Bill eventually came to the conclusion that only the communist LNC could be trusted and he sided with them, by the spring of 1944 the Germans were close on their tail, Bill had been ten months in Albania and though he was far from tired of it he was weary of the anomalous position of the British effort and support, belatedly the British command realised the Balli's were not worth supporting and so they decided to support the Royalist Zoggists. For Bill this was academic as on the 22nd May he was evacuated from Grava Bay and of the Albanian missions he later wrote that he was convinced that the British support for the communist LNC was just and expedient, however the goodwill from such support was lost by the British support for the other factions, Bill always believed that the only people worth backing in Albania were the LNC, this support though got Bill the sack.

By August 1944 Bill had received another offer, a chance to fight with the Italian partisans in Northern Italy where the Germans were continuing to hold on, someone had clearly noticed that Bill got on with the communists and the Italian partisan movement was largely communist-inspired.

Bill spent a couple of years in north-east Italy with the partisans and this episode of warfare was the one that he looked back on with fondness, if that is an appropriate word for warfare, at the friends he made, and kept in touch with for the rest of his life. After the war Bill was given the freedom of the city of Belluno in recognition of his efforts in liberating the citizens from their German oppressors. There is a street in the city named after him and a trekking path named in his honour, Bill clearly left a good impression on the local populace.

The British and Americans dropped many men behind the enemy lines to aid the partisans as German resistance was strong, the Germans wished to concentrate the allies efforts on Italy in the hope that they could weaken their efforts in the French and low country campaigns.

On the 31st August Bill and a companion were parachuted behind enemy lines in a mountainous region of northern Italy, unfortunately Bill made a bad landing and hurt his back again, his companion thought that the reason for the bad landing was that Bill had stuffed the pockets of his parachute suit with books to read for the coming winter. What was worse none of their supplies and kit made the drop successfully, and for the next four months they had no other successful air drops so they had to rely heavily on the generosity of the partisans, they were not found wanting in that regard.

Bill's two companions, John Ross and Victor Gozzer, were probably the two people who got closest to Bill as a person in his whole life. Indeed Bill kept a close correspondence with the two of them for the rest of his life and there was a deep mutual respect and affection between them all, warfare can do that. Their objective was to act as 'liaison officers' between the various factions of the partisans though it was hard to have any real say as their lack of equipment and weapons did not exactly lend them an air of authority. It was only after the first air drop that their ideas began to take root with the partisan's and the 'hit and run' method of attacking the German defences and blowing up bridges rather than to stand and fight began to prove more effective.

Difficulties did on occasion arise, one time a group of partisans whom Bill was attached to wanted to attack a group of German's who had overrun one of their supply depots, it was all Bill could do to persuade the partisan leader to flee while they still had a chance as the German's were making efforts to surround them and when it was agreed to retreat Bill chose to lead them up the North face of Le Vette.

They found a gully and settled down for the night in the bitter cold autumn air, with one blanket between sixteen of them it was not a warm night. The next morning they watched the German's a few hundred yards beneath them frantically searching for the missing partisans and the much needed wireless set. They dare not move and had to spend two nights in the open, unable to light a fire to keep warm and in constant fear of discovery by the German's who were firing in the forest below. Bill wrote:

By the end of the third day we had to move whether or no. No one had eaten for seventy two hours, some had frozen feet, and all were stiff with cold. The start was not auspicious. Having gone to the top of the gully at dusk to reconnoitre I was recalled by wild cries from below. Since for three days no one had dared to raise his voice above a whisper, it seemed something important must have happened – perhaps they had found some food. In fact one of the ex-prisoners-of-war had slipped. I found him lying dazed with a severe gash in the head, on a ledge 60ft below our 'gite' on the lip of a straight drop of a like distance. His hands were lacerated too, but securing him to the tail of my coat, I eventually dragged him to the top of the gully where the remainder were now waiting.

They eventually made it back to safety at a farm where they had their first hot meal in several days while waiting for a re-grouping of the partisan leaders who had survived the German reprisals. The Germans shot or hung anyone suspected of being a partisan or indeed anyone who harboured such men, they burned the farms and pillaged food, it was a difficult time to be a man on the run. Bill describes a local partisan leader:-

Deluca, a local businessman in the fur trade, used his business as a cover for his partisan sympathies and assisted the partisan's right up to the end of the war and often taking part in battles himself. He always carried with him as corroborative details a couple of moth-eaten marten skins to give 'artistic verisimilitude to an otherwise bald and unconvincing narrative'. Deluca was an able, active and influential man, and the greatest help to the mission and the partisan cause; among his many accomplishments were the ability to skin, dress and cook anything that walked. His spiced kid [goat], spitted and roasted, was perfection.

They moved from place to place, avoiding the Germans and on one occasion while they were hiding in the forest they came under bombardment from a German artillery division. Bill horrified his fellow soldiers by donning his Royal Artillery cap, standing up and observing the enemy guns, John Ross thought he was being crazy and dragged him back down under cover whereupon Bill merely said that 'an Artillery Officer should be properly attired when coming under fire from the enemy'.

Bill only managed to send one letter home to Adeline during his whole time it Italy, he wrote :

I sent off one note about six weeks ago. I wonder if you have not received it? I hope you are getting the regular fortnightly messages [from HQ]. Have had no mail, or anything else, since we arrived last August. A lot of mail was sent but unluckily it fell into enemy hands. I expect there were books and possibly a pipe amongst it. Life is a good deal harder and more harassed than it was in Albania, but I have no doubt we shall get through the winter all right if that should be necessary. There is a lot of snow here now [It was Dec]. A few weeks ago I had half an hour on skis and fell about all over the place. It seemed to me to be worse than skating. Hope you are battling along and that Joan, Pam and Anne are all well.

Bill was clearly missing his sister and nieces and what with the poor communication between them it must have left him feeling lonely at times. Life was not dull however, Bill and his team had to and wanted to keep in touch with all the various partisan factions and so, often travelling by night, they visited the many men holding out against the German enemy. This was dangerous work for Bill and his team and if they were ever caught they would be shot for certain. One time they had to be hid in a lorry under a load of wood while they were driven through a German checkpoint, through a gap in the wood Bill could see a German soldier prodding the pile of old timber with his bayonet, thankfully he missed them all. The Italians took many risks to protect those who were there to help them.

On Boxing day 1944 they finally got their first air drop of weapons and now Bill, with his team, made his way through the mountains to join the Belluno division and contact was established on the 9th January 1945, the war was going to get interesting now. Bill did not totally forget his climbing and managed to 'sneak' an ascent of Mount Serva (7000ft) during the winter which astonished his partisan comrades. Although the war was coming to an end there was much hatred and bitterness with many reprisals taken by the Germans on the Italian citizens of Belluno and the surrounding villages.

On one occasion Bill and his men were trying to blow up a bridge when they suddenly found themselves being shot at, the sniper was actually a fellow partisan and when confronted by Bill he was no doubt mightily relieved to hear that they were impressed with his dedication to duty and even more impressed with his poor aim.

In April 1945 the Americans broke through to Verona and the war in Europe was nearing its end at long last. The American breakthrough was crucial as it held the key to the Brenner Pass which is the way the Germans would have to beat a retreat and the partisan forces moved quickly to close the roads. Slowly but surely the Germans were surrendering but Belluno was still holding out and the partisan leader, Deluca, with Bill alongside him tried to negotiate with the German Leader in the city to surrender however there was a reluctance to surrender to 'mere' partisans though the Germans did indicate a willingness to surrender to the British forces working their way up the valley. There was a brief fight between the German and British forces however on the 2nd May 1945 the Germans surrendered and Bill wrote:

That morning three of us went on another of Deluca's motor-cycles into Belluno, for so long the goal of our ambitions. I should like to report that were wrenched from the cycle by an enthusiastic crowd, borne shoulder-high to the Piazza del Duomo and there crowned with laurel leaves to the prolonged and deafening 'Viva's' of the assembled multitude. We were too soon for that. The streets were nearly empty, most of the people wisely remained indoors until after the situation cleared.

A mere three weeks later Bill became a freeman of the city, the first freeman had been the legendary Garibaldi and Bill was only the fifth man to be given the honour and it was one he rated very highly, even more than the DSO he received from the British for his efforts in Albania and Italy.

Never one to rest on his laurels Bill tried to get a posting to the far east where the war still raged but was unsuccessful, he produced his report on his time in Italy for his superiors and stressed the respect, decency and hard work of the communist / Garibaldi partisans he fought with. The war was now over for Bill and as a bonus he found out that he been awarded the DSO to his Military Cross and retained his rank of major which was a title he liked to keep about him.

The war was now over, Bill was forty-seven, a single man who liked exploring and a man who had no idea what the future held for him, just like the time after the First World War he needed something to keep him occupied and it was to be mountains again that were his saviour from domesticity and seeming stagnation.

(L.) Frederick Gardiner (centre) with Lawrence & Charles Pilkington.
(R) St. George Littledale.
Below: Highfield House in Old Swan Liverpool , the early home of St
George Littledale

The Walker Family and their guides

South Park Lodge, the Walker family home

Mount Elbrus first climbed by H. Walker & F.Gardiner

The Grandes Jorasses, first climbed by Horace Walker in 1868.

Godfrey Allan Solly

Bill Tilman (wearing hat) and Eric Shipton outside Seacroft in
Wallasey shortly before leaving for Nanda Devi in 1935

Left - John Menlove Edwards

Below Left - Colin Kirkus

Below - Andrew 'Sandy' Irvine

Above - Bill Tilman aboard Mischief

Right - K2   the second highest
mountain in the world

Memorial plaque outside Bill
Tilmans last home near Barmouth

The author on Menlove's classic
'Crackstone Rib'

The Mountains again

After the first war he went to Africa to seek solace from the horrors he'd seen and this time he had but one goal, the Himalaya.

In 1946 Bill went to Scotland and climbed Ben Nevis, while descending he slipped on some scree and broke his arm, he had to be helped down the mountain by a group of Boy Scouts though the injury was not serious and later that year he made a short trip to the Swiss Alps.

In 1947 he received an invitation to climb Rakaposhi (25,500ft) from a Swiss expedition, this was to be the first of many trips that Bill would make over the next four years in the mighty Himalaya. There are suggestions that Bill may have been acting as a spy for the British in the sensitive Himalayan border areas where both Chinese and Russian nations had a seeming interest. Bill was well versed in travelling fast over rough mountain terrain, he could live off the land and was familiar with the local peoples and could engage in 'idle gossip' with them. He had spent two years during the last war engaged behind enemy lines and he was thus well trained and best of all Bill could keep his own counsel, most obvious though is that such an endeavour would appeal to his sense of adventure and doing something of worth. A trip to the Himalaya with an expedition from a neutral country was perfect cover for him as well.

The expedition to Rakaposhi failed and after the trip Bill felt he was getting a little bit too old for the demands made upon the body by climbing at great altitudes, he still loved the mountains and the atmosphere, he wrote:

I felt uncommonly happy at trekking once more behind a string of mules with their bright headbands, gaudy red wool tassels, and jingling bells, over a road and country new to me with the promise of sixteen such days ahead. I felt I could go on like this for ever, that life had little better to offer than to march day after day in an unknown country to an unattainable goal.

After the expedition split up Bill headed north to Kashgar and to a meeting with his old friend Eric Shipton who had been the British consul there since 1940. They proposed to climb Mustagh Ata (24,388ft). Bill left Kashmir on the 1st August 1947, an auspicious day in that it heralded the end of the British Empire in India, he met Eric and his wife Diana in the small town of Sarikol. They made their attempt on Muztagh Ata from this town and Diana Shipton accompanied them to their base camp at 17,000ft with a local Sherpa, however they failed to climb the peak as Bill came down with altitude sickness and then both he and Eric discovered their feet were becoming frostbitten, only a quick descent would save their toes.

Bill decided to make his way back to Pakistan via China and Afghanistan, a circuitous route and one which lends credence to his possible espionage duties, a slight problem however was that he had no visa for Afghanistan. He was duly arrested, on suspicion of being a Russian, and imprisoned at one point and after long and protracted negotiations was allowed to enter Chitral and safety. He felt that his 'expedition' was a failure though he did deduce that the Afghans were very suspicious of the Russians though more disposed towards the British.

Another trip was made to Kashgar to meet Eric where they planned to climb in the Bogdo Ola Mountains, Bill flew out to China and then 'endured' a twelve day bus journey to the town on Urumchi where he finally met Eric and the Sherpa Lhakpa who had been with them the previous year on Muztagh Ata. It was a journey Bill did not enjoy as he lamented the passing of the old methods of travel by mule and horse, only to find them replaced by the bus and truck.

They stayed at the American consulate at Urumchi and although they failed to climb any peaks they did spend a few days together in the mountains, it proved to be the last time they were to climb together as their lives were soon to take vastly different paths though they continued to keep in contact for the rest of their days.

Bill left Kashgar on the 1st October 1948 and made his way to Chitral by a less troublesome route than the previous year and eventually made his way back to England. For the first time he did not go back to Wallasey but to a house his sister had bought in Barmouth, North Wales which was to be his home, in Britain at least, for the rest of his life.

By 1949 the many changes to the Himalayan nation's status forced Nepal to open her borders to westerners for the first time. It was a fortuitous opening of the floodgates for Bill as he made three visits to this wonderful mountain kingdom between 1949 and 1950, he wrote:

There can be no other country so rich in mountains as Nepal. Apart from Everest and Kanchenjunga and their two 27,000ft satellites, there are six peaks over 26,000ft, fourteen over 25,000ft and a host of what might be called slightly stunted giants to 20,000ft and upwards, which cannot be enumerated because they are not all shown on any existing map. It should be understood that, except for Everest and those peaks on the Nepal-Sikkim border, most of which (except Kanchenjunga) have been climbed, this enormous field has remained untouched, un-approached, almost unseen, until this year (1949) when the first slight scratch was made.

One can imagine Bill's excitement at having so much country to explore and he did not waste his time when he got underway on his first expedition. The Nepalese government restricted the first British expedition to the Langtang Himal and a condition was attached to the expedition in that they had to do some scientific work - a prospect which filled Bill with dread.

Bill and three fellow Britons left Kathmandu on the 29th May, the weather was foul with near constant rain which seemed to make the many leeches even hungrier, they had to stop frequently to remove them before they took too much blood. The party surveyed the Langtang Valley and the many mountains that surround it including the elusive Gosainthan which they measured at 26,291ft. They found a 'forgotten' pass into Tibet, a country which they could no longer visit due to the Chinese incursions. Bill with Peter Lloyd only managed to climb one small peak, Paldor (19,451ft) as the weather was so poor however, Bill delighted in exploring this new country which he had looked longingly down upon from the north col of Everest in 1938. Despite his seeming disinterest in all things scientific Bill did make an accurate record of the many plants, trees and even some of the insects he encountered which added to the overall knowledge of the flora and fauna of this previously forbidden kingdom.

However as he had only climbed the one peak Bill regarded the trip as something of a failure and when he met the Maharajah of Nepal he asked for permission to return the following year to the Annapurna range. Bill selected Annapurna IV and he was able to select his own team unsurprisingly lacking any scientists and including a fellow Merseyside man, Dr Charles Evans, who would later come to prominence on the successful Everest expedition a few years hence. He was accompanied by four others including Major Jimmy Roberts and a New Zealander by the name of Packard.

They set up a series of camps eventually reaching an altitude of 22,400ft where first Charles Evans and Packard tried for the summit but were defeated by bad weather (the same storm that caused the French team on Annapurna I such immense suffering). They tried again with Bill on the 19th June and Bill wrote:

The sun shone bleakly through a veil of high cirrus which it had painted, as upon flimsy canvas, an iridescent halo. Climbing even at the height, which was by no means extreme, our pace seemed fully as slow as that of a glacier; unhappily, one feared, without the glacier's inexorability. Having climbed for nearly two hours we paused at a small rock outcrop to take stock and to compare our height with that of Machapuchare, whose fish –tail seemed to make a rude gesture at us from above a bank of cloud. It is difficult to judge by the eye alone, but the most helpful among us dared not affirm that we were much, if anything above it: which meant we had risen only 500 feet. After another hour, during which we gained height quicker owing to the steeper slope, the altimeter put us at a height of 23, 400ft. Packard was going strong, Charles Evans panting a little, while the combined effect of age and altitude threatened momentarily to bring my faltering footsteps to a halt. In fact, my goose was cooked.

Bill later reflected that it would be unlikely if he could ever go so high again.

They beat a retreat from Annapurna IV and decided to explore the region around the mountain, on one such excursion Bill fell and badly hurt his troublesome back again. He had to lie still for five days before he could move whereupon the whole party decided to return to Kathmandu. It was now late September and another opportunity was to present itself to Bill and it proved to be one that he would be unable to resist, a chance to see Everest from its southern side. This came about when a chance meeting occurred with Oscar Houston, the father of Charles Houston, the American from the successful Nanda Devi ascent, in Kathmandu. Bill describes the meeting best:-

At Kathmandu, where we were lapped in comfort at the Embassy, we did not take long to wind up our affairs. I felt I could leave safely but perhaps undeservedly murmur: 'Now my weary eyes I close, Leave, ah leave me, to repose'. But it was not to be. I there met Mr Oscar Houston, the father of Dr Charles Houston a companion from my Nanda Devi days, who had everything in train for a journey to Solu Khumbu, the district on the Nepal side of Everest and the home of the sherpa's. He invited me to join his party, and refusal to do so would have seemed ungracious. Moreover the journey would be of supreme interest; apart from viewing the south side of Everest there was the fun to be expected from seeing sherpa's, as it were, in their natural state. Mr. Shipton and I had often discussed such an unlikely happening, and here it was offered to me on a plate.

In 1949 the Himalayan Committee had asked the Nepal Durbar for permission to send a party to reconnoitre the south side of Everest, but this had been refused and the Langtang Himal offered in its place.

Two weeks later Charles Houston arrived and a party of five, including Betsy Cowles, made their way to Solu Khumbu. This was to be the only occasion when a woman would be on an expedition with Bill, he later wrote rather laconically:

'Besides the Houstons, father and son, there were two old friends of theirs, Mrs E. S. Cowles, an American climber of note, and Anderson Bakewell who was then studying at the Jesuit College of St Mary's near Darjeeling. Hitherto I had not regarded a woman as an indispensible part of the equipage of a Himalayan journey but one lives and learns'

The journey to Namche Bazaar was special in that they were to be the first westerners ever to visit the Sherpa town. Bill was warming to Betsy and she to him, they were to remain great friends for the rest of their days.

From Namche Bill and Charles Houston went further up the valley to investigate the western Cwm of Everest, they only had six days and made their way to Thyangboche monastery and then onto the foot of the Khumbu Glacier which united Bill and Charles opinions that Everest could not be climbed from the south. If they had had more time to reconnoitre then they may have considered otherwise as this was to prove the key to the successful ascent some three years later.

The party enjoyed a Thanksgiving dinner in the Himalayan wilds and for once Bill seemed more relaxed than for a long time, he later wrote:

The best attainable should be good enough for any man, but the mountaineer who finds his best gradually sinking is not satisfied. In an early English poem attributed to one Beowulf we are told:

Harder should be the spirit, the heart all the bolder,
Courage the Greater, as the strength grows less.

If a man feels he is failing to achieve this stern standard he should perhaps withdraw from a field of such high endeavour as the Himalaya.' .

Bill never again went to the Himalaya, he spent the next three years in a sort of wilderness. He obtained a position as a diplomat in Burma which proved a somewhat miserable existence. He received the prestigious Founders Medal from the RGS while in Burma but it did little to lift his gloom. His letters home were full of questions to Adeline about Bodowen, their home in Barmouth, and it was clear he was missing the place. In March 1953 he came home to a new life and a new career. Bill was going to take up sailing.

Mischief heads South

In 1954 Bill bought an old Bristol Pilot Cutter and it has been remarked that she was his first, true and only love though when he first saw her in a boatyard in Palma she was in a rather sorry state. Bill clearly took pity on the old boat and spent a not inconsiderable sum in repairing her and making her seaworthy. Bill being Bill however, he was not interested in making mundane voyages to frequented waters, for him the challenging southern ocean was to be his first target. Mischief was a mere 45ft in length, 13ft in beam and 7 ½ ft deep, she weighed fourteen tons and was originally designed to be operated by a crew of two. When Bill bought her she was in need of an extensive refit. While this was being done Bill went on a number of sailing trips in the Mediterranean while keeping an eye on the refit of his boat, he noted with satisfaction that although the Spanish (who were carrying out the refit) took many siestas they were only half the price of a British yard.

The refit complete Bill began to try and muster a crew to get her back to England, Bill always had difficulty with his crews, more often than not because of his somewhat spartan habits. He got as far as Gibraltar with Mischief's previous owner and his wife who had agreed to come along much to Bill's regret at having a woman on board. He cobbled a crew together and embarked on the journey back to England through the Bay of Biscay, no easy task for a good sailor never mind one who had little experience and an even less experienced crew. Bill had to endure his first 'mutiny' on this maiden voyage and dropped two young NCO's off at Porto as they refused to go any further with him.

However they did finally make Lymington, which was to be Bill's home port for the next twenty years. Mischief needed more work on her and while this was being done he ploughed ahead with his plans to head south on the first of what would be three very successful explorations to Patagonia and the Crozet, Kerguelen Islands. Bill needed a crew and placed an advert in the yachting press and later 'The Times.' On this, his first voyage, he was fortunate to get a good crew mainly men from the military and in particular ex gunners who Bill would have trusted above all others.

Bill had been fascinated by the Patagonian Ice Cap for many years, the glaciers flowing out of the mountains penetrated to the sea and as Bill put it 'a mountaineer can step from his boat and begin his climb at sea level'. The Spanish maps for the area were peppered with the word 'inesplorado' and while the Ice Cap had been climbed from the Argentinian side it had not been traversed from the Chilean channels, tucked in behind the Andes. Bill wrote:

The adventure of crossing an ocean, the seeing of new lands and little known coasts, and the setting foot on hitherto unvisited glaciers were for me sufficient reasons for travelling so far afield

On June 27th 1955 Mischief sailed out of Lymington with her crew of five and they sailed to Las Palmas in the Canary Islands, Bill was still learning to navigate on this trip and after a bad landfall of the north coast of Spain he wrote:

The navigator can always attribute his errors – unless, of course, they are fatal – to abnormal tide set or the perverse behaviour of currents, whereas a man who leads his party into the wrong valley or onto the wrong ridge has no such scapegoat and is written down an ass. We should have to do better after taking down our departure for the Canaries, for it would not do to miss them.

With an improving navigation technique they made their way across the Equator heading for Montevideo which they reached on the 1st October 1955, however the pace slowed and they then only made an average of 56 miles a day as they left Montevideo towards Punta Arenas in Chile which they reached on the 9th November. They spent three weeks here in preparation for the difficulties that would lie ahead and on the 26th November they sailed out, the adventure proper was about to begin. The waters of the Magellan Straits are treacherous with fast currents and many unmarked islets, they were seeking the Peel Inlet and the Calvo Glacier which was the departure point for the climbing party who hoped to make the first ever crossing of the Patagonian Ice Cap, Bill wrote:

It was fascinating sailing: rounding miniature capes, peeping into hidden coves, tacking between rocky wooded shores, backed by sombre fells of yellow heath and grey slabs, and over all the low driving clouds. Desolate and forsaken as the scene was, it had the powerful appeal of an un-trodden land and the bracing challenge of unsparing harshness. Today [2nd December] is a horrible day of cold rain. Made good about 7 miles and had to use the engine for an hour at either end. We got into a rocky inlet about 5pm and anchored in Kelp in 7fms and about 30 yards offshore. Everything on deck is sodden and no chance of doing any work on the sails or sheets. However it is nice to get down below after such a day to the cabin where the stove soon makes it warm.

The area they were sailing in had originally been in-habited by the now extinct Patagonia Indians who wandered naked in these lands living off mussels and fish, they had nothing to fear only the coming of western man with his disease and religion. Now their settlements lay abandoned as a cruel testimony to the hand of a so called better man trying to educate and civilise a people who were in no need of such perceived niceties.

They reached Peel Inlet threading their way through the myriad of small icebergs and ice floes which ground into Mischief's hull much to Bill's concern, he wrote:

After some six miles of threading our way through patches of ice and occasional stretches of clear water we at last turned into a small bay to reconnoitre the approach to the next 'sea-level' glacier. Waterfall Bay, as we called it, was magnificent if nothing else. Quite near and high on our left a great white stream of ice swept round the foot of a black ridge to break into myriads of cracks, seracs, and crevasses, many of them scintillating with a vivid blue, as they plunged steeply to the ice-strewn water. On one side was bare rock; on the other, almost as steep, evergreen forest.

Bill and two of his crew were to set out from this bay while those remaining behind on the boat were to retreat out of the bay to find a safe anchorage away from the ice, though they were to return to the glacier on each Sunday till the 19th February to meet the returning climbers. If by that date they had not returned then Mischief and the remaining crew were to return to Punta Arenas, Bill and his climbing party had fifty days food with them and there was little room for error or mishap.

The crossing of the Patagonian Ice Cap was accomplished successfully though not without incident. Bill decided to bathe in the icy glacial waters of Lake Argentino on the far side of the Ice Cap, Charles Marriott suffered an infected foot, Bill fell into a crevasse and on their way back over the glacier and they nearly missed finding a crucial food dump when they were overtaken by a blizzard. A typical entry from Bill's diary reads thus:

Still blowing hard but sun shining. Visibility about ½ mile 10am. Started out to look for dump....... gave up partly because I think the snow is so deep we could not find anything...... Charles complained of the cold. Decided to start at noon. Job of packing tents. Jorge said we ought to try to go back to Argentina. Charles agreed. Vetoed. Started at 12.50 in high wind and plodded up to crevasse which marked the dump (Bearings compass left in glove in dump). When abreast dumped loads and went searching – Jorge very reluctant to leave loads scared of getting lost. No good very thick went on with Jorge leading very slow. When passed the crevasse Charles suggested another look. Off again on slope, finally un-roped with Charles and Jorge scattered. Jorge again staying by loads when Charles spotted a black thing 200 yards away, sure enough cheers all around. We'd saved my photos and possibly our lives. I doubted if I could have got these two over the pass to camp VII. Was really getting very worried and have been since the storm which has been with us for four days now.

When they were picked up Bill was angry to discover that Mischief had become grounded at one point while they were away and the crew had worked hard to save her, she had sustained some damage and Bill decided to head north to Valparaiso to get the repairs carried out and also for Charles Marriott to get some urgently required medical treatment for his infected feet.

They left Valparaiso in March and sailed through the Panama Canal, the Caribbean and Bermuda to arrive back in England on the 9th June 1956, a year and day after they had left.

After this expedition Bill believed he had found the perfect way to marry his love of climbing and sailing and so he began to look for his next objective, it was clearly going to have to be the southern wildernesses to which he would turn again. Bill decided on the uninhabited Possession Island, part of the Crozet group of Islands deep in the southern ocean.

It was however an unhappy trip in that Bill suffered a recurrence of his back problems, his crew seemed to be spending more time ashore partying than wanting to sail and to compound matters further the weather and big seas began to make a damaging impression on Mischief's old rigging. In one such storm they lost their dinghy which meant that they could not attempt a landing on Possession Island, another storm flooded the galley and Bill's health was a constant cause for concern, eventually he realised that they had to return to south Africa without even reaching the longed for islands. Bill wrote:

I wondered weakly how many more such battering we would receive in the course of those 2,000 miles away in Lat 49 S, whereas a man of more robust mind would have argued that the weather had done its worst, that we had come through in tolerably good shape, and that since the summer was advancing we were unlikely to meet with any more such breezes lasting for three days. Another worrying thought was that besides myself only two of the crew could be relied upon to steer safely in bad weather, and the prospect of that long haul under those conditions so daunted me that prudence decided me to give up and sail back to Durban.

They returned to England via the Red Sea, the Suez Canal and the Mediterranean and while Bill was feeling slightly better he was still far from 100 %. This failure to reach and accomplish their objective hit Bill hard and he was determined to try again in 1959 and set about getting another crew and placed an advert in the Times newspaper.

His advert was to famously read *'Hand (man) wanted for long voyage in a small boat, No Pay, No Prospects and Not much Pleasure'*, despite this honest advert, placed only a month before he was due to sail, he had many replies more often from inexperienced romantics rather than experienced hands. He selected a crew of five and they set sail on the 30th July 1959 on what would prove to be an expedition as successful and as well received as his crossing of the Patagonian Ice Cap three years previously.

They arrived in Las Palmas a happy crew and went straight onto Cape Town where they had a good journey watching the Dolphins playing around their bow. In later expeditions Bill was renowned for a spartan diet though on this trip they ate well:

For lunch we rang the changes on cheese, sardines, herrings, bully beef or 'spam', with dates, marmite or peanut butter as 'afters'. The cheeses were whole ten-pound Cheddars...... For tea we had biscuits and jam, sweet biscuits and occasionally cake, pancakes or soda bread...........

But the evening meal we regarded as our main hope and stay, like so many gross rustics 'whose principal enjoyment is their dinner, and who see the sun rise with no other hope than that they shall fill their belly before it sets'. It consisted of whatever dish the skill and ingenuity of the cook might concoct from ingredients limited to bully beef, sausages, spam, rice, beans, lentils, peas, macaroni, spaghetti, potatoes and onions, helped out with dried vegetables and soups for flavouring by stewed prunes, raisins or apples, or a massive steamed pudding.

On the 1st November they reached Cape Town, where Bill had friends to greet and many social activities in which to indulge. Bill seemed to prefer the 'colonial settings' in which he found himself rather than the formality of English social engagements which seemed to him class ridden and out dated.

Mischief needed some more work carrying out which delayed them longer than Bill would have liked and it was not till early December before they left for his second attempt to reach the Crozets. Thankfully there were no serious gales to bother them this time and on the 20th December they sighted Marion Island, the first of the sub-Antarctic Islands, and sailing onwards through Christmas Day, where they indulged in lots of mulled wine, they finally saw their longed for objective on the 27th December, Bill was mightily relieved and wrote:

Perhaps the earlier sighting of Penguin Island had taken a little off the edge of this landfall but not much. For here was the long looked for prize at the end of a 10,000 mile voyage, a prize with a true romantic flavour – a lonely island set in a stormy sea, and Mischief borne towards it on the crest of great following seas, with albatross wheeling in her wake.

The party landed easily on a sandy beach and began to reconnoitre the island and her mountains, they came across some huge sea elephants where Bill was disappointed to note that they just grunted and did little else. They found the two main mountains of the island to be much lower than marked on their map though they managed to climb them both, the first time they had been climbed. All were amazed by the wildlife on the island especially the penguins and elephant seals. Bill wrote to his sister later:

Roger and I cleared up what peaks there were. They were disappointing. We were led to believe in 5000ft snow covered mountains...........in fact the height was only 3200ft and the little snow only temporary. There were two others of 3100ft and 2700ft but there was no climbing. The wild life compensated for this. There was a penguin rookery (king penguins)of several thousand on the beach, one had to brush them off with one's feet to get anywhere. On the beach, too, were hundreds of elephant seals, great creatures like slugs, hardly bothering to open their mouths and bellow unless one kicked them. On the grass slopes above the albatross and giant petrels were nesting. Roger ringed over 200 of them. Their eggs and penguin eggs make good omelettes, and we also knocked off the odd penguin to eat. The meat is not bad. The vegetation is very scant, but we collected what there was.

From Possession Island they sailed onto Kerguelen and were suitably entertained, wined and dined at the French Research Station. They left for Cape Town on the 2nd February 1960 and reached Lymington on the 30th June eleven months after they had sailed out.

Mischief goes North

The long trips south were proving tough going for Bill, the miles sailed per ratio to the mountains climbed was very low and so he looked to the north to try and redress the balance. Each trip south had involved a year away from England and by 1960 he was ready for a change and wrote:

A voyage to northern waters, unlike one southwards, has little to offer in the way of pleasure to a yachtsman beyond a bracing climate and spectacular scenery. Instead of the crew delighting in the freedom of shorts and a shirt, or complete nudity, they may be pent up in winter woollies. As for basking on deck, only the helmsman will spend any time there and he will be well wrapped up in sweaters and oilskins.

Above all else Bill craved remoteness and inaccessibility and so after much study he decided Greenland could offer what he needed and the length of time it would take to get there would prove to be considerably less than when heading south. The fact that the waters are more difficult to negotiate clearly did not put him off.

Greenland belongs to Denmark and in 1960 had approximately 30,000 inhabitants living largely in small settlements on the west coast, It is the largest island in the world and if placed over Europe would completely cover it. This was what Bill was looking for and he made a total of thirteen trips north between 1961 and 1976.

Bill planned to make his first trip in the summer of 1961 and a rather pressing matter was the replacement of Mischief's engine from a now badly rusted petrol one to a Perkins marine diesel. This eased his very real fears of having to carry so much petrol with the obvious danger of fire given that most of his crews were smokers.

He managed to gather a good crew and set sail from Lymington on the 14th May 1961: Bill later wrote:-

The first voyage to Greenland seemed to me a less momentous undertaking than the three voyages southwards. The time involved did not amount to more than a long summer cruise, nor did so many ominous question-marks hang over the enterprise as they had, for example, over the voyage to the Crozet islands. On the other hand I was not happy about the Atlantic crossing and the expected head winds to which I was unaccustomed. In Davis Strait, too, we might expect trouble with fog and icebergs. Unknown perils loom the larger. I had never seen an iceberg; my experience of ice was limited to the small floes we had encountered in the Patagonian Fjords.

Navigation was most difficult for Bill in the English and Irish channels as he refused to update his maps, he much preferred unknown waters where he could rely on his 'instinct' and observations of an ethereal nature such as the flight of birds, sea temperature etc.

A month out of Lymington they reached Godthaab in Greenland, their first port of call and Bill rowed ashore to try and find the harbour-master who allowed them all ashore 'provided no-one had Veneral Disease'!. Bill and his crew were greatly enamoured with the numerous icebergs they encountered:

We never tired of looking at bergs. At first we counted and logged all those in sight but north of Disko Island they became too numerous to count. If some particularly nasty or grotesquely shaped monster hove in sight we sometimes went out of our way to have a closer look at him. According to the light their colour varied from an opaque dazzling white to the loveliest blues and greens. Some had caves or even a hole clean through them in which the blue colour was intense and translucent.

They made their way to Upernivik Island where Bill and Charles Marriott climbed a 6370ft peak and came to within 200ft of the summit of a 6500ft peak. One must remember that these were climbed from sea level and compared favourably with some of the Alpine giants of Europe given that many ascents there start from a considerable height. One must also take into account Bill's age, he was now sixty three.

Unfortunately Bill's back problems returned due to a slip on deck and Charles Marriott had a bad foot yet again so they returned back to Lymington on the 26th September after a journey of some 7000 miles and only four months away from England. A pattern now developed in Bill's life, he would spend the summer away and return to England to write a book of his trips and while it was being published he would go away on his next adventure. This suited Bill as he was not one for publicity and this life allowed him to keep going doing what he believed to be important.

Despite Greenland's west coast being sparsely populated Bill considered it an untrue wilderness, however the Canadian side of Greenland *'is as desolate as a man could wish, more or less uninhabited, and besides that mountainous'*. He garnered another crew and on 23rd May 1962 headed back to Greenland to arrive on the 15th June after a much quicker journey than the year before. On the Greenland coast Bill, with a fellow crewman Roger Tufft climbed Agssaussat at just under 7000ft and another peak Amausuaq at 4620ft as well as another un-named lower peak.

They then sailed to Baffin Island but found the ice too thick to penetrate in such a small boat and so they returned back to Greenland to await await more favourable conditions. In due course better conditions presented themselves, they made an anchoring in Exeter Sound off Baffin Island and Bill, with Roger again, climbed Mount Raleigh. This last peak had been called 'False Mount Raleigh' which had been incorrectly identified on the existing maps and was duly officially renamed 'Mount Mischief'. After yet another successful trip they returned back to Lymington on 28th September.

The following year Bill voyaged to Bylot Island which was further north than they had previously been and there was a very good chance that they would at some point encounter pack ice. The aim of the expedition was to make a crossing of Bylot Island and to reach the Island they had somehow to get past the Middle Pack, a band of sea ice, and this they did by heading north to open water where they could then track west to reach the island. Bill later wrote:

At midnight we came up with the ice that earlier had been betrayed to us by the 'blink', a yellowish-white appearance of the sky produced by the reflection of pack-ice on the clouds. It proved to be another projecting cape which we presently rounded and resumed our westerly course. Throughout that next day we met many scattered floes, so widely scattered that for the most part we could maintain our course. Seals were fairly plentiful, sticking their heads out of the water or basking peacefully on the floes, and since we were under sail they took little notice of our passing. The crew seemed anxious to have one shot and equally in favour of casting me in the role of murderer. I must have been talking too much of my misspent youth in East Africa, of elephants and rhino, for they evidently took me for Buffalo Bill.

Bill shot his seal though with a single shot!

The party reached the Island and Bill with Bruce Reid made the first ever crossing in a total of fifteen days hard going in soft snow and with a high pass, measured at 5700ft, to cross en route. They had travelled only fifty miles but Bill was later to write that they were the hardest he had ever done. The fun was not over either, they needed to be picked up by the crew who had remained behind on Mischief, Bill had arranged for them to keep an eye out for smoke signals however there proved to be no kindling to start a fire and they even considered burning their tent to attract attention. They burnt some heather but no-one came and were it not for some Inuit hunters they would have been in serious trouble as their food had run out, two hours after their rescue they were back on Mischief where Bill berated his crew for not seeing his fires.

On the 26th September they made it home where Bill reflected on the success of the expedition and began planning his next trip but not before spending a lot of money on strengthening Mischief and replacing a lot of the now rotten oak frames. They sailed from the Faroe Islands heading for Angmagssalik in Greenland via the newly formed volcanic Island of Surtsey where Bill became the first Englishman to stand upon its shores. The ice was heavy and thick this year and Mischief joined a convoy of steel hulled ships forcing their way through the pack ice but given their greater speed and the need to keep a safe distance from these ships eventually they became boxed in and only reached Angmagssalik after sustaining further damage which caused Mischief to leak badly.

Emergency repairs were carried out to make her seaworthy and there was little choice but to abandon their objective and return home, however they were further trapped by pack ice which afforded Bill the opportunity to climb Poljemsfjeld and a small peak just under 4000ft.

In 1965 Bill tried again to make for Skjoldungen though this time he was successful as the ice was not so bad as their previous expedition, he attempted an ascent of an unclimbed 5000ft peak and climbing a couple of lesser peaks before making a fast journey back to Lymington.

South Again

Bill was now getting old but he was not yet ready to give up his life of adventure and in 1966 he headed south again, despite the colder weather and rough seas he had a deep affection for the challenges they presented. His objective was the south Shetland Isles and in particular Smith Island which was more mountainous than the other islands though sadly, he noted, they were inhabited. A crew was gathered including a scouser 'from my home town', John Ireland, whom Bill had great difficulty in understanding such was the thickness of his accent and he often had to repeat himself so he could be understood.

They left Lymington on the 14th July 1966 bound for the Antarctic via the Canaries, Montevideo and Punta Arenas, sixteen days later they arrived in Las Palmas and after a week of stocking up on essential supplies and carrying out some minor repairs they set sail for Montevideo. In five days they made an incredible 520 miles though on the sixth day they managed only 25 as the winds slackened, as compensation though it proved easier to catch the flying fish which made a hearty breakfast and which Bill thought as good as fresh Herrings. On Bill's sailing trips, especially those to the southern oceans his books are full of descriptions of the meals they ate and when the cook produced a good 'duff' [pudding] Bill writes as though his spirits have been lifted to unimaginable heights.

On the 27th August disaster struck. Bill came on deck at 7.40am to find the ship on course, the helm lashed but no sign of the helmsman, David Shaw. Bill raised the alarm and all hands were soon on deck scanning the rough seas but no sign was ever found of their friend despite sailing back seven miles and 'tacking back and forth' for several hours. Bill 'hove to' for the night, reluctant to leave the scene and unsure as to whether continue or turn home, clearly Smith Island would not now be possible as there was no-one experienced enough to stay aboard Mischief while Bill climbed his mountains.

They decided to continue however and on the 2nd September they crossed the Equator once again though for Bill and the crew the journey had gone on long enough, they longed for Montevideo, especially as supplies were running low and Bill had to ration the tea and coffee. The winds increased and they began to make good time again and after 60 days from Las Palmas and 5,300 miles they arrived in Montevideo where Bill's problems really began.

The crew became restless and bemoaned the lack of safety equipment (Bill routinely failed to carry a life raft, radio or distress signals) and the seemingly poor condition of the rigging. Three of the crew announced that they would not be continuing and this forced Bill to scout around for other crew members. A few came but really it was a case of making do and one could not be fussy about who came along, such was Bill's desperation for more crew that he eventually had to go to the sailor's home run by the Salvation Army. Also Bill had to report to the British Consul the loss at sea of David Shaw which necessitated a further delay and trouble with reporters keen to get a scoop.

With a makeshift crew they sailed from Montevideo on the 28th October aiming for Punta Arenas some 1200 miles further south though all was not well with the crew, Bill noticed that the weather was changeable and the cooking consistently bad. On the 20th November they entered the Magellan Straits and four days later Mischief and her crew finally made it to Punta Arenas. Continuing unrest with the crew caused Bill some concern but as they were not yet mutinous he decided to continue to the south Shetland Isles and perhaps carry out a reconnaissance for a future expedition. Bill did not totally rule out the prospect of doing something on the remote Livingstone Island if he could find a decent anchorage.

Bill continued to have problems with his makeshift crew, increasing unrest with conditions on board, difficult seas and the spartan diet forced Bill to quote Byron 'Comfort must not be expected by folk who go a-pleasuring'. Whether the crew thought they were 'a-pleasuring' is not known but one can deduce that they thought pleasure a distant memory.

On the 24th December the barometer dropped alarmingly and Bill became worried as to their whereabouts as the fog was thick and good sights could not be taken. On Christmas day the weather cleared slightly though the cold was penetrating and snow began to fall. When trying to get the cabin heater to burn they did too good a job and the whole thing caught fire forcing the crew onto deck while the fumes disappeared. They noticed on the horizon a land mass which eventually proved to be Smith Island, this discovery helped to lift the gloom which had descended on Bill and the crew. They made landfall and enjoyed a bottle of beer and buns for a somewhat indifferent Christmas Dinner.

The next morning they started the engine as there was no wind and they were intent on making Deception Island that day, in a heavy fog they found the entrance to Port Foster and Whalers Bay where the British base lay along with an abandoned whaling station.

The party received a cool reception from the base leader when Bill went ashore to show the ship's papers and crew's passports. There were no supplies to be bought which surprised Bill as normally the base stations are well stocked and he usually had no difficulty in procuring supplies. Thankfully the captain of a local ship, the Shackleton, was more obliging and allowed Bill and his crew aboard to share a good meal, however this hospitality was soon withdrawn and Bill decided to head for south Georgia where he was assured further supplies could be bought. Two of Bill's crew needed to see a doctor for some ailment or other and Bill was told the Chileans had a good doctor at the next base.

Bill made the short sail to the Chilean Base on another part of the Island where he enjoyed better hospitality than that given by the British. The crew were becoming more fractious and on one occasion a fight broke out amongst two of them, even the kindly Chileans were becoming fed up with Bill and his angst ridden crew and when the crew had been treated by the doctor it was clearly best to be away.

At 7.00pm on the 6th January Mischief finally sailed en route to south Georgia where they hoped to be rid of their most troublesome crew member before sailing onto Cape Town and then home. Although it was late at night the peaks of Livingstone Island glistened in the pale sunlight as they motored round in the calm sea followed by swimming penguins and a school of porpoises. The crew worked their way through the many channels avoiding the icebergs and were thankful for the good visibility. For the next week the weather remained fair and where it not for the strained atmosphere on board this section of the trip would have been most enjoyable. By the 20th January Mischief was some 100 miles from south Georgia and the next day the crew sighted land. It had taken them fifteen days to cover the journey from Deception Island to south Georgia. When one considers Ernest Shackleton et al in the James Caird taking a day longer to cover only a slightly shorter distance in rougher seas, one can only marvel at the fortitude and strength of those intrepid Antarctic explorers.

Mischief shortly arrived at the whaling station of Grytviken and the British settlement on King Edward Point. At last Bill, his crew and Mischief got a warm welcome from the local in-habitants, they were given free use of Shackleton house where they enjoyed a good bath, Bill's first since leaving England some six months earlier. There was no way that Bill could leave his most troublesome crew member in south Georgia, even after he had apparently threatened Bill with a knife and had to be locked up in the local jail. It became clear to Bill that he would have to be taken back to Montevideo and they would have to sail back to England from there, sadly Cape Town would have to be missed. What was worse for Bill was that he seemed enchanted with south Georgia and with a more amiable crew he would have happily stayed and explored / climbed to his heart's content, as it was they had to leave for Montevideo. They left south Georgia on the 28th January for the 1700 mile trip north-west when they could finally drop off the worst crew Bill had ever had on any voyage.

On the 15th February they sighted the high buildings of Montevideo and relief was shortly at hand for Bill, four of his crew left immediately though one further calamity soon became apparent when a book of travellers cheques disappeared. Bill managed to cash a cheque and spent a week repairing the mainsail and jib which were both in a bad way, a crew of sorts was cobbled together though it now became clear who the thief was as the cash that Bill had received when cashing a cheque had disappeared and he had now lost yet another crew member. Thankfully another cheque was cashed and with three very inexperienced crew members Mischief sailed from Montevideo on the 21st March 1967 on the long trip back to England.

A reasonably straightforward journey followed and on the 15th July Mischief could be seen sailing up the Lymington River a year and a day after her departure after a journey of some 21,000 miles, Bill wryly noted that to undergo such a journey with four misfits in a crew of five was just too many.

North Again

By 1968 Bill had sailed over 115,000 miles in Mischief and despite the frustration of his last trip south he was determined to seek another adventure in the Arctic and found a suitable objective in Scoresby Sound, the biggest Fjord in the world, Bill wrote:

By leaving at the end of June and going direct one should arrive off the sound at about the right time early in August. It would be a pity, however, to lose the whole of June, a pleasant month to be at sea, when the crew might enjoy some real yachting weather, the sort of weather that would do little to inure them to the rigours ahead but would at least afford some compensation. Moreover, with time in hand, we could call at the Faroe's, Iceland and Jan Mayen Island.

Bill did not know it but this plan would be the undoing of Mischief.

A shorter trip meant less difficulty in getting a crew as they would be away for a much shorter period than from when they headed south. Bill was persuaded to take a life raft but only because it was free, he wrote with some prescience *'Strangely enough, at the sight of this white blister installed on Mischief's deck my mind was filled with foreboding'.*

They left England in early June and made for the Faroe Isles and from there they sailed to the east coast of Iceland and Akureyri. Bill and some of the crew climbed a couple of lowly peaks which unsurprisingly he found quite tiring given that Bill was now seventy years old.

Next they sailed on to Jan Mayen Island where Bill hoped to climb an extinct volcano, the Beerenberg and at 7677 feet high a respectable objective given that one would have to climb from sea level. In the early morning of the 21st July Bill was roused from his slumbers by a terrific crash and he rushed onto deck only to be told by the watchman that they had struck a rock pinnacle and had run aground. They managed to free themselves from the pinnacle of rock but not before doing serious damage to the hull and consequently Mischief was leaking badly. They managed to motor into a sheltered bay and Bill was able to go ashore and speak to the Norwegian commandant of a nearby base to advise of his predicament and see what help could be sought. The crew managed to beach Mischief and carry out emergency repairs that Bill hoped would see them back to Iceland or maybe England where proper repairs could be carried out. A further problem arose when the ice floes and small bergs began to enter the bay and pressed hard against Mischief's now fragile hull causing further damage and all hope was near gone if they could not get Mischief well away from the shore. However it was not to be and despite a valiant effort from the crew and the Norwegians Mischief was lost, Bill later wrote:

For me it was the loss of much more than a yacht. I felt as one who had deserted a stricken friend, a friend with whom for the past fourteen years I had probably spent more time at sea than on land, and who when not at sea had never been far from my mind. Moreover I could not help feeling that by my mistakes and by the failure of one of those who were there to see her to safety we had broken faith; that the disaster or sequence of disasters need not have happened; and that more might have been done to save her...... 'I shall never forget her. The world was all before her, where to choose her place of rest, and providence her guide.

Bill clearly felt the loss of Mischief deeply, she was probably the only true love of his life but the chain of events were not to put Bill off sailing and within a few days of his return to England he began looking for another boat. He bought another Bristol Pilot Cutter called Sea Breeze which proved to be as not as good a boat as Mischief but one that would allow him to keep sailing which was all that clearly mattered to him.

Sea Breeze required a lot of work to be done and was in need of a major refit. However she would be ready for the 1969 season and so Bill decided once again to attempt to reach Scoresby Sound and set about finding a crew.

On the 19th June 1969 Sea Breeze sailed from Lymington to the sound of the now familiar Royal Lymington Yacht Club starting gun, however a fault with the boat soon became apparent as she started to leak and they had to sail into Yarmouth for some emergency repairs. The repairs were to prove so extensive that they had to sail back to Lymington and lost a week only finally getting away on the 30th June. Further problems arose and another call to port was needed for more repairs, awaiting these two of his crew decided not to return seemingly having little faith in Sea Breeze or of its Master. A replacement crew was found and they made a good, fast passage to Iceland where Bill and Brian Potter, a more reliable crew member, climbed Strandertinder at 3310ft.

Sea Breeze crossed the Arctic Circle and on the 7th August the dense fog thinned to reveal a startling landscape of glacier and mountains, they were just off Cape Brewster at the southern entrance to Scoresby Sound. Unfortunately ahead of them was solid pack ice and the crew refused to go on with the exception of Brian Potter, Bill wrote:

Brian, John [Murray] and I argued, standing for some odd reason round the foot of the mast below. I knew it would be no use. I am not eloquent and it would have needed the fiery eloquence of a Drake or a Garibaldi to stiffen John's spine..... To give up when so near, in an able boat with ample supplies, was hard enough to stomach, but with an unwilling crew there was nothing to be done.

They sailed back to Lymington where they arrived on the 9th September, Bill was very disillusioned on the back of three years bad sailing and having not achieved any of his objectives. He was now nearly seventy two yet his thirst for more adventure was still strong and so on the 5th June 1970 he set sail again heading for Greenland and the port of Faeringehavn which they reached on the 14th July despite being delayed in pack ice, two successful climbing trips were carried out on this trip and some of Bill's earlier enthusiasm comes to the fore in his writing, he wrote upon arrival back in Lymington on the 27th September:

For my part it has been a good voyage, if not the most successful then certainly the happiest which is almost as important

Bill continued to make voyages north to Scoresby Sound in 1971 & 1972 in two somewhat troublesome trips with sea / ice conditions, weather and crew against him. In 1972 he sailed to the same bay where Mischief was lost and were becalmed, Bill went ashore to see the Norwegians and was greeted on the beach with the words 'Mr Tilman, I presume?'

They finally sailed for Scoresby Sound where on the 3rd August they met their first ice floes and Sea Breeze's engine decided to stop working, it would have been foolish to continue without an engine but Bill was determined and so headed to Angmagssalik with the thought of giving his crew the slight satisfaction of having set foot in Greenland. There was still a lot of ice and when an opening appeared he sailed straight for it – a serious error of judgment as the fjord they were heading into had a huge glacier at its head and massive ice floes were calving away covering the fjord in huge icebergs which the crew fought manly to keep away from their fragile ship. One such floe forced them onto a rock and Bill gave the order to abandon ship, he and the crew had to spend the night on some rocks and by next morning only the top mast of Sea Breeze was showing above the icy water.

Bill had now lost his second ship and they were in potentially serious difficulty with little food and no shelter, perched upon a small rocky islet within the Arctic Circle. However they were fortunate in that a local boat spotted them the next day and they were able to be rescued. The sailors were penniless, had no passports and had to rely on Her Majesty's Consul in Reykjavik to get them back to England.

Bill was now seventy four and one would imagine that he had packed enough adventure into a single lifetime, however he clearly thought otherwise and began hunting down another boat. At the end of 1972 he found Baroque, his third Bristol Pilot Cutter and bought her on the spot. Bill was later to say that cruising to northern waters every summer had become almost essential as breathing.

As he became older Bill grew more parsimonious and Baroque suffered as a result, his indifference to harsh conditions and a spartan diet caused his crews much anguish and morale was often low, but still to the north Bill felt compelled to go each year.

In 1973 Greenland was again the object of Bill's desires and they left Falmouth where Baroque had been refitted, almost immediately they encountered problems which necessitated them putting up in Cork for repairs.

Eventually, after many trials, they reached Greenland where Bill made a solo ascent of a small unclimbed peak while two other crew members, one of whom was Simon Richardson, made an ascent of Mount Change. Baroque leaked constantly and the crew had to continually re-invent ways of channelling the water away from their bunks while the pump ran day and night.

Bill became quite close to Simon Richardson who was in essence a young Tilman, energetic and keen for adventure. He was good at problem solving and practical in his approach to any difficulties, unbeknown to both of them they had both embarked on a path that would ultimately bring them together in four years time for a final voyage into the southern oceans.

The arrived back in Lymington on the 6th October where much work remained to be done on Baroque and although Bill thought the voyage troublesome he had enjoyed himself.

In 1974 Bill decided on Spitzbergen as his next destination and Baroque left Lymington for Bear Island via the North Sea on the 1st June 1974. They arrived on the 7th July, heading north through the Hinlopen Strait which was passed on the 31st July. Then heading east they encountered pack ice and Bill wrote:

The breeze having died we were again under engine when at 4 am I took over the watch from Alan. What followed is not easy to explain and still less easy to excuse. Perhaps, having spent the last three days mostly on deck and enjoyed only disturbed nights, I was not as bright as I should have been. Zeiloyane, the two islets mentioned above, where in sight ahead and with the west-going ebb under us we were rapidly approaching them. We had already discovered that west of Cape Heuglin along the north coast of Edge Island the water was shallow and we intended passing north of the Zeiloyane islets. I had my eyes fixed on one but the northernmost looked to me like a spit of land projecting from the coast of Barents Island. What with the engine and the tide which, as we neared the islets seemed to gather speed for its rush through the channel, we must have been making 7 or 8 knots over the ground. Before I had really hoisted in what was happening we were heading between the two islets which are a mile or so apart. To attempt to pass between unknown islets however wide apart that may be, is always a hazardous proceeding. A shoal extended the whole way between the two and the rate we were going ensured our being carried right up on the back of it before we ground to a halt.

They were now in trouble, they had to remove ballast from the boat, thankfully the seas were calm and Baroque remained steady though the rudder received two savage blows. Eventually the crew managed to break free and sailed home to a sad homecoming as Bill was to learn that his beloved sister, Adeline, had died on the 7th September after shortly hearing that Bill had safely arrived back in British waters. Bill did not hear of her death till 24th September when a close friend broke the news to him, he said nothing but later wrote:

By the Autumn of 1974 circumstances had changed for the worse. I had now to face life entirely alone like a Himalayan ascetic in his mountain cave – a spacious cave, I admit, far too spacious for one man. Instead of making it easier, this made it harder to get away either for long or short periods, what with the dogs who shared master's cave and other considerations.

One of these considerations was Bill's age and declining health, he was becoming increasingly deaf, he began to suffer from arthritis and a near constant flu which proved really debilitating. After this last Spitzbergen trip Bill did think maybe it was time to call it a day though the call of north continued to be heard and in 1975 he made an attempt to get to Ellesmere Island and having failed he tried again in 1976 though Baroque and the skipper were clearly not up to the task and the crew forced Bill to turn back.

In his seventy ninth year Bill was beginning to seriously recognise his increasing frailty and inability to endure a hard voyage as skipper.

Bill's doctor, Dr Robert Haworth, a fan of Bill and his life came up with an idea after a meeting with Bill of an annual three peaks race. The idea was to sail from Barmouth in Wales to Fort William in Scotland and ascend the highest peak in Wales, England and Scotland along the way. No mechanical transport was to be allowed and two crew members from each ship must climb Snowdon, Scafell and Ben Nevis from the nearest port to the mountain and the winner of the race would be presented with a trophy. The first race sailed from Barmouth on the 25th June 1977 and only four teams managed to finish the race though those that had dropped out made their way to Fort William for the final celebrations.

There was one more trip on a boat for Bill however...............

Bill was approached by Simon Richardson, the young man who had been north with him a few years previously, to join him on a long trip to the southern oceans and in particular a visit to Smith Island where Bill had encountered one of his worst failures. He had a boat, which he had named En Avant, and wanted Bill along as he respected and admired him for what he had done in his incredible life. He probably also knew that Bill liked him and that a chance to return to the southern oceans would prove irresistible to him.

En Avant had undergone no serious sea trials since her conversion from a semi wrecked tug to a sailing ship, she did have a steel hull which Richardson thought useful in the icy seas they would no doubt encounter. However the conversion was done 'on the cheap', many believed the tug was not suitable for such a conversion and that her subsequent loss confirmed their views, essentially En Avant was changed completely from one type of vessel to another, using a different method of propulsion and was hoping to sail in seas for which she was not designed.

On the 9th August 1977 En Avant sailed from southampton initially to Las Palmas and by the end of August they had arrived off the south American coast, they had been granted a fine crossing which pleased Bill and the rest of the crew.

They sailed onto Rio and Bill wrote:

I am having a very easy time doing little or nothing beyond watch-keeping.........In fact I begin to doubt whether I am really worth the run of my teeth. The gear is too heavy for me and I find it difficult getting about the wide deck with nothing to hang on to. After leaving here I imagine we shall rig some lifelines. Still it would have been a mistake to refuse Simon's pressing invitation.

On the 1st November 1977 En Avant sailed from Rio intending to make for the Falkland Isles to meet a party of climbers, nothing was ever heard or seen of En Avant ever again and it is assumed that she was lost in a storm sometime in November or December of that year.

Bill Tilman was seventy nine years of age when he died and into those years he had crammed so much adventure as well as a fair smattering of hardship endured by his participation in the two world wars. He eschewed all publicity and praise that was rightly his due given his considerable achievements and yet it is sad that he is so little known outside mountaineering and sailing circles where he is considered a legendary figure.

Bill never married nor did he form any real close relationships other than with his sister and nieces. He was financially independent, in part from his father's legacy as well as the income generated by his writings and lectures and so he could conveniently come and go as he pleased.

The 1978 Three Peaks Yacht Race, as it had become known, had a trophy made in Bill's honour to be presented each year. It would be presented to the best finishing team that wrote the most descriptive account of their trip in the ship's log. The committee felt that this would be most appropriate to Bill as it took into account sailing, mountaineering and writing and that as such the H. W. Tilman Trophy was certainly worthy of his name.

Most appropriately the first winner of the trophy was the boat 'Cannonade' crewed by 103 Air Defence Regiment, Royal Artillery.

H W Tilman deserves to be better known by the people of Liverpool and it would be heartening if the powers that be in our city could find some way to honour and commemorate this remarkable and inspirational man.

Andrew 'Sandy' Irvine

Andrew Irvine is probably the best known of our mountaineers amongst the general public and casual readers for his heroic association with George Leigh Mallory on Everest in 1924. Sandy, as this was the name he would always answer to, was born on the 8th April 1902 at 56 Park Road South in Birkenhead, in a house that still stands overlooking the beautiful Birkenhead Park. He was the fourth child of Willie and Lillian Irvine who were strict archetypal Edwardian parents believing in the doctrine of 'a child should be seen and not heard' however they were very loving in always wanting what is best for their children. It was clear from an early age that Sandy was a brave, daring and fearless child. Academically Sandy was not the brightest family member but he did show an aptitude for all things mechanical and he managed to persuade his father to let him have a workshop at the family home where he could disassemble a multitude of things 'to see how they worked'.

The family had a great love for North Wales and frequently holidayed there each year, the children were allowed to wander free on the hills and lanes, developing an independence and self reliance that would set them in good stead in later life. Sandy initially attended Birkenhead Prep School before following his elder brother into Birkenhead School in 1911. He worked hard in school though he did worry he was not good enough.

A family holiday in 1915 involved the Irvine children visiting a cousin in Glasgow and it was on this holiday that Sandy went on a voyage down the Clyde where he was amazed at the Battle Cruisers being built and longed to be able to go on one. His cousins christened him 'Sandy Andy' on account of his blonde hair one assumes, and he liked the name so much that he insisted everyone call him 'Sandy' including his family. The name stuck and only rarely did anyone call him Andrew thereafter.

In September 1917 Willie decided to send Sandy to Shrewsbury School, the same school attended by St George Littledale half a century earlier, it was here that Sandy really thrived.

He settled in well and while still struggling academically he excelled in sports, he had a particular love for rowing and worked his way up the lower ranks of the school rowing team to eventually become one of the best rowers the school had known, winning for the first time at Henley Regatta the Elsenham Cup in 1919. The following year they tried to win the coveted Ladies' Plate, although they managed to make the final they lost in a close race to Christ's College, Oxford.

Sandy's interest in all things mechanical led to some interesting 'experiments' at home one of which resulted in his younger brother getting a perforated ear drum when Sandy blew him off a pile of bricks when studying the effects of his home made gunpowder. Whilst at Shrewsbury Sandy continued to be captivated by mechanical objects and by some quirk of fate the school had come into possession of a German Machine Gun, Sandy dismantled it to see how it worked and came across a solution to a problem that had beleaguered the British equivalent which kept jamming. Another problem Sandy managed to solve was when he invented, from scratch, an interrupter gear that would allow a machine gun to fire through the propeller without damaging it. He sent the design off to the War Office who were surprised to receive such detailed drawings from a mere schoolboy, sadly another inventor had been working on this problem and arrived at a similar solution though the War Office did thank him for his efforts and suggested he keep trying.

After Shrewsbury Sandy finally managed to get into Merton College, Oxford though it took a re-sit of the responsions entrance exam. Within the first week of attending Merton Sandy was offered a place in the Oxford boat which made him something of a celebrity, he would have to train hard for the boat race with Cambridge on 1st April 1922 though one big advantage was that they were relieved of their studies which pleased him no end. Sadly they lost to Cambridge though some of the local press did notice Sandy as 'quite promising but needs more experience'. After Easter Sandy had to get back to his studies but his main passion always seemed to be the rowing and he was selected again the following year for the boat race. This time he had ample opportunity to train and anticipation was running high for an Oxford victory as they had not won since 1913. While the preparations were moving apace Sandy was selected for the Oxford University trip to Spitsbergen, on this expedition would be Noel Odell and Dr. Tom Longstaff, two stalwarts of the Alpine Club who would later recommend heartily for the inclusion of Sandy in the 1924 Everest Expedition.

On the 24th March 1923 the boat race took place with the Oxford crew in a newly designed boat and in a very close, hard fought race Oxford triumphed though they would not win again till 1937. The following day Sandy met Noel Odell for lunch in Whitehall to discuss the forthcoming trip to Spitsbergen and Odell noted Sandy's obvious enthusiasm for the project.

Sandy with Odell and other members of the forthcoming trip to Spitsbergen went to North Wales for a few days climbing during Easter 1923. It is a popular misconception by many people to assume that Sandy was an inexperienced climber and that George Mallory only decided to take Sandy on their last fateful climb as he knew better than anyone how to make the Oxygen apparatus work. What is generally not known is that Sandy was a capable climber and proved to be so on this short break when he led the crux pitch of 'Great Gully' on the brooding Craig Yr Ysfa in such poor conditions that had defeated Odell himself.

While Sandy may have lacked any real mountaineering judgment on Everest, given his lack of experience at altitude, and he no doubt trusted George Mallory in the decision making he was certainly capable and fit enough to be considered a worthy partner for him. On this trip they also climbed on Cadair Idris and the almost alpine east peak of Lliwedd climbing Route 2, a 1000ft Severe climb.

The rest of the spring and summer of 1923 were largely taken up with studying and the increasing preparations for the Spitsbergen trip which was due to depart in mid July. They left Newcastle aboard the SS Leda and while the expedition members had to endure 'filthy' Second Class cabins Sandy had recently struck up a relationship with a married woman who had decided to accompany the expedition on the first stage to Tromso and so he enjoyed better night-time accommodation in the First Class cabins than the other members.

The boat pulled into Lodingen harbour, this enabled Sandy and Noel to make a dash for the highest peak just south-west of the town where they were afforded marvellous views from the summit. The next day they arrived at Tromso and enjoyed a farewell dinner with the ladies who had accompanied them before unloading the crates from the Leda onto The Terningen, a sloop which was to be their home base for the next six weeks. At 1.00am on the 23rd July they sailed out of Tromso towards Spitsbergen in a rough sea that debilitated many expedition members for a couple of days till the seas lessened.

One member wrote on a particularly fine morning;

All were soon on deck, even the worst sailors among us, to see the wonderful first glimpse of a mysterious land of ice and snow and jagged mountain peaks. The first impression to the mind of a newcomer to this strange part of the globe is one of awe at the grandeur of the ice and snow, and the thought that it is all new and thousands of years behind the world we know in geological formation and development. The mountains are reminiscent of the Alps but the barrenness and bareness is new. Glaciers bigger than the biggest in Switzerland sweep down right into the sea.

The sloop sailed around the coast and whenever they could Odell and Sandy, perhaps with one or two other members, would leave the main party and climb a small peak or cliff. On the 28th July Sandy fell into a crevasse on the first occasion he had ever walked upon a glacier. They finally landed at Cape Duym after their initial objective of landing at Whalenberg Bay was not possible due to heavy pack ice. Sandy with Odell , and another pair of surveyors, left the sloop on the 30th July to begin their epic trek across the icy wastes of Spitsbergen. They pitched their first camp in glorious sunshine at 4.15am, the daytimes were often misty and so they elected to travel overnight and sleep during the day, in August this is possible due to almost 24 hours of sunlight.

It was hard work pulling the two sledges each of which weighed over 500lb though they got lighter as they ate their way through the food supplies. It was Sandy's job to check that all the crampons and ski bindings fitted each other's boots and he took on the responsibility of ensuring that each days camp was correctly stocked and that nothing had been left behind. He was meticulous in his approach and frequently made notes of how things could be improved for the next expedition. The party lived on a diet of pemmican (a type of dried meat paste) and dried fruit, biscuits formed a frugal pudding.

Initial progress was slow due to the soft snow of the lower glaciers and after a few days Odell suggested they try the skis, despite Sandy never having used them before he threw himself into learning on the job and soon became competent though not without the occasional hilarious mishap especially when they encountered a slight downhill section. Sandy and Odell were primarily interested in making geological observations of the landscape while the other two members concentrated on surveying the island, it worked well and often Sandy with Odell could be seen climbing a local peak from camp just for the sheer fun of it.

After 150 hours of near constant sunshine the snow conditions became worse and it was all the party could do to make camp with one sledge of supplies abandoning the other some four miles further back. The next day Sandy and Milling went back to try and recover it, the snow was very 'sticky' and the sledge often sank deeply into the snow but they finally managed it. It was this effort to see the task through that convinced Noel Odell that Sandy would be an ideal member of the Everest team due to leave for Tibet early in 1924. The next day the team managed to shoot an arctic fox for the pot but only Odell and the chef would eat it, Sandy preferred the pemmican.

On the 16th August Sandy & Odell climbed an unnamed peak some 5500ft high by a difficult rock face which had several difficult pitches, Odell compared the climb to the Tower ridge on Ben Nevis. They had a superb view in all directions from the summit which Odell described as being as fine as the high Alps, a quick descent by a snowfield led them back to their skis and camp. Some thirty years earlier a Russian team had climbed Mount Chernishev for the first time and Odell now realised that the map they had produced was inaccurate and so the Oxford party set about correcting it.

The weather now began to take a turn for the worse and for two days they were confined to their tents by blizzards and hurricane force winds. While trapped in their tents Odell began to relate some of his past adventures and told of one story when walking on the mountains of North Wales with his wife he was approached by a lone motorcyclist asking the way to Llanfairfechan, it was Sandy and he produced a newspaper cutting from his wallet to prove the point. This caused no end of hilarity amongst the party and lifted their spirits especially as Sandy was becoming concerned over the length of time available to the party to get back to the boat. Odell also mentioned the forthcoming Everest expedition and the problems they were having with the oxygen apparatus, this was something Sandy could really get his teeth into and he discussed the matter for hours with Odell and made many notes and sketches in his notebook for future reference.

On the morning of the third day the party had to move and while the weather had improved slightly the conditions underfoot had not and they had a frightful struggle with the sledges in the deep soft snow. Matters were made worse by an injury to Odell's shoulder that prevented him from helping in the pulling of the sledges. Sails partly helped and the party fought its way to Klass Billen Bay, the glacier now became smooth and most of the big crevasses were filled with snow so faster progress could be made. They pitched their final camp on a rocky outcrop above the bay in glorious sunshine surrounded by magnificent mountains reflected in the golden evening sunlight. After they retired to bed for the night the storm blew in again and collapsed Sandy and Odell's tent such was its force, with help from the others they managed to re-erect it but sleep was not possible. Thankfully by 9.00am the next morning the storm had blown itself out and all that remained was a short final march to the comforts of the Terningen, a party from the boat met them and made this last pull more bearable.

Once on board they enjoyed a sumptuous meal prepared in honour of their safe return, four days later they arrived back in Tromso where Sandy could finally have a bath in the Royal Hotel. All was not over however as Odell wanted a final climb and had decided to tackle a serious climb on the Jaergerrasstind. A party of four, two ropes of two, with Odell and Sandy leading saw them get to within 300ft of the summit before turning back, Odell stressed the importance to Sandy of having a sensible turn-around time and making sure that one had enough energy for the descent. Such was their tiredness after a seventeen hour day the party fell asleep on the shore while waiting for the boat back to Tromso.

Odell was impressed with Sandy's fitness, attitude and ability to fix things, he was especially impressed with Sandy's aptitude with regard to the on-going oxygen apparatus and he would subsequently recommend Sandy to the Mount Everest Selection Committee without hesitation. He told Sandy so and suggested that he get some practice skiing and learn about snow conditions. Upon arrival back in England Sandy was all aglow at the prospect of getting a chance to climb the highest mountain in the world.

Everest 1924

Sandy needed two recommendations to be considered by the Mount Everest Selection Committee and he went to the Lake District in September 1923 to meet with George Abraham whom Odell had recommended, they had dinner and it must have gone well as George wrote to Mr. C. E. Meade on the selection committee putting Sandy forward.

The next day Sandy and his old school friend Dick drove from Keswick to Langdale to try and make the first ever double crossing of the Hard Knott and Wrynose passes in a motor car. George Abraham and his daughters came along also to assist in the photographing of the enterprise.

On the 24th October 1923 Sandy received his longed for invitation to join the 1924 Everest Expedition, subject to a rigorous medical which he duly passed with flying colours. From this date on Sandy was near bombarded with paperwork from the Mount Everest Committee and one of the first things he did was contact Percy Unna to request one of the oxygen sets used on the 1922 Everest Expedition.

Once this was received Sandy spent many hours in his room at Oxford taking the apparatus apart and seeing how it worked, how it could be made lighter, more efficient and thus more practical for use high on the mountain. He made many observations and drawings and showed them to Percy Unna who agreed they should send his revised plans to Siebe Gorman [the manufacturers of the oxygen apparatus]. It was a very disappointed and indignant Sandy who, upon arrival in Darjeeling in 1924, noticed that his designs and modifications had been ignored.

Sandy had many meeting with Unna who gave him permission and money to buy additional equipment and tools for the expedition, Sandy knew there would be problems with the oxygen on the mountain and was determined to be well prepared to deal with them when they arose.

Odell had also told Sandy that he needed to learn about snow conditions on the mountains and to ski. Sandy wrote to another friend of Odell's, Arnold Lunn, in Switzerland who promptly invited him to Murren over Christmas and New Year. When Sandy arrived he had no real experience of skiing and although he had been on skis in Spitsbergen that was mainly on the level terrain of a glacier dragging a sledge. Sandy was a diligent pupil and soon picked up the basics of skiing though he did acquire the nickname of the 'Human Avalanche' such were the frequency and spectacular nature of his falls.

Sandy also managed to join a party of guided skiers who were to descend the largest glacier in the Alps, the Aleitsch. They took the train up the inside of the Eiger and from the top station, the Jungfraujoch, they skied down to the small hut just before the onset of a blizzard. The following morning they skied down the rest of the glacier to arrive at a small village where the party got rather drunk.

When Sandy returned back to Oxford in the January he wrote to Arnold

Lunn thanking him and he further stated;

'When I am an old man I will look back on Christmas 1923, as the day when to all intents and purposes I was born. I don't think anyone has lived until they have been on ski'

One other piece of training Sandy undertook was to fly to 20,000ft in an aeroplane, to get a feel for the air at that altitude was his excuse.

The 1924 expedition to Everest, like the preceding two, were huge logistical operations run with an almost military precision. Each member of the expedition was given a list of personal items they needed to acquire for the trip and Sandy spent three days in London at the beginning of February acquiring his many items of equipment and being fitted for the boots he would use high on Everest above the north col.

A mightily relieved Sandy returned to Birkenhead for the final month before departure though he did make further trips to London to speak at length with Percy Unna over the oxygen set and stoves. Sandy continued to work at home in his small workshop on the oxygen apparatus he had brought back with him from Oxford. He was also becoming more concerned over not hearing from Siebe Gorman but hoped they had made use of his plans.

Before departure Sandy, George Mallory and two other expedition members were guests of honour at the Exchange Club in Fenwick Street, Liverpool for a meal given by the Wayfarer's Club on the 28th February 1924. The Liverpool Post had earlier printed the names of the expedition members and ran the headline:-

'MOUNT EVEREST EXPEDITION – TWO BIRKENHEAD MEN IN THE PARTY'.

I feel that George Mallory's link with Birkenhead is somewhat tenuous in that he was not born in the area and was living and working elsewhere in the country. It is true to say that he spent a fair amount of time in the area as his father was a minister in St John's Church. All that said however on the 26th May 1924 in a letter home to his mother Mallory wrote;

Irvine is the star of the new members. He is a very fine fellow, has been doing excellently up to date & should prove a splendid companion on the mountain. I should think the Birkenhead News ought to have something to say if he and I reach the top together.

Perhaps George Mallory had a closer affinity to Birkenhead than we give him credit for however his story has been so well told in countless books it would seem superfluous to repeat it here.

The next day Sandy, George Mallory together with Benthley Beetham and John Hazard boarded the SS California bound for Bombay, as they were boarding a reporter shouted to Sandy and asked how he felt about climbing Everest. Sandy replied *'It is the duty of the Alpine Club to climb as near as it can to Heaven'*, he also knew that his family had reservations about his relative inexperience though they also encouraged him to live up to his reputation and not let the family down.

Life on board was not without its comforts and dinner was a formal meal where the expedition members were expected to wear a dinner jacket though they could dispense with the starch collars and ties. Mallory thought Sandy rather quiet though he correctly assumed that he would be one you could rely on, the quietness can only be attributed to Sandy's initial shyness and that would change in time. Sandy in turn respected Mallory's mountaineering experience and equal determination as his own to reach the summit of Everest, though his determination did not seem to gnaw away at him as it clearly did at Mallory.

Sailing south through the Suez Canal onto the Red Sea the team noticed a marked increase in the temperature that left them feeling all limp and languid and it was with some relief after several days to finally land in Bombay where they were glad to leave the ship after three weeks at sea and re-discover their land legs.

The party took a train from Bombay across India to Darjeeling which took five long hot days with the team sleeping and eating on the train all the way. The journey from Siliguri to Darjeeling was the highlight of the railway trip for Sandy as the railway left the hot and arid plains of India and rose into the mountains into an entirely different, cooler world. Sandy noted in his diary:

The last bit of train journey 6am – 11.30am climbing 7000ft up to Darjeeling in a motor rail coach on a 2ft gauge railway doing most terrifying curves and traverses of cliffs & swaying about the whole time was most delightful. Starting up through very impressive & terribly thick jungle quite impossible to penetrate without the greatest difficulty & all hung with creepers some quite smooth just like hundreds of cords hanging from the branches & some thick & wound together like enormous cables. All the way just enough clearance for the train and a cart track.

On the 23rd March the party arrived at Darjeeling and met up with the rest of the team, they spent four long and hard days checking everything had arrived and re-packing the mountain of supplies ready for the long march into Tibet. Sandy also spent some time in examining the stoves and acting as a guinea pig for the expedition doctor, he was pleased to note that he could hold his breath at 7000ft for twenty seconds longer than any other expedition member.

The expedition could not rely on regular supplies throughout the long trek into Everest's base camp and so carried some 3000lb of food, tents and equipment which had to be carried by ponies and mules. The expedition leader, General Bruce, wanted to get his men to Everest as fresh and in the best health possible so all expedition members were to ride the majority of the 300 miles across the arduous Tibetan plateau. The journey to Kalimpong was one of new experiences for Sandy and he marvelled at the flora and fauna of this remarkable landscape and despite the effort of such a journey it is clear that Sandy's sense of humour remained strong. He developed a novel way of stopping his horse by merely putting his long legs onto the floor and standing up lifting the pony with him. In the end the riding of a small pony proved too much for Sandy and he ended up walking some two thirds of the three hundred miles to Rongbuk.

He wrote frequently to his mother telling her about the wonderful scenery and how well the expedition is doing on the march. He tells her about their accommodation in the dak bungalows and how well appointed they are, it was clear he wished to assuage his mothers fears. Upon arrival in Kalimpong, the end of the first stage, Sandy once again checked the oxygen stores and stoves, something he would have to do regularly over the next five weeks. The team had to split up into two parties as each stage could only provide accommodation for half the team at a time though after they had reached the village of Phari they could march as a single unit as they would be sleeping tents from thereon in.

The next stage of the march was amid wonderful scenery though partly obscured by the mist of several forest fires caused by an exceptionally dry season, Sandy wrote to his Spitsbergen colleague, Milling;

It's perfectly wonderful being able to go about in a bush shirt and shorts all day and get every damn thing done for you and be able to ride whenever you get tired of walking and through the most pricelessly wonderful glades in the jungle. We are under 6000ft here so the forest is pretty thick still; the only pity is that the visibility has not been good just lately – not for distances over 2 miles or so, otherwise the scenery would be just wonderful. This is a remarkable place: it's pitch dark now & it was bright sunlight when I started this letter – at least very nearly!..........I say old man Odell is just the same as ever! He longs to have you here and the other members are getting quite fed up with our side illusions to you & Spits. They get such a lot of them.

Sandy had now 'opened up' a bit and lost some of his initial shyness and reserve, talking more with Mallory than any other member, he knew he would have to win his confidence if he were to have any hope of getting on the summit party. While he was building bridges with Mallory he did not totally ignore Odell and spent a lot of time with him working on the oxygen apparatus but there was certainly a switch in allegiance to some degree with Sandy clearly having his eyes and heart set on the summit of Everest. This section of the march was proving a delight, the team could bathe regularly in the rivers and streams met en route and they took almost every opportunity to do so for once on the stark Tibetan Plateau there would be little likelihood of anything other than an air bath. Sandy was having to spend an increasing amount of time with the oxygen apparatus which clearly had not been improved to his design and thus he essentially had to largely re-build the whole system en route to the mountain and at base camp, it was fortunate that he had the foresight to bring sufficient tools for the job despite their weight.

On the 1st April they crossed from Sikkim into Tibet by crossing the Jelap La pass at 14,500ft, Sandy noticed a slight headache after climbing 3000ft in a morning and he was glad to sit down for a few minutes and rest, after all this was an altitude record for him. They reached the village of Yatung and met up with the first party who had arrived a day earlier. The son of the British trade agent laid on a party where the members were given seats of honour and treated to a performance of Tibetan Devil Dancers – it lasted four hours and were it not for the Chang and Rakshi they were repeatedly plied with they may have found it a trifle long however they appeared to enjoy the performance and agility of the dancers. The next day General Bruce was not well and so delayed his departure but sent his second in command, Col. Norton ahead instead. Sandy spent the rest day repairing the oxygen and going for a walk with Mallory in the hope of finding something to climb.

The next stage to Phari was through impressive gorges leading out onto the Tibetan Plateau proper, from here-on in the march would become tougher as the near constant winds and dry air play havoc with one's eyes and throat. At Phari it became clear that General Bruce could go no further and Col. Norton was appointed the new leader in Bruce's absence. The team had hoped that Bruce may recover and meet them further on the march at Kampa Dzong but it was not to be as he had suffered a recurrence of a malarial infection and to continue would have been foolish. Mallory also was suffering from stomach pains and Beetham from dysentry.

The Tibetan Plateau is one of the highest land masses in the world and lies at about 14,000ft with many passes of 17 or 18,000ft to be negotiated, vegetation is at best scarce and all around them were numerous unclimbed and unnamed snow peaks. Walking or riding across such terrain is hard work, the wind blows constantly and at the end of each day's march one has to set up camp. The altitude was starting to affect some members of the party now though Sandy and in particular Mallory seemed to be dealing with the adverse conditions better than most.

The nights became colder and on the 8th April, Sandy's twenty second birthday, it fell to minus 18, the clothing they had bought in London was now starting to be put to the test though Sandy wrote in his diary that it severely restricted his movement which is not surprising given that he was probably wearing twenty pounds in weight of clothing.

The long trek was taking its toll on the equipment and every night Sandy was up till past midnight fixing a multitude of essential things and spending longer on the oxygen apparatus than he ever thought possible. Eventually he would re-design the whole system five times en-route until satisfied he'd found the right solution that minimised leaks and was practical and simple enough to be carried and used at altitude, his efforts alone made the oxygen apparatus viable and it is sad to wonder that had he not been so efficient he may not have found himself at the top camp with George Mallory on the 7th June 1924.

The terrain became harsher and the going rougher though Sandy now had a pony that he could ride however an altercation with the owner, who wished him to change it threw Sandy into a rage and the owner backed down. Sandy was clearly 'fired up' as he crossed a 17,500ft pass later that day and was feeling much fitter and stronger than at any point on the long march.

Two days later on the 21st April 1924 Sandy and Mallory climbed a small hill behind camp and for the first time Sandy saw Everest which both thrilled and awed him. That evening Mallory, who was now the climbing leader, told Sandy that he would be on the third summit team with him,

Norton & Somervell were to go first and try to climb Everest without oxygen. The next night Sandy finally hit upon the solution to the oxygen apparatus, he would in all probability get a chance to use it himself and the next morning it was a very tired but happy Sandy that set off on the days march.

At Shekar Dzong Mallory, Somervell, Odell and Sandy tested the new oxygen apparatus which was a vast improvement on the previous designs. Sandy now started to feel unwell, hardly surprising that he was spending every night fixing things in his tent to the small hours and then, after a few hours sleep, making the long march required each day. The wind now began to blow even stronger hurling small stones onto Sandy's blistered and sunburnt face causing a lot of pain. Upon arrival at Tashi Dzong he went straight to bed only to be woken an hour later by Mallory with a box of crampons which required attention and fitting to boots. The next day, the 28th April, they arrived at the longed for Rongbuk Monastery, the last outpost of civilisation before base camp some eleven miles away. At the head of the Rongbuk valley Everest could be seen in all its imposing majesty and while the other members were 'sightseeing' Sandy was again ensconced in his tent this time fixing Beetham's camera. The next day the team walked to base camp which Sandy described;

'Bloody morning, light driving snow, very cold and felt rather rotten.....Walked all the way from Rongbuk Monastery to the base camp 1 ¾ hours over frozen river and very rough terrain. The base camp looked a very uninviting place'

The temperature at base camp was always below freezing and a strong wind usually blew down off the Rongbuk glacier making life hard and rest difficult. There was to be no rest for Sandy and Odell who were busy with the oxygen apparatus modifications which at 17,800ft was doubly difficult to complete but it had to be done. Another anxiety was that while Sandy was in base camp fixing the apparatus, which would shortly be needed by the first climbers going up to the north col, he was not getting any acclimatisation training and he feared he may lose his chance at the summit.

The 2nd May was Sandy's last day in base camp which he spent working flat out on the apparatus, it was a great relief when all the sets were finished and there was no more soldering to be done. In addition that day he fixed a cooker, shortened Mallory's crampons by half an inch and pared down his toolkit which was to be taken up to camp three beneath the north col and the last possible camp where small repairs could be made. Sandy wrote in his diary:-

I hope to put up a good show when the altitude gets a bit trying. I should acclimatize well at [camp] III the time we will spend there,'

The lower camps I & II had been established and stocked by local Tibetan's hired for such purpose and without their help there was simply no way a huge expedition could attempt Everest or indeed any Himalayan giant.

Early after lunch on the 3rd May the climbers set of from base camp intending to spend the night at camp one which was supposed to be the most comfortable of camps, upon their arrival Sandy decided that is was rather unpleasant and was glad to move on the next morning to camp two. Sandy wrote;

The going from I to II was very rough. Mallory and I kept to the lateral moraine as long as possible. After crossing the glacier just opposite a side glacier we found a lovely frozen lake surrounded by seracs where we rested for about half an hour – photographing and studying the map. When we moved on a devil must have got into Mallory for he ran down all the little bits of downhill and paced all out up the moraine. It was as bad as a boat race trying to keep up with him, in spite of my colossal red corpuscles.

This latter reference is to some blood tests carried out at base camp where Sandy was deemed to have a higher red blood cell count than all the others.

On arrival at camp two they put up their tents and then helped the porters build their stone shelters, called Sangars, with a tarpaulin over the top to keep them warm. While helping build the stone walls Sandy developed a nose bleed, a sure sign of the altitude taking effect, so he took a break while Mallory and Odell went further up the glacier to prospect a route to camp three. Sandy was still full of optimism and was looking forward to moving up to camp three the next day, some 2500ft higher than he had ever been before. The next day they left at 11.00am and Sandy was entrusted with six porters to shepherd up the glacier the same as Odell, clearly Sandy was considered a full member of the climbing team. At one point a porter fell behind and Sandy carried his load a short way to give him a rest. They reached the site of camp three at 6.00pm very cold, tired and hungry though the food at this camp was not very well organised yet and the climbers went without the vital liquids that are necessary at this great altitude.

The next morning Mallory was up at 6.20am to the criticism delivered by Sandy of being 'an energetic beggar' but Mallory was keen to ensure that all the supplies, including food, were brought up before they went any further. The day was spent ferrying some of the loads from camp two that had not made it the day previously, this was not an ideal situation as the climbers needed to conserve their energy for the summit push. Their second night at camp three was even colder than the previous as the thermometer dropped to minus 30 Celsius, in addition the wind blew ever stronger and snow fell most of the night. Yet another day had to be spent in trying to ferry the remainder of the loads from camp two, and all the time the climbers and porters were becoming more drained, Sandy himself was feeling wretched and stayed behind at camp three while Hazard and Odell reconnoitred the route to the north col though they had to return later in the day with the news that the weather was bad and the winds very strong. The backlog of supplies was seriously hampering the progress of the expedition every bit as much as the weather and Mallory with Sandy had been at the thick of it at camp three in rallying the porters, Norton decided that they both needed to rest and ordered them to descend to camp two. Sandy was severely dehydrated and on the descent was near collapse, he tried to help himself by piling snow onto his head and when he did finally get to camp two he drank six cups of tea and a couple of glasses of melted glacier water to restore his spirits until he began feel much better.

camp three was still being battered by storms and so there was no other alternative but for the leader to order a retreat to lower altitudes, indeed all the way to base camp, while the storm would hopefully blow itself out and all the men could recover. Sandy reached base camp on the 11th May where the now seemingly thick air of 16,500ft was a tonic to what they had endured only a few miles away. The expedition doctor arrived in base camp after tending to General Bruce and pronounced that many of the porters were not fit enough to continue and some were very seriously ill with one dying during an evacuation to base camp from camp one.

Sandy enjoyed a rare rest day before returning to his seemingly normal duties of fixing things in his workshop / tent. Mallory was concerned over the delays encountered and revised his summit day to May 28th 1924. His fear was that they were getting perilously close to the oncoming monsoon season which would render the mountain un-climbable and more dangerous than ever. The morale amongst the porters was low, especially given the death of one of their own men, and Norton sent Karma Paul, the head porter, down to Rongbuk Monastery to see if the head Lama would grant them an audience, this Norton knew would mean a great deal to their men and so it proved as on the 15th May they all went to the Monastery to receive their blessing, Sandy wrote;

After sitting for an hour and a half eating meat and macaroni with chop sticks (well-chewed ends), drinking Tibetan tea and eating radish with very strong pepper in an ante-chamber, we were ushered into the presence of the Lama who sat on a red throne on an iron bedstead just inside a kind of veranda....we sat on beautifully upholstered benches on either side of an alcove in the roof. Noel [Capt. JBL] had his camera about 30ft away on the edge of the roof. After being blessed and having our heads touched with a white metal pepper-pot (at least it looked like that) we sat down while the whole damn lot of coolies came in doing 3 salams-head right onto the ground and the presented the caddas and offerings and were similarly blessed. Next bowls of rice were brought and the Lama addressed the coolies in a few well-chosen words and the said a prayer or prayers – it all sounded the same, ending on a wonderfully deep note.

After the ceremony the porters seemed much happier to continue and their spirits soared, Sandy however was feeling less than well and for the next few days he was troubled by diarrhoea. This did not stop him from doing all that he could for the expedition and he made sure that the porters knew how to use the stoves and repairing various items of equipment that had become damaged during the retreat from camp three.

The only real worry now for the expedition was the aforementioned monsoon which had arrived on the 1st June 1922, the year of the last expedition, however the monsoon was usually preceded by two weeks of warm, clear and stable weather and it was this 'window' they would hope to use for their assault on the upper slopes of Everest. Therefore it was vital that everyone should be 'in position' when this weather window came. On the 18th May Sandy left base camp heading up for camp one though still feeling rotten from his diarrhoea he made good progress and the following day, feeling much better, he made his way up to camp two in record time. On the 20th May Sandy made his way up to camp three again and in good enough time to carry out the numerous repairs left for him in his tent by the advance party of Mallory et al. That morning Mallory, Odell, Norton and a porter called Lhakpa Tsering had attempted to fix a line of ropes up to the north col, a major camp as Everest summit could be seen along with the ridge they were to climb, though this party had had several close shaves throughout the day with the difficult terrain before establishing a feasible route to the north col. At one point a tired Mallory had fallen into a crevasse on the descent and only just managed to extricate himself though the effort had left him exhausted.

While Mallory and the rest of the party recovered Sandy with Somervell and Hazard went up to the north col with twelve heavily laden porters. The terrain proved too difficult for the porters and so Sandy and Somervell hauled their loads up a 200ft Chimney so they could climb un-encumbered and thus all climbers and porters safely reached camp four on the north col. They dumped the loads and as there was insufficient room for everyone Sandy and Somervell returned back to camp three '*very tired and thirsty*', Sandy wrote home to his mother '*that he'd been to the north col in a blizzard and never want to do it again*'.

Another night in camp three followed and the next day Norton told Sandy that six oxygen appliances were needed for early the next day to be taken up to camp four in readiness for a summit attempt. Sandy worked till midnight to complete his task although it was bitingly cold and he began to feel unwell again. Odell and Norton left that morning but could not get to camp four as the newly fallen snow had rendered the route unsafe and so they turned back. Hazard and the porters in camp four however decided to descend as no-one had come up to relieve them and a disaster would surely be imminent if they did not get help in descending the by now treacherous slopes. Such was the state of the snow four of the porters turned back and Norton knew he would have to mount a rescue. As Norton, Somervell and Mallory headed up to the north col Sandy with Hazard was ordered to descend again leaving only Odell and Capt. Noel (the cameraman) behind to help them. Norton, Mallory and Somervell managed to rescue the four stranded porters and descend safely to camp three much to the relief of all concerned. One must remember the death of seven porters in 1922 and Norton was anxious not to see a repeat of such a tragedy. Another bad night was endured in camp three before the bedraggled party limped into camp two, the following day they all descended to be greeted by the bad news that another porter had died because of his badly frostbitten feet.

Given that so many of the porters were now out of action another revised summit plan was discussed and to Sandy's great dismay it would not include him in either of the two parties, though he would be included as a reserve member. Mallory chose Geoffrey Bruce to be his partner for the first attempt and Somervell with Norton would make up the second party, notably neither party would be using oxygen as they considered the apparatus to be too heavy and besides there were not enough porters to carry it high up the mountain.

Sandy, while upset at not being chosen, still played his part and made a rope ladder for the porters to negotiate the formidable ice chimney on the way to the north col above camp three.

On the 31st May the four climbers, the reserve party and fifteen porters made their way up to the north col making good use of Sandy's rope ladder and upon arrival at camp four Sandy set about making a meal. Sandy and Noel Odell had been appointed by Norton as the official support team, this 'support team' were to cook the meals and look after practically every need of the lead climbers, Norton later wrote for the Times dispatch;

Since 1922 we have recognised the necessity of this role, picturing the comfort to a returning party of weary climbers such support might afford. The most optimistic imaginations fell short of the reality, as produced by that 'well-known firm [Sandy & Odell]. For over a week those two have lived on the north col (23,000ft) and have cooked every meal – and only those who have done it can appreciate the recurring hatefulness of this operation. They have gone out day and night to escort and succour returning parties of porters and climbers over the intricate approaches to the camp, carrying lamps, drinks, and even oxygen to restore the exhausted. They have run the camp and tended the sick. Whether we reach the top or not, no members of the climbing party can pull more weight in the team than these two by their unostentatious, unselfish, gruelling work.

Mallory and Bruce succeeded in establishing camp five despite Bruce straining his heart in ferrying a dumped load and despite Mallory's and Bruce's best efforts to persuade the porters to move higher and establish a further camp they had to beat a retreat back to the north col and camp four. Mallory had decided however to mount a further attempt with oxygen and to this end he decided that Sandy was the only man capable of accompanying him.

On the 2nd June Sandy was up again early to prepare breakfast for

Norton & Somervell's heroic attempt on the summit. They left at 6.00am, as Sandy watched them leave he noticed the returning party of Mallory and Bruce and set out to meet them, Mallory told Sandy of his plans and Sandy immediately rushed back down to camp three to prepare the apparatus in readiness for his attempt. Mallory had also descended to see how many porters could be mustered for this final assault. Mallory desperately wanted to be 'done' with Everest as he disliked being away from his wife and children for such long periods.

Using oxygen, Mallory and Sandy made quick and satisfying progress back up to the north col and heard the news that Norton & Somervell had managed to establish a further camp at 27,000ft, camp six as it became known. On the morning of the 4th June they left their shelter and made slow, painful progress up Everest where Norton noticed that he had to take eight or nine breaths for each upward step made. At 28.000ft Somervell could go no further and Norton continued on his own till he too could go no further, he had reached an altitude of 28,126 ft before turning back to join Somervell for the long descent back to the north col. Somervell was so debilitated by his throat that he soon fell behind Norton and finally had to stop while his cough became worse, eventually he managed to perform some 'compressions' and dislodged a part of his larynx that had become frostbitten, after that he was able to breathe properly again and continue his descent in the dark towards the welcoming site of camp four on the north col.

When Norton arrived at the north col Mallory put to him his plan for a further attempt with Sandy and with oxygen, Norton reluctantly, as he thought Mallory should have taken Odell, agreed and the die was cast.

Sandy and George Mallory left camp four at 7.30am on the 6th June 1924 with packs weighing 25 pounds, considerably less than the 35 pounds they would have weighed prior to Sandy's mechanical genius in reducing weight and delivering a more effective oxygen apparatus.

Odell, before the pair left snapped a photograph of them both, Sandy with his hands in his pockets and Mallory fiddling with the oxygen set, nobody realised it would be the last photograph ever taken of them alive. The weather was good though it did cloud over later in the day, Mallory and Sandy made it to camp five at 25,600ft where they sent back their porters with a note saying there was little wind and they were hopeful of the summit. The next day Odell moved up to camp five while Sandy and Mallory moved onto camp six, again they sent the porters down with a note from Mallory which read:-

Dear Odell,
We're awfully sorry to have left things in such a mess-our Unna cooker rolled down the slope at the last moment. Be sure of getting back to IV tomorrow in time to evacuate before dark, as I hope to. In the tent I must have left a compass-for the lord's sake rescue it; we are without. To here on 90 atmospheres for the two days-so we'll probably to go on two cylinders-but it's a bloody load for climbing. Perfect weather for the job!
Yours ever G. Mallory

Odell found the compass and sent the rest of the porters down to camp four, he was glad to be on his own as he could spend more time studying the geology on his way up to camp six the next day.

As Odell sat outside his tent on the evening of the 7th June 1924 he reflected on both Mallory's and Sandy's absolute desire to climb Everest.

We can never truly know what happened on the afternoon of 7th June at camp six, Mallory preferred to prospect the route ahead for next day and it is known he had a preference for the ridge rather than Norton's lower route across the face. Modern climbers take this ridge route and the infamous difficult second step is overcome by an aluminium ladder left by the Chinese on their successful ascent however Mallory and Sandy were finding their way and it is not certain whether they found an alternative route up this rocky face and ridge above camp six. Mallory left a note for Odell in the tent at camp six suggesting he keep an eye out for them on the skyline from 8.00am.

Sandy made breakfast on the morning of the 8th June 1924 while Mallory got himself ready for the climb, Mallory preferred an 'Alpine' start and it is possible they left under a clear moonlit sky as the weather was good. Odell left camp five early full of joy and optimism for the day ahead, he climbed a 100ft cliff just to test his powers at this extreme altitude. He found the first fossil on his walk up and at 12.50pm he wrote in his diary 'At 12.50 saw M & I on ridge nearing base of final pyramid.' Moments later the clouds rolled in and he made his way up to camp six arriving at 2.00pm finding the tent in a usual 'Sandy Irvine' mess of discarded tools and other apparatus.

The weather had now got worse and a blizzard was blowing in, Odell became concerned that Mallory and Sandy may have difficulty in locating the tent in such conditions. He climbed some 200ft above the tent and began to shout though the force of the storm eventually forced him to seek shelter in the tent. Thankfully the storm eventually blew itself out and mindful of Mallory's insistence that he return back to the north col, as there was not enough room in camp six for three climbers, he made his way back down. Odell stopped frequently on his descent to see if he could see either of his two friends but given the scale of the mountain it was simply not possible to see anything in the now fine evening.

He arrived back at camp four by 6.45pm where he was welcomed by Hazard with mugs of soup and tea. It was a clear night but nothing could be seen of Mallory or Sandy and the same blank, lifeless landscape was present in the morning. Come midday Odell decided he would go back up to both camp five and camp six, in itself a herculean effort after what he done previously, to see if there was any sign of the now missing climbers. However before he left he advised Hazard to train the binoculars onto a patch of snow and once at the camps he would lay sleeping bags on the snow to signal if there was anything that could be done. He struggled up to camp five that afternoon but there was no sign of Sandy or Mallory. His porters could go no further so he spent a bitterly cold night at the camp before climbing on up to camp six on the 10th June 1924 where, much to his distress there was again no sign of either of them, the tent was exactly as he had left it. Odell made a search of the surrounding area, following a route he guessed that may have taken but still there was no sign and after two hours he gave up the struggle in the increasing wind, towards evening the wind lessened and Odell could lay the sleeping bags out in the snow in a simple 'T' shape to demean that no trace can be found.

With a heavy heart Odell descended straight back to camp four knowing full well that if Sandy and / or Mallory were up there alive there could be no hope of surviving another night out in the open above 27,000ft. The wind howled as he descended and Odell had to frequently seek shelter behind some rocks from the stronger gusts of wind, his had been a heroic effort perhaps unparalleled at the time in mountaineering but it was of no avail Sandy and Mallory were lost.

We will never know what truly happened on that last climb, many people believe that they did make it to the summit and died on the descent. Edmund Hillary, upon reaching the summit in 1953 confessed to looking for signs of them but he saw nothing. The finding of George Mallory's body in 1999 only added to the mystery and perhaps we will only ever know what happened if the body of Sandy Irvine is ever found as it is believed he had the camera that could contain a photograph from the summit.

For many years it was assumed that Sandy Irvine was only taken by Mallory as he knew and believed in the oxygen apparatus. While there is no doubt this played a part in Mallory choosing Sandy it is clear that he performed as well as any man on this expedition. He worked tirelessly repairing and building things, he carried his fair share of loads and helped in carrying out the many chores that needed to be done.

The only thing that Sandy perhaps lacked, and this was no fault of his own given his youth, was mountaineering judgment. He proved capable of leading the respectable rock climbs of the day and even 'outshining' Noel Odell on the infamous Great Cave Pitch on Craig Yr Ysfa. He was certainly as fit if not fitter than many of the lead climbers and it surely leads one to the conclusion that Sandy was an equal with every other climber on this expedition.

There were many memorial services held for Sandy including one at Shrewsbury School and in Oxford, a service was also geld in St Paul's Cathedral. However the service held in St John's Church in Birkenhead and presided over by Mallory's father was the one that meant the most to Sandy's family.

In the official account of the expedition, The Fight for Everest, Norton wrote the following about Sandy;

He shares with Odell the credit of having shown us all how to 'play for the side' stifling all selfish considerations, for nothing in the record of 1924 was finer than the work these two put in as 'supporters' at Camp IV.

Sandy Irvine's cheerful camaraderie, his unselfishness and high courage made him loved, not only by all of us, but also by the porters, not a word of whose language could he speak. After the tragedy I remember discussing his character with Geoffrey Bruce with a view to writing some appreciation of it to The Times, at the end Bruce said: 'It was worth dying on the mountain to leave a reputation like that' Men have had worse epitaphs.

In 2001 a climbing wall was built in Birkenhead School where Sandy was once a pupil and it was named in his honour 'The Sandy Irvine Climbing Wall', and was officially opened on the 16th November by his great niece and biographer, Julie Summers, who also unveiled a portrait of her Great Uncle in the Bushell Hall of the school.

Colin Kirkus & Menlove Edwards

'I grew up exuberant in body but with a nervy, craving mind. It was wanting something more, something tangible. It sought for reality intensely, always as if it were not there... But you see at once what I do. I climb.' John Menlove Edwards

Over time it began to be appreciated by the early mountaineers that in winter the British mountains afforded a splendid opportunity to get some good practice and exercise for a summer alpine excursion. In due course the British mountains began to be enjoyed year round and a new sport, if that is what it can be called, developed and flourished initially in the English Lake District and then gradually elsewhere.

It is generally accepted that Rock Climbing began to be seen as a distinct activity in its own right with W P Haskett Smiths ascent of the Napes Needle in Wasdale in 1886. This slender pinnacle of rock in the Lake District is dwarfed by the mass of Great Gable behind it yet its ascent really marked a departure from the climbing of a mountain by any feasible route to that of seeking out difficulties for difficulties sake.

The early rock climbers tended to stick to gullies [steep fissures in a cliff face] or chimneys though as confidence grew they ventured out onto the steeper faces between the gullies and found that although they often looked blank from a distance upon closer inspection the climbers realised they were often peppered with small cracks and ledges that would happily accept a foot or hand.

Equipment was rudimentary in the beginning, a simple hemp rope was all that was taken and even that could have been the proverbial washing line pilfered from the hotel they were staying at. Specialised equipment did not come till much later, footwear was invariably a pair of simple nailed shoes or boots. The belaying techniques deployed were often quite simply dangerous, the climbers usually moved together and merely draped the rope that stretched between them over any convenient flake of rock or other protuberance, it is remarkable that fatalities were so few and it must be attributed to their overall caution and ability in not only the actual climbing but in finding a way up the cliffs.

I have already mentioned the first or early ascents of many climbs carried out by the likes of 'The Walkers' etc towards the end of the 19th century and I choose not to go into any great detail here again but instead to concentrate on a handful of those who advanced the sport in the 20th century.

By the 1930's equipment and belaying techniques had advanced but not in any way remotely like what we enjoy today. The rope was still of hemp that kinked terribly when wet and weighed considerably more as a consequence, whereas modern nylon ropes stretch when loaded by a fall the hemp rope didn't, a fall could be disastrous and the rope could simply snap, the age old maxim of the leader must not fall was never truer than in these early days.

Harnesses were simply not heard of and it was usual to just tie the rope around your-self with a simple bowline before setting off on a climb. Footwear had hardly changed either though on the more difficult climbs one would climb in socks or wear a pair of black Woolworths rubber plimsolls such as some of us used to wear in school PE lessons until very recently. Occasionally a spare loop of hemp line would be carried for a sling in which to thread the rope through a chock-stone or over a flake but that was essentially it. When one compares the paraphernalia of a modern rock climber with his sticky rubber boots, lightweight karabiners, alloy nuts and various camming devices these early climbers were amazingly under-shod so to speak.

There were social changes to take into account as well, whereas the Victorian mountaineers were almost always very well heeled by the 1930's more people than ever from differing backgrounds were making for the British hills and moors. These new climbers were invariably from the burgeoning middle classes, and as more of them made their way onto the hills and mountains of Britain so to did the standards of difficulty increase proportionally.

Two men from Merseyside in particular raised the standard of British rock climbing to such an extent that even today their climbs are very popular and widely respected.

Colin Kirkus

Colin Kirkus was born in Liverpool in 1910, the family home in Croxteth Grove was but a stone's throw away from the old homes of the Walker's and Frederick Gardiner though it is unlikely the Kirkus family were aware of their famous old neighbours. Colin was introduced to the mountains of North Wales by his parents at an early age, he was lucky as both his parents had a deep love of the countryside and in particular North Wales which proved to be within relatively easy reach for any comfortable Edwardian middle class family. Colin initially attended Caldy Grange Grammar School then went, as a day boarder, to the Liverpool College school, near to Mossley Hill, were he was to prove above average academically though sadly not quite good enough to be considered suitable for a university education.

At the family home hung a picture of Cwm Idwal by Peter Ghent and the wildness of the scene apparently captivated the young schoolboy who expressed more than a passing interest in mountains and climbing even at the age of eleven. His fervour grew each summer with the annual family holiday in North Wales where he often went for walks and climbs with his brothers or, as he got older, on his own. He developed at an early age a considerable toughness and resilience which would stand in him in good stead as his climbing and mountaineering career thrived. In 1927 Colin persuaded his family to switch their usual holiday destination from Carrog to Betws Y Coed, the advantage of the change being that Betws Y Coed is much nearer the bigger mountains of Snowdonia and thus Colin could indulge his passion for climbing on the these magnificent mountains and crags.

He lacked a climbing partner and so climbed on his own, he later wrote in his classic instructional work 'Let's Go Climbing' :

'I spent practically the whole of this holiday in continuously breaking a rule that is constantly hammered into beginners – climbing alone while still a novice. But what else could I do? I did not know any climbers, and it was only occasionally that I could get my father or brothers to accompany me. There was only one alternative – not to climb – and that was unthinkable. The ambition of my life at that time was to do some recognized rock-climbs; not just casual little scrambles, but real routes that

had names and were described in the guide-book.'

' Though wrong as a policy, this early solo-climbing taught me an immense amount. I knew that if I made a mistake I had no-one to help me; I had to rely entirely on my own skill and my own judgment.'

Colin subsequently had a number of close shaves on his solo exploits, on one occasion only avoiding coming to grief after he had somehow managed to stop himself after a fall at the edge of a huge drop in a gully. However the more Colin climbed the better he got, once he managed to extricate himself from a very steep climb by lassoing a bollard of rock with some rope he carried for such a purpose, and then hand over hand he swarmed up the near vertical rock to a ledge and safety.

Although Colin was far from working class he was not representative of the class of men and women climbing in North Wales at this time, the public school and university background was much more prominent, Colin would have to work for his living.

After the summer holiday he went to work for the Royal Insurance in Liverpool where he worked for thirteen years until he joined the RAF for the Second World War. He also had by this time joined the prominent Wayfarer's Club from Liverpool and was able to make regular weekend trips to North Wales and, perhaps more importantly, he now had no need to climb on his own all the time. The club enjoyed strong links with the Climbers Club who had a hut 'Helyg' in the Ogwen Valley. As well as weekend trips Colin was able to climb on the sandstone outcrop of Helsby of an evening, here he honed his technique to a high degree and it would only be a matter of time before he got the opportunity to transfer these skills onto the bigger cliffs of North Wales and elsewhere.

In 1928 Colin began his climbing career properly with two new ascents, one a delightful easy climb in the Moelwyns above the town of Blaenau Ffestiniog and a particularly vicious climb in the Carneddau range which even today is still graded Very Severe. This climb gave Colin one of his closest shaves as, climbing solo, he had to make a wild lunge near the top in the hope of finding a hold to save him-self from falling.

Later that year he met Alan 'AB' Hargreaves, who was to become a solid regular climbing partner and together they shared many adventures and difficult climbs.

During the winter of 1928/29 Colin & AB wrote a new guidebook to Helsby, which was now recognised as one of the most important outcrops in the country. The standard of some of the climbs was far in excess as to what had been achieved at that time on the big mountain cliffs of North Wales and the Lake District.

At Easter 1929 Colin and AB went to Helyg and they made a number of new climbs that were as hard as anything done before. Shortly afterwards they made their way to the Lake District and repeated some of the hardest climbs that had been done in the area including Botterrill's Slab on Scafell which is still graded Very Severe today. One can be sure that Colin gave the impeccable Flake Crack on Central Buttress a wistful stare. The standard of Lakeland climbing was considered by many to be superior than that of North Wales though it would not be long before the balance would be addressed. AB was later to write that this trip was where Colin really found himself as a climber, although he had only been climbing a couple of years he was able to climb some of the hardest routes in the country.

In June 1929 Colin led a party staying at Helyg up Belle Vue Bastion high on Tryfan and a short walk from the hut, it's a superb climb, which had only been climbed two years previously, still graded Very Severe today it has a wonderfully exposed second pitch. Colin then led the party over to the north facing crags of Glyder Fach. He had espied a narrow groove to the left of an established route, he led on up it establishing a superb climb now called Lot's Groove which is still graded Hard Very Severe, only one other member of the party was able to follow him up the climb and it would be two years before anyone else could repeat it, many considered it to be one of the hardest in the country. As if that was not enough the next day on Tryfan's East Face Colin climbed Central Route which while lacking the purity of line was to prove just as hard and technical as Lot's Groove.

On June 29th Colin climbed Longland's Climb on the west buttress of the mightily impressive Clogwyn Du'r Arddu, a huge sombre north facing crag on the flanks of Snowdon. Cloggy, as it is affectionately known to climbers today, is the most impressive crag in North Wales if not the whole country and his second ascent of this climb moved him into the top echelons of climbers operating in the country at the time. Today this climb is still considered a tough Very Severe with an occasional loose hold, lots of exposure and no mean technical difficulties, when you consider that the climbers of the day had little more than rubber pumps and a stiff hemp rope it was a remarkable climb. Modern climbers have it so much easier and can fall to their hearts content, this was a 'luxury' denied to these early pioneering climbers where a fall would invariably prove fatal not just to the leader but also other members of the party who could be dragged from their belay by a long leader fall.

After this impressive week's climbing in North Wales Colin rode home to Liverpool on his bike, anxious to catch the last ferry from Birkenhead at 11.00pm and a final ride up out of the city to Sefton Park where his family now lived.

Colin lived for climbing now, AB used to meet him at his office on a Monday morning where he often found Colin asleep, tired from his cycle back from the mountains the night before no doubt. Colin used to keep photographs in his desk of various cliffs and would mark on them the existing climbs that had been done, the gaps in-between these climbs were what interested him and he would 'pencil-in' possible climbs which would prove the objective for the following weekends.

In September Colin, AB and another talented Liverpool climber, Ted Hicks, went to the Lake District and climbed Central Buttress on Scafell. This superb climb first done in 1914 was many years ahead of its time and was undoubtedly the hardest climb in these Isles. The main difficulty was the huge flake half way up the cliff which had to be overcome by tying a man to a chock-stone which had become wedged between the flake and the main bulk of the cliff, then the leader simply climbed over the man to grasp a good hold near the top of the flake. This chock-stone has now sadly gone making the ascent of this famous climb significantly harder and is good value for its present grade of Hard Very Severe. The party also made the fifth ascent of Gimmer Crack on the magnificent cliff overlooking the beautiful Langdale valley.

At the end of the month Colin returned to Wales climbing a couple of easy new climbs in Cwm Idwal and making an early attempt on what became known as Suicide Wall an audacious route when it was finally climbed and one that leaves one amazed at the confidence and ability of the climbers of this period for even considering attempting it.

Colin was now at the forefront of British rock climbing, advancing standards and pioneering new routes of impeccable quality, present climbers can be forgiven any jealousy for the 'blank canvas' Colin and others enjoyed on these virgin cliffs. Getting to the mountains every weekend was not easy and being a member of the Wayfarer's Club gave Colin the chance to meet many men from a higher social standing who had transport. One such man was a Scot living and practicing in Liverpool as a Dental Surgeon, Graham MacPhee was a hard climber with many first ascents to his credit, including the aforementioned Gimmer Crack.

After a Wayfarer's dinner in late November MacPhee took Colin and AB out to Helyg where they arrived at 1.30am. The weather was foul but that did not stop them climbing on the delightful Idwal Slabs and Holly Tree Wall, it was bitterly cold when they reached the top and the rain was turning to sleet. Two weeks later they were back again when Colin made the second ascent of Heather Wall on the East Wall of the Idwal Slabs in difficult conditions where the rock was found to be very greasy. The climb is still graded Very Severe – even in good conditions with modern equipment, that afternoon they made another new climb on the East Wall just for good measure.

As the 1930's dawned Colin continued to climb and form new friendships, one notable friend was Marco Pallis who was to broaden Colin's outlook on life and mountains generally, ultimately Colin would visit the mighty Himalaya with Marco and his friends.

January 1930 was particularly cold though that did not prevent Colin and AB cycling to Helsby to get some practice in for the coming summer. They frequently drove out in MacPhee's reliable Sunbeam to Helyg where they walked and scrambled in blizzards or torrential rain, they were a keen lot.

February 1930 was a momentous month for the Wayfarers as they opened their own hut in the Lake District. The Robertson Lamb Hut (RLH) in Langdale is situated close to the crags and was frequently used by Colin and the other members when in the district. One such visit was an Easter trip to Dow Crag where Colin & AB were trying the classic Great Central Route, Colin missed a crucial hold and took a big fall of seventy feet where thankfully AB had constructed a good solid belay and was able to hold the fall thus saving Colin's life. The hemp rope cut deeply into AB's hands and he was burnt to the bone as the shock came onto the rope. The injury was quite serious while Colin was largely unscathed save for a broken toe and some bruising, a year later Colin returned and led the route properly without incident.

A month later Colin was staying at RLH with Marco Pallis and Ivan Waller when they began a five mile walk to the crags of Scafell. Colin had espied a possible route on the East Buttress and eventually climbed the classic Mickledore Grooves, an unprotected and exposed climb today graded Very Severe, but is considerably harder in anything but perfect dry conditions, Colin led it when the rock was wet and slimy. When he got back to Liverpool Colin telephoned AB to let him know about his first major new route in the Lake District, AB repeated the climb in August 1931 and enjoyed it so much he went straight back to the bottom of the cliff and soloed it.

In early June 1930 Colin went back to Cloggy and made the fourth ascent of Piggot's Climb but he made it in a better style than any of the previous ascents dispensing with the shoulder from his companions and climbing the whole crux pitch entirely free. Even though he was not even twenty years of age he was one of only a handful of people to have climbed both existing routes on the cliff and yet more was to follow.

In the middle of June Colin again went to Cloggy, this time with MacPhee and they first climbed Longland's in the very fast time of 2¼ hours before indulging in a swim in the lake at the bottom of the cliff. The west buttress is a steep cliff undercut along most of its length with beetling overhangs. Colin thought he saw an entry through them though not by climbing the overhangs direct but by out-flanking them with a slightly descending traverse which led to a narrow and steep looking slab. This appeared to lead upwards to the great slab which formed the most prominent feature of the cliff.

They scrambled up to the start of the steep initial wall beneath the overhangs and Colin led off on the steep and blank looking traverse to outflank the dark overhangs. It proved a severe effort as all the holds were sloping the wrong way and Colin had to remove his rubbers as they would not grip – he climbed in his socks. After the traverse Colin found himself on a small grass ledge feeling rather small and dwarfed by the immense wall of rock in front of him. He climbed a thin narrow slab with much loose rock, so loose in places he had to throw every other hold away, to his right he espied a thin ribbon of grass, rather like a long and ragged caterpillar, and hoping this would prove easier he stepped onto it. Unfortunately it began to peel off and slide down and so he took to the rocks again after only a few feet and climbed onto the very edge of the buttress where the rock was firmer though his position more exposed. After 120ft a shout from below made Colin pause while MacPhee tied on another 100ft of rope, with this done he continued with the ascent to eventually reach a grassy recess and a belay where he could tie on and bring MacPhee up to him. With the party re-united Colin led off again aiming for the big slab over to his right, the traverse was difficult and incredibly exposed. Colin later wrote :

I got a long way across, and then stuck. The next move might be possible, by a kind of jump. It would be dangerous, but – well, a new climb was worth the risk. I looked at it a long time. It seemed to grow more terrifying and I was a long way from my second. I came back.

Colin eventually found another way and climbed into the corner at the foot of the huge great slab where he could belay and bring Macphee across to join him.

The corner was a near vertical wall of grass, Colin made a mad rush at it climbing more quickly than the grass could fall down and digging his nails and toes into the grass before reaching the belay. The next pitch was less steep but still covered in grass and as Colin climbed the grass began to unfurl rather like a roll of carpet, difficult and at time unpleasant climbing led to the next belay but the climb was nearly in the bag. The next two pitches led up the great slab itself, sun warmed rock and delightfully easy (for the day) climbing led them upwards to the top left hand corner of the slab and the cliff itself. The climb, named The Great Slab (Very Severe) is one of the best routes of its grade anywhere and as the passage of many feet have removed much of the grass and loose rock it is one of the most highly coveted climbs in the whole of North Wales. Colin and MacPhee were the first men to complete two climbs in a single day on this most magnificent of cliffs. Colin now concentrated more than ever on seeking new climbs and was without doubt the best climber in the country.

The following weekend Colin was again in Wales and looking at a new climb on the nose of Dinas Mot in the Llanberis Pass. The Direct Route goes straight up the middle of the smooth sweep of rock and the final corner proved to be the crux with Colin needing a shoulder from his second to surmount the final crack. This final pitch he had to climb in socks and Colin cut his feet badly, above the route he tied his blood stained socks to a small ash tree where they remained for several years.

Another quality Very Severe climb was thus added to Colin's climbing CV, such was his ability that in later years Colin used this climb as his descent when climbing other routes on the cliff! Later in the summer of 1930 Colin went to the Alps for two weeks with the Wayfarer's Club and while not climbing anything spectacular it possibly laid the seed for Colin's future ambitions in the higher mountains.

The weather in 1931 was largely poor though while this held Colin back to a degree in his quest for new climbs it was not always the case and many believe that this was Colin's most productive and best year.

In late May Colin with MacPhee made their way to lonely Cwm Silyn, after climbing an easy route the day before they had used the opportunity to assess the big central mass of rock where he managed to climb a superb new Very Severe called simply Kirkus's Route, MacPhee wrote later that they had to race back to the car as it started raining again after the nineteenth wet Sunday in a row.

In late June Colin again with MacPhee made his way to Glyder Fach where he climbed an impeccable new route called Lot's Wife which proved slightly easier than his previous contribution on the cliff. The following day he climbed alone in the Carneddau on the brooding Craig Yr Ysfa and produced one of nicest climbs imaginable. Pinnacle Wall is a severe climb on perfect rock with a beautiful aspect and the confidence with which it was approached by Colin is testament to his judgment and ability.

Come August Colin was back on Clogwyn Du'r Arddu with a new second, John Menlove Edwards, another iconic figure in the climbing world and together they pioneered a new route up the East Buttress. Chimney Route had been looked at earlier but never climbed and proved to be another worthwhile Very Severe climb though the last pitch, known as the 'Ricketty Innards' is now avoided due to much loose rock making its ascent dangerous. Later on that year Colin returned to Cloggy and added a direct finish to Chimney Route as well as climbing another new route Pedestal Crack which proved to be the hardest technical climb on the cliff to date and is still a good Very Severe climb.

In September Colin with Ivan Waller went to Dinas Mot again and actually failed to make the second ascent of a superb line first climbed by Menlove Edwards. Western Slabs proved too difficult but he did add a test piece of his own West Rib which provided some very bold protection-less climbing with a fair smattering of exposure and delicate climbing that nowadays warrants a Hard Very Severe grade, a full grade harder than Menlove Edwards climb. A few weeks later saw Colin with MacPhee on Cloggy trying to wring another new route from its forbidding precipices and they succeeded in climbing Bridge Groove which for many years was considered a Very Severe climb but is now acknowledged to be Extremely Severe (E1), this ascent marked a great leap in difficulty for Colin and rock climbing in general, it was certainly the hardest climb on Cloggy even if it was not recognised as such at the time.

At Easter 1932 Colin attended a Wayfarer's meet in Scotland and stayed at the CIC hut beneath the impressive north face of Ben Nevis, conditions were good and many routes were climbed. Colin not only rock climbed but was a good winter climber and was equally happy going on a long walk with friends. With the summer fast approaching Colin trained hard on Helsby usually cycling there from Liverpool, a journey of 20 miles each way which he did in less than an hour and a half, on one such occasion he did 42 routes and lost 4lbs in weight.

Soon after he was back on Cloggy with Maurice Linnell and they climbed a new route called Birthday Crack, so named as it was both Colin's twenty second Birthday and Maurice's twenty third. They then turned their attention to a line of cracks and chimneys to the left of Pedestal Crack and after an impressive solo effort by Linnell on the first pitch they forced the classic Curving Crack (Very Severe) which is still one of the cliff's 'must-do' climbs. A week later the party were back and Colin led another new route The Direct Finish to the East Buttress which is a superb and relatively easy climb graded Hard Severe though positioned as it is high above the East Buttress the exposure can make it seem harder. This climb was destined to be Colin's last major new route in North Wales though he was not to know it at the time, he made other new climbs but none had the impact as his previous climbs.

The British had recently been given permission by the Tibetan government to mount another expedition to Everest in 1933 and it was clearly expected by many that Colin would go given his overall fitness and mastery on the rock. Colin trained hard, frequently cycling from Liverpool to Helyg and back at weekends and on occasions even walking from Liverpool. Colin's younger brother Guy recalls one instance where Colin was forced to drink rain water from puddles on his walk back from North Wales after a particularly hot weekend.

Sadly, despite much lobbying on Colin's behalf he was not invited onto the 1933 Everest expedition and it was stated that he lacked sufficient climbing experience outside of the UK. Colin's friends argued that the Alpine Club allowed Sandy Irvine to go in 1924 and he had less experience than Colin. Alf Bridge even wrote to the Alpine Club and suggested that they expected Everest to be climbed from the playing fields of Eton. Colin was bitterly disappointed at not being selected though this disappointment was short lived as Marco Pallis was planning a similar trip to the Himalaya for the Wayfarer's Club and room was soon found for Colin.

Whereas the 1933 Everest expedition was a huge logistical operation the Wayfarer's Gangotri Glacier Expedition was a much smaller, intimate affair intent on proving the theory that it was possible to climb in the Himalaya with a small party and still climb peaks of a respectable height. Colin's employer took an enlightened view on his request for extended leave to visit the Himalaya and permission was granted, Colin threw himself into the logistical necessities of organising a trip to the far side of the planet in the 1930's.

They sailed from Liverpool on the 1st April 1933 and by the end of the month had landed in Calcutta. From Calcutta a 600 mile train journey across the dusty and humid plains followed till they arrived at the rail head at Dehra Dun and Mussoori where a week was spent sorting their supplies into manageable loads to be carried by the porters into the mountains.

On the 10th May the climbing party with 70 porters left Mussoori amid warnings that the path had been swept away by winter avalanches. Colin's main worry was over the cook as a bad cook can break even the strongest of expeditions though Colin need not have worried as their cook proved to be first class. A week later they arrived at Harsil at an elevation of 8830ft where it was cooler and they could rest for three days while fresh porters were sought for the next stage into the high mountain pastures and a base camp. On the 24th May and a little over seven weeks out from Liverpool they approached their base camp below the moraine of the Gangotri glacier and with fine views of the Satopanth peaks and the mighty Shivling, a true Matterhorn of the Himalaya.

The very next day Colin was up and away scouring the nearby glacier for a camp, their initial forays were more of an exploratory nature rather than seeking pleasure in climbing the peaks as this was such a rarely frequented corner of the Himalaya little was known of the topography of the area.

However by early June Colin clearly had had enough and climbed a small peak in front of Satopanth II with Ted Hicks. He also got to within 800ft of the summit of Kedarnath with Ted Hicks and Charles Warren though turned back due to the lack of food and the possibility of an oncoming storm – which duly came!

After a single day's rest Colin climbed back up to advanced base camp to meet Charles Warren again, who in the meantime had worked out a viable route to the summit of Central Satopanth Peak (now known as Bhagirathi III). It was too irresistible for Colin to ignore and the next morning he and Warren left camp with everything they would need for the next few days on their backs, this was truly 'alpine style' climbing with no porters or sherpas to help them. They made three camps on their way to the summit with Colin having to do some really difficult rock climbing at altitude on the last day, the first time such difficult climbing had been attempted at altitude. On the 18th June 1933 the pair reached the summit at 22,060ft, the summit itself was so narrow that there was insufficient room for both of them to stand together. The monsoon had now arrived rendering climbing dangerous and difficult but they made it back to base camp without incident save for Charles becoming slightly snow blind. Colin now had to return back to England with Ted Hicks though he could and did take great pride in an impressive first expedition to the Himalaya. Not only did he manage to climb a difficult unclimbed mountain but the climb had involved some very difficult rock climbing at altitude, surely this would persuade the Alpine Club of his suitability for any future Everest expedition. Colin returned to Liverpool in late August 1933 and shortly thereafter was back at his desk in the offices of the Royal Insurance on Dale Street.

The Himalayan expedition had broadened Colin's mountaineering mind however he still had a love for the British hills and rock climbing. In early 1934 Colin climbed a small corner on Stanage Edge in Derbyshire, a small corner on a buttress not 40ft high, but one of impeccable quality that waited nearly twenty years for a repeat ascent by a party that included a youthful Joe Brown, its modern grade of Extremely Severe (E1 5b) is testament alone of its difficulty and a clear indication of Colin's prowess on rock.

In the Easter of 1934 Colin together with Maurice Linnell and other members of the Wayfarer's Club went to Scotland for some winter climbing. Colin travelled up north with Maurice on his motorbike and sidecar into which were crammed rucksacks, tent, ice axes and even ski's, they arrived in Fort William after an overnight drive on mid morning the 30th March 1934.

That day they walked up to the halfway lochan on Ben Nevis and set up camp, the afternoon was spent resting and skiing until Maurice broke one of his skis thus ensuring a relaxing evening. The next day was not cold though there was still much snow on the ground so they decided, or at least ended up climbing, on Castle Buttress. Colin later stated that they had almost reached the top of the buttress after the difficult climbing had ended and he was beneath the cornice [essentially a snow overhang] when the snow slipped beneath him and he fell. The next thing Colin remembered was coming to some 300ft lower from where he had fallen, he followed the rope above him where he found Maurice Linnell on the other end, some eighty feet higher up. The rope had caught over a ridge of snow with Maurice and Colin on either side of it, when Colin found Maurice the rope had slipped itself around Maurice's neck and had apparently strangled him but later investigations suggested that the fall itself had resulted in Maurice's death. Colin did what he could despite being seriously injured as he kept drifting in an out of consciousness. Eventually Maurice's body was recovered and Colin himself was stretchered off the mountain such was his condition and, one would imagine, distress.

Colin was in hospital in Fort William for three weeks with inter alia a fractured skull, the whole incident affected him greatly, 'AB' said that he was never the same man again, one must remember that Colin was still only twenty three at this time and the whole matter was a great burden upon him. He still had a deep love of mountains and climbing and took great pleasure later in the year taking a novice cousin, Wilfrid Noyce, climbing in North Wales.

Colin was now seemingly focusing more on taking people who had little or no experience out into the mountains, either walking up the hills or rock climbing. In modern times it is now possible to dedicate oneself totally to climbing, either guiding or in retail and it is clear that this was something that Colin was ideally suited to however for someone of Colin's modest background in the 1930's this was simply not possible. Travel to the mountains at weekends was not easy either and Colin relied heavily upon his friends who had cars, though he had shown his true mettle in the past by both cycling and walking to North Wales if he had too.

There used to be, on a Friday evening, a Crosville bus from Woodside in Birkenhead to Bangor and this 'Ramblers Express' would call at Ogwen Cottage / Idwal Youth Hostel en route. Most weekends it would be packed with young people eager to leave the dreary city behind and all for just a few shillings return.

In March 1935 Colin went to the Lake District with MacPhee, who had nearly completed his iconic Ben Nevis guidebook, a remarkable achievement given that he was based in Liverpool for most of the time and frequently drove the 800 miles to Fort William to broaden his knowledge of this renowned peak which offers some of the best winter climbing in the world. They climbed on Gimmer Crag on the Sunday, doing easy climbs and generally 'loafing about', their seemed to be a change in Colin's approach to climbing after his accident.

Throughout 1935 Colin spent most weekends in North Wales, climbing with MacPhee or Bob Frost, a fellow Wayfarer and an excellent climber who many believed to be just as proficient and capable as Colin. Colin had been approached by the Climbers Club to produce a guidebook for Glyder Fach and he threw himself into its writing with vigour and passion, visiting all the cliffs and checking grades and making a few additional new routes along the way.

Another Everest expedition was being planned and many of Colin's friends thought his inclusion a mere formality given that now he had proven himself at altitude, while it is not known what Colin himself thought of his chances he did begin cycling back out to North Wales from Liverpool and so one must deduce that he at least hoped and wanted to be included. Colin went to Zermatt with Frank Smythe and Eric Shipton who were to assess the prospective members of the expedition, he climbed the Matterhorn in a very fast time however an invite to join was not forthcoming for Colin though he could take solace in that Bill Tilman was not offered a place either. Colin's friend Alf Bridge perhaps summed it up best over a drink with him when he said :

'The trouble is Colin you're not a "good chap" who can talk about things other than climbing. As a bloke who eats, drinks and sleeps rock climbing, you've no chance! What use would you be in a little tent at Camp 5 or 6? Instead of being able to discuss the life and works of Leonardo Da Vinci to take your companion's mind off the howling blizzard outside, you would only be able to tell him about some dreadful route on Cloggy. You'd frighten the poor bugger to death'

The reality was that the chance of a working man going on a Himalayan expedition would be twenty years away, only by Joe Brown's selection and brilliant performance in 1954 on Kangchenjunga could the door be opened to the masses.

Colin continued to climb regularly at Helsby, often with Bob Frost who had recently updated Colin's guide in the Wayfarer's Journal, he made the first lead ascent of Morgue Slab which is still graded Extremely Severe (E1 5b). Having been denied a chance at Everest in 1936 Colin concentrated his efforts on the Glyder Fach guidebook and a trip to the French Alps in the summer. Colin also made his first return to Ben Nevis though sadly suffered another injury in a rock-fall when attempting to reach Glovers Chimney high on the mountain, thankfully no-one in the party was seriously injured and they were rescued by some Scottish climbers operating in the area who escorted them to the CIC hut. Colin returned to his tent that Sunday evening where he had a bad night as his ribs were badly bruised, he was back in work on the following Tuesday though.

With an upcoming trip to the Alps Colin frequently visited North Wales with MacPhee and Frost, repeating old favourite routes and still adding the odd new climb here and there till finally the day arrived for their departure on the 3rd July 1936. Two weeks in the Alps were not to be sniffed at and both climbers had grand plans however the weather that summer was poor though that did not stop Colin and Bob attempting some good climbs. They climbed the Forbes ridge on the Aiguille Du Chardonnet and had an exciting time descending in the teeth of a ferocious storm to reach the hut after a nineteen hour day.

They also managed an ascent of the Ordinary Route on the Aiguille Du Moine and a fast ascent of the classic south-west face and Main ridge of the Grands Charmoz.

When back in England Colin spent the rest of the summer working on the Glyder Fach guidebook which was now finally nearing completion. Although Colin was not pioneering as many new routes he seemed to take as great a joy with climbing at a more moderate level than when he was advancing standards. On the 20th December 1936 Colin climbed his final new route in North Wales Pinnacle Edge high up in the Nameless Cwm above the Ogwen valley, he was climbing solo and the route, while hardly worthy of a mention in the modern guidebooks, was climbed in the manner at which Colin started his climbing some nine years previously.

In the spring of 1937 the Glyder Fach guidebook was published, it was, and is still regarded as, a classic work though for Colin, after its publication, it meant that he could climb for pleasure again. However his pleasure, as previously stated, seemed to be derived from the instruction and fellowship of those less talented than himself. He climbed more often with people he met at Idwal Youth College than Helyg. Colin also visited the magical Isle of Skye with Alf Bridge and it was here that he uttered a remark that has passed into climbing folklore, it stands as true today as then on the summit of Sgurr Alasdair in the summer of 1937.

"You know, Alf, going to the right place, at the right time, with the right

people is all that really matters. What one does is purely incidental."

In the autumn of 1937 an event happened that caused Colin great sadness in that his good friend and staunch climbing partner Bob Frost was killed in a motorcycle accident while travelling to the Blackpool Illuminations on a friend's motorbike. Bob was only twenty five and was coming to the height of his powers as a climber and many wonder at what both he and Colin could have achieved on British rock had fortune shined upon them both. Many at the Idwal Youth Hostel commented that Colin had no real desire to undertake serious rock climbing with anyone else and an air of sombreness hung over their weekends for many a month after Bob's death.

Colin was now in his late twenties and yet his love of mountains and mountaineering were not diminished one iota as for many a weekend he continually went to North Wales irrespective of the weather and walked, climbed, scrambled whenever and wherever he could. In early 1938 Colin became interested in a small cottage in Nant-Gwynant called 'Hafod Owen', it was remote and perhaps better known for the tenant Colin let it to during the early war years which we will come to in due course.

In August of 1938 Colin took his annual holiday at the newly leased Climbers Club hut in Cornwall. Here he climbed the classic Black Slab for the first time and it's still the best known of Colin's new climbs in the area. Colin was also approached by the BBC to take part in a new radio programme about the British hills and mountains, the programme was intended to draw a wider public attention to the increasing interest in the outdoors and also to garner support for the forthcoming Access to Mountains Bill going through Parliament. Colin was clearly well thought of and was at the height of his influence in British mountaineering.

In 1939 Colin was approached by the publishers Thomas Nelson & Sons to produce a book on climbing, one that was to be aimed at the younger reader and one that fitted into its *'Let's Go'* series. Colin signed the contract in July 1939 and undertook to complete the book by the following October but the war put paid to immediate publication and the book did not appear till 1941. When *'Let's Go Climbing'* was published it was very well received though Colin was at that time in the RAF and taking part in regular night time bombing raids over Germany. It is a delightful book and full of the joy and sheer passion that Colin so clearly had for the mountains and climbing. Even today many climbers regard it as their favourite mountaineering book, it is still in print today such is its popularity.

The situation in Europe was now worsening and it was clear that war with Germany would be inevitable. Colin became engaged to a local Heswall girl, Eileen Foster, and they were to marry in 1940. Early in the war Colin's younger brother, Nigel, was killed on a RAF bombing raid while attacking two German destroyers, the war was barely three weeks old and it was this family tragedy that almost certainly led Colin to joining the RAF at nearly thirty years of age.

A weekend after Easter 1940 Colin married Eileen Foster at Heswall Parish Church, shortly afterwards the French capitulated and Britain with her Commonwealth forces stood alone, it was against this sombre background that Colin attended his medical with the RAF. After the accident on Ben Nevis Colin's eyesight was out of alignment however, given the long queue for the medicals, Colin was able to memorise the order of the letters on the eye-test and passed without difficulty. Colin underwent training with Bomber Command and passed as a navigator and started his first flights over Germany in March 1942. He proved a top class navigator and took part in the famous 'Thousand Bomber' raid on Cologne in May 1942. What Colin saw that night was enough to persuade his other younger brother, Guy, to find some other squadron of the RAF in which to serve and consequently Guy entered into the Coastal Command.

The bombing raids were not as successful as Bomber Command had hoped and so they set up an elite 'Pathfinder' Force to provide better intelligence for the main bomber force. The Pathfinders were to consist of volunteers and it says much of Colin's character, and perhaps desire to avenge the death of his brother, that he was among the first volunteers. One must remember that the raids Colin had taken part in to date where highly dangerous with a high casualty rate, Colin had frequently stated in his letters home and to friends how frightening they were and yet he still volunteered for a more dangerous mission. The odds were 1 in 20 in not returning from a mission and these volunteer forces were to fly fifty missions at a time instead of the normal thirty.

On the 13th September 1942 Colin and his elite crew flew out to Bremen in their Wellington Bomber on yet another bombing raid sadly flight BJ 789 never returned that night. Colin's friends and family hoped that they had been captured and made Prisoners of War but nothing was ever heard of them again and it is presumed they ditched into the North Sea after sustaining damage to the plane over Germany.

Even today many of Colin's routes in North Wales and the Lake District are cherished climbs and while they lack the difficulty of modern routes they possess something special and are often the best 'lines' on the cliff. Though we are not merely left with his climbs, he wrote one of the best instructional books with 'Let's go Climbing' and his 'Glyder Fach' guidebook is a wonderful example of clarity and simplicity.

John Menlove Edwards

Considered by many to be the greatest of all the pre-war rock climbers 'Menlove' was a complex individual, in later life he would be beset by bouts of severe depression and angst over his homosexuality. He often felt a social inferior to many of his contemporaries and ultimately his professional career as a psychiatrist would suffer as he was to develop a seeming persecution complex over his repeated failure to break into the ranks of psychoanalytical theorists. In climbing though he was amongst the first to see the possibilities for superb climbing on the cliffs of the Llanberis Pass, which are now the most popular crags in the whole of North Wales. He was also a gifted writer and wrote the first ever guidebook to Clogwyn Du'r Arddu as well as some of the best known essays ever written on the sport of rock climbing.

John Menlove Edwards was born on the 18th June 1910, the fourth and last child of Rev. George Zachary Edwards and his wife Helen. They came from Crossens near Southport where George was the vicar. His father was a compassionate man who once predated Orwell and his road to Wigan Pier by disguising himself as a tramp and wandering on the road for two weeks seeing the 'real' world and reporting on it in a pamphlet entitled 'A Vicar as Vagrant'. The Edwards household had a deep social conscience, some may perhaps say with heavily Socialist leaning tendencies.

The Edwards family was not a wealthy one but they did have a maid and nurse, Polly, whom Menlove adored, she went with them when in 1912 the family moved to Ainsdale just to the north of Liverpool. It was a hard, new, parish in which to work and the Edwards family only relief came on their annual holiday to the Lake District. On one such holiday George Edwards had an accident which would debilitate him for the rest of his life.

In 1917 the stress and strain caught up with George and he had to retire, at only 43, on a small clergyman's pension and the family moved further down the coast to Formby. Given the strained finances Helen Edwards had to return to work and managed to get various posts as an Art Mistress in several of the private schools in Birkdale. It was hard and stressful work for her especially as now George had developed Parkinson's Disease and was declining rapidly.

The annual holiday was still something to look forward to and George encouraged his children to walk, swim and explore the area around themeven if he couldn't. Menlove was growing big and strong and in 1923 he won a place in Fettes College just outside Edinburgh, it was to be his first time away from the family and home.

Menloves time at Fettes was not a happy one but he muddled through and hoped to become a medical missionary when he was older. In 1928 he won the Begg Memorial Prize of £60 per annum and in addition he applied to the Church Missionary Society for a grant where he was awarded £100 per annum on the condition that he would work as a doctor in one of their hospitals for a number of years after completion of his training. He left Fettes and enrolled as a medical student in Liverpool University, he was glad to be returning home able to spend time with his mother and, sadly declining further in health, father.

Menlove was introduced to climbing by his elder brother Stephen at the end of June 1930 when he went to Helyg. Stephen was at Cambridge University and a member of the university mountaineering club and so access to Helyg was not a problem for them. On the 27th June they climbed the girdle traverse of Idwal Slabs and then Idwal Buttress, the following day they wandered round Gallt Yr Ogof admiring a pair of Peregrine Falcons. A short holiday in the Alps followed in which nothing of great merit was done however upon his return to England Menlove went to Wales again and climbed a new route on Lliwedd with a fellow Liverpool University friend, Sandy Edge. The Ochre Slab is essentially a variation on Shallow Gully though in the modern guide it is graded Very Severe due to its loose rock and poor protection.

On the 25th November 1930 Menlove was elected secretary to the newly formed 'Liverpool University Rock-Climbing Club', the formation of this club caused something of a stir as rock climbing was still considered by nearly everyone as a branch of general mountain craft and not a separate and distinct discipline. Maybe it was Menlove's socialist tendencies that led to the naming of the club as, with the developments on the Peak District hills and Gritstone Edges by 'working class' men, rock climbing was perceived as something that could be done by the working masses who worked longer hours than their middle / upper class compatriots and they could never afford the luxury of an Alpine holiday where, so called, real mountaineering could be practiced.

The clubs first meet was at Helyg in December 1930 and most of the members took the old Crosville bus from Birkenhead to Bangor which conveniently would stop on request anywhere in the valley. Their first morning at the hut dawned grey and wet and snow could be seen down to 1000ft but this was no foil to Menlove who was anxious to be out, he persuaded a colleague to join him on a climb on Glyder Fach, they chose the Direct Route which is now graded Hard Severe and, given the inclement weather, a brave choice but they managed it well and returned back to Helyg where their friends had spent the day playing cards and drinking endless cups of tea.

The next day Menlove went to Lliwedd again and found a better start to the Far East Arete which A B Hargreaves, who made the second ascent the followjng year, described as fairly severe. The weather was again foul and Lliwedd is no crag to be on when the rain falls heavily but this did not seem to affect Menlove's ability or enthusiasm. The following day was fine and Menlove with his friend Geary went up onto Idwal's East Wall and repeated Colin Kirkus Grooved Wall despite the fact that there was a waterfall coming down it. He then espied an unclimbed section of rock and promptly led a climb that he named Route V, a poor easy climb but an unclimbed one at that. The following day he added a new finish to the direct route on Glyder Fach, a pattern was clearly forming now in Menlove's climbing activities and unclimbed rock was a clear attraction to him, this new finish is now invariably the one taken by most parties climbing the route. Their last day was spent on the East Face of Tryfan where Menlove soloed up the North Buttress before joining his friends for an ascent of the classic Terrace Wall Variant. It had been a very good weeks climbing for Menlove who was now the star climber in the club though clearly he wished to progress further as early in 1931 he acquired a motorbike which made it easier for him to get to Wales at the weekends and Helsby during the week.

One weekend in March 1931 Menlove was out in Wales staying at Helyg when he met 'AB' Hargreaves who invited him up to the Lake District where he had recently moved to. On the first day they did Tophet

Wall Direct, an exposed and steep climb now graded Hard Severe and 'AB' anxious to look after his friend suggested he change into socks or rubbers. Menlove shrugged his shoulders and said he'd be fine in his boots, which were new and studded with something like marbles – according to 'AB'. Menlove floated up the climb and the next day they made their way to Pillar Rock where 'AB' was keen to bring the young upstart down a peg or two on the difficult Walkers Gully. The climb was wet and 'AB' had to retreat from the top pitch and announced to Menlove that they had better descend, Menlove was having none of that and promptly led the pitch in fine style, 'AB' was impressed.

Like Kirkus before him Menlove trained regularly on Helsby on fine midweek evenings and became very strong. I doubt they looked upon Helsby as a training crag in those days though and it was probably just an opportunity to go climbing. Menlove got to know Colin Kirkus quite well and they became good friends.

In the Easter of 1931 Menlove was back at Helyg and climbed the Very Severe Belle Vue Bastion high on Tryfan and then he soloed the Very Severe Long Chimney on the Terrace Wall of the same mountain. The next day he repeated Jack Longlands climb on Lliwedd Purgatory which is still graded Very Severe and calls for a cool head as protection is sparse, clearly within a very short space of time Menlove had established himself as a climber capable of climbing the hardest routes in the country. However he was not like Kirkus in that he chose to totally concentrate on a particular crag until he felt it was worked out, he favoured the East Wall of Idwal and Lliwedd in that regard.

In early July, after a wet weekend, Menlove made the second ascent of Colin Kirkus's great climb, Lot's Groove on Glyder Fach. He mentions that the climb is quite technical but not unjustifiably so and no great feats of strength are required, clearly the 21 year old Menlove was proving to be some climber in being almost dismissive of possibly one of the hardest climbs in the country to date.

The weather in 1931 was far from perfect but this did not stop Menlove teaming up with Colin Kirkus on the 6th July to force one of Cloggy's best lines in Chimney Route which I have already described.

Over the next few days Menlove climbed three of North Wales's best routes.

On the 12th July he soloed the magnificent Sub Cneifion Rib, an impeccable and easy 400ft climb high above Llyn Idwal. The next day, in the rain, together with Stewart Palmer he climbed the delightful East Wall Girdle, still a good value Very Severe climb in the dry so heaven knows how difficult it would have been in big hob-nailed boots in a downpour. On the 14th July Menlove climbed Outside Edge, a Very Difficult climb on the Great Slab of Cwm Silyn. This was, and still is, a stunning climb up an impressive piece of steep rock, but thankfully the holds are as big as the exposure, for its grade it has to be one of the best climbs in the country. Menlove, despite his relative youth, was clearly developing an eye for good climbs in the most unlikely of places.

On the 6th August Menlove went to Dinas Mot on the north side of the Llanberis Pass and climbed the delightful Western Slabs, a climb Colin Kirkus would retreat from some weeks later and climb West Rib instead which is now considered the harder climb. Menlove also took his many partners up the now classic Kirkus route The Direct before doing the girdle traverse of the Nose of Dinas Mot, Menlove described this climb 'as about Difficult standard' – it is now graded Very Severe.

The weather continued to remain dire and a day was spent in Helyg trying to catch the by now infamous rat without success. As food and reading matter ran out Menlove beat a retreat back to Liverpool and his impending studies.

During this early summer Menlove had added four classic climbs to his North Wales repertoire: Western Slabs, East Wall Girdle, Outside Edge and Sub-Cneifion Rib. All of these climbs are delightful, open and delicate and perhaps a reflection of Menlove's state of mind at this time. His later offerings would show a darker, lonelier, mysterious and more tragic side to his character.

Menlove trained hard, even going to the gym in the Adelphi Hotel and at the end of August 1931, after climbing nearly every day for the past two months, he was in the Lake District with Marco Pallis and Bill Stallybrass heading up to Scafell Crag and in particular the brilliant 'Flake Crack' of Central Buttress. Bill takes up the story as Menlove moves onto the hardest part of the climb;

Our party was soon on the Oval. As last man on the rope, I was carrying a spare 100ft line. In my haste to catch up with the others, I had left my rubbers behind and was climbing in stockinged feet. At the foot of the Flake, Menlove quickly arranged some slings, called to Marco and me to change places on the rope and brought me up to him. Our whole performance was hair-raisingly chaotic. For some reason, I was still carrying the spare line. I gripped hold of Menlove's shoulders and we both swung out from the rock. He seemed to be only very loosely tied-in. My strength was by then running out. I seized hold of a spare rope which Menlove had secured to the chock-stone and lowered myself until I could jam my body into the crack and take a rest. Menlove meanwhile was make fresh arrangements with the rope. Suddenly he called out: 'I'm going back to have a go!' Next moment he was lay-backing steadily up the crack, un-belayed, and was soon at the top. It was an astonishing feat of courage after witnessing Alf Bridge's near-disaster. Marco and I both had ignominiously to be hauled up like sacks of coal.

Later Menlove admitted somewhat shamefacedly that he had been determined to do the climb unaided, but had felt obliged at least to make a show of giving Bill a chance to climb over him in the orthodox manner.

On hearing of the first successful 'clean' lead of the Flake Crack Colin Kirkus wrote to congratulate Menlove on a superb lead that he would probably have 'funked', the letter clearly meant much to Menlove as he kept it for the rest of his life. Within the space of two years Menlove had become one of the best and strongest climbers in the country while still only in his early twenties.

It is surprising to note that Menlove never climbed as intensively again as he did during this period in 1931, this was due partly to the need to develop more time to his studies and partly due to his continuing anguish at his burgeoning homosexuality and the implications that would have against his religious beliefs. One must remember that in 1930 it was a criminal offence to form a physical relationship with someone of the same sex and the church was particularly condemning on that point. One must also remember that Menlove, the irony of his name and sexual leanings must have borne heavily on him, came from a deeply religious family. His father was a Vicar and his elder brother, Hewlett, was now also a minister in St Helens. The seeds of Menlove's future troubles were clearly being sown at this time. A further difficulty for him was his promise to act as a medical missionary after he had passed his exams, the CMS had made Menlove a grant to enable him to go to university and the prospect of it all weighed heavily upon him.

In December 1931 however Menlove was back in Wales with the University Rock Climbing Club and produced two of his most well known and popular climbs in the Llanberis Pass. Spiral Stairs & Flying Buttress are nowadays very easy climbs but when Menlove climbed them they were heavily vegetated and had a fair share of loose rock. After the meet was over he did not visit North Wales for six months and the only climbing he did was in Scotland on a Wayfarer's Club meet.

In early 1932 Menlove wrote an interim guidebook for the East Wall and Holly Tree Wall of Cwm Idwal for the British Mountaineering Journal. By June Menlove had finished his exams and went back to Helyg where he climbed badly when attempting Colin Kirkus climb Nose Direct on Dinas Mot and his partner, Bill Stallybrass, had to near haul him up the difficult pitches. Menlove spent the week of 19th – 26th July 1932 at Helyg where Colin Kirkus was also in attendance but he had no enthusiasm for climbing merely preferring to swim in the lakes that could be walked to from the cottage. Menlove seemed to have lost the urge to climb and during August at Helyg he seemed to spend an inordinate amount of time trying to catch the many rats that frequented the small cottage. However by the 17th August 1932 he forced himself to do something and walked to the Upper Cliff of Glyder Fawr to produce a hard new climb, Procrastination Cracks which is still considered a good, though stiff at its grade, Very Severe climb. A week later he climbed the brilliant Grey Slab with the twelve year old son of one of the climbers staying at Helyg, this is one of the great routes of North Wales both bold and delicate and situated high up on the mountainside above Llyn Idwal, it still warrants a grade of Very Severe in modern guidebooks.

The elder climbers staying at Helyg introduced Menlove to the steep dank, loose and vegetated cliffs of Clogwyn Y Geifr in Cwm Idwal and it was here that Menlove seemed to find a mirror to reflect his feelings of angst. 'AB' Hargreaves turned up at Helyg and they climbed a horribly wet and loose route up Craig Y Rhaedr on the North Side of the Llanberis Pass before visiting Cwm Silyn the next day and repeating Colin Kirkus climb on the Great Slab. Menlove climbed this route in his hob nail boots much to 'AB's consternation as he found the climb hard enough in stockinged feet.

Nothing much else was done in 1932 as December was a cold month and Menlove only climbed the Central Gully of Glyder Fawr under snow and ice conditions. On the annual University Rock Climbing Club meet held this year in the Idwal Youth Hostel, Menlove met John Sheridan and shortly after Christmas they went up to Skye on his motor bike intending to have some fun sailing across to the Island from Mallaig. Menlove wrote a charming essay for the Wayfarer's Journal about this trip called 'Little

Fishes'. They had a number of close shaves as two relatively inexperienced 'sailors' taking to the wild waters of Northern Scotland during Winter is not everyone's idea of fun or a sane activity. They braved storms and choppy seas as well as the condemnation of the local fisherman, Menlove rode above all this and one may suppose that his affinity with water began here.

In early 1933 Menlove did his last climb with Colin Kirkus, Neb's Crawl proved to be a poor route up the magnificent cliff of Dinas Cromlech in the Llanberis Pass, a cliff whose great future in the sport of rock climbing would not be truly realised until the 1950's. A further trip to the Llanberis Pass at Easter saw Menlove again at Dinas Cromlech where he climbed a wandering Very Severe climb, Pharaoh's Passage and a poor Very Difficult route.

Later in the Easter break Menlove went to Scotland with an old school friend from Fettes, Alec Keith and after meeting some other friends went for some easy walks and climbs in the southern Cairngorms. On one such excursion they frequented the raging torrent of the Linn of Dee, the place where Lord Byron once nearly drowned. The party were impressed though Menlove thought it was a pleasant enough place, he believed it possible to swim down the river and given that there was so much melt water such an escapade would be quite safe as the water would carry a swimmer over the hidden rocks. The River Dee at this point is channelled through a rock gorge little more than four feet wide and consequently the force of the water is impressive and almost deafening. The next day, as the weather was too poor for climbing, Menlove proposed to do it and despite the protestations of his friends they all made their way to the bridge from where he could access the torrent, he agreed to tie a rope to himself so his friends could help him if he got into difficulty. He then simply tied one end of the rope to a tree and jumped in to the broiling waters, he fought against the whirlpools and freezing waters to emerge on a ledge slightly winded but none the worse for wear.

Later in 1933 Menlove made the second ascent of Colin Kirkus classic climb Great Slab on Clogwyn Du'r Arddu with his brother and 'AB' Hargreaves. The climb passed easily enough but 'AB' later noted Menloves enormous strength in that he managed to lift their third man, who weighed fifteen stone, who had slipped on the slab traverse of the first pitch back onto a ledge from where he could retreat. A few days later they were back at Cloggy making the third ascent of Curving Crack before dragging 'AB' off to Dinas Cromlech for a new route, Pharaoh's Wall, a steep and enjoyable Very Severe climb. After all of this Menlove returned back to Liverpool University to study for his by now imminent exams.

He was back in Wales by mid-May climbing 'Dives' on Dinas Cromlech before returning again to the rotten cliffs of Clogwyn Y Geifr high above Llyn Idwal where he made two new climbs on poor rock and abundant vegetation. Today these climbs are rarely ascended and one must wonder as to what forces drew Menlove onto them.

Menlove passed his exams with credit and met his brother Stephen, who had come over from his St Helens parish, for lunch and enjoyed himself immensely, no doubt glad that the worst of his studies were over. Later that same day his other brother, Hewlett, was involved in an accident on his motorbike, Menlove and Stephen rushed to Liverpool Infirmary but to no avail as Hewlett died soon after, the irony that one brother had become a doctor while the other was beyond medical help was not lost on Menlove or the family. Menlove tried to lose and console himself in poetry while offering support to his frail father and tired, overworked mother.

Hewlett's death affected Menlove deeply and especially so given his rising devotion to his faith and Menloves declining belief. After the funeral Menlove went to Wales for a few days and visited his now beloved cliffs above Llyn Idwal. He pioneered four new climbs in three days, one of which, the Devil's Pipes, is even now considered almost suicidal given the looseness of the rock and abundant vegetation. He spent most of the summer at home in Formby and only made the occasional foray into Wales climbing such poor routes as Grass Route on Glyder Fawr and an offering or two on the Kitchen cliffs. Menlove returned home to discover his father had fallen and broken his hip which required a six week stay in Southport hospital and so he stayed in Formby looking after his mother and sister. One further problem on the horizon was Menloves commitment to join the CMS as a missionary, his rapidly declining faith made this a near impossible prospect to endure. In the end the CMS realised that Menlove could not go and withdrew the offer of a missionary placement though they did demand the £500 he had received towards his education which Hewlett's widow paid off for him without his knowledge.

George Edwards died in January 1934, twenty years after his initial accident in the Lake District and shortly thereafter Menlove took leave from Liverpool and went to the Isle of Wight to study for his Diploma in

Psychological Medicine. He spent six months there only making one or two visits to Wales. On one such occasion he climbed the Slow Ledge Climb on Dinas Mot in the Llanberis Pass, the climb so called as one would slowly slide off the ledge in question if it was sat upon. Menlove began to frequent the Gorphyswfa Hotel at the summit of Pen Y Pass and the scene for the famous 'Pen Y Pass' parties hosted by Geoffrey Winthrop Young. The hotel was near to his 'columnar cliffs' in the Llanberis Pass and was a convenient stopping point as Menlove disliked hill walking and once said that he *always go to a cliff where there's a downhill path if possible*.

He came back to Liverpool late in the summer of 1934 and duly passed his Diploma in December of that year. Now that he was qualified he could set up his own practice which he duly did by taking rooms in Rodney Street however life in Liverpool had changed as most of his friends had left the university and were scattered throughout the country and even the occasional visit to Helsby seemed insufficient recompense for a changed life. When he needed company Menlove could often be found at Helyg where he continued to climb regularly putting up the occasional new climb or repeating an old favourite. In January 1935 he visited the cliffs of Tremadog and was not overly impressed so he retreated to Black Rock Sands for a bathe in the sea. The Tremadog cliffs would receive much attention from climbers after the war.

His practice was doing well in Rodney Street and Menlove's affection with water came to the fore again early in the year when he kayaked from the Cumberland coast to the Isle of Man during the night in a collapsible canoe. He covered the forty five miles in sixteen hours and the endeavour was reported in the Liverpool Daily Post. A few weeks later he, with Colin Kirkus, set out from Conwy in a rowing boat aiming to row across the Irish Sea. They endured a stormy night, only managing to keep their boat afloat before returning back to Conwy on the wind and tide. A days rest saw Colin Kirkus head off into the mountains while Menlove rowed the boat back to Liverpool alone, a distance of some fifty miles.

At Easter 1935 Menlove was staying at Helyg when Wilfrid Noyce, a seventeen year old public schoolboy and a cousin of Colin Kirkus, came to stay. He had done some climbing previously and was madly keen to try something harder and so on the Easter Sunday Noyce was with Menlove on the first ascent of Dead Entrance on Carreg Wastad which is still quite a tough though poor route at a Very Severe standard. They also climbed another poor route Scramblers Gate before trudging back up to Pen Y Pass for tea with Geoffrey Winthrop Young.

The next day found Menlove and Noyce on the Milestone Buttress where they climbed, with no real ease, one of the classic climbs in the district, Soapgut. Now it is a polished horror with the passage of many hands and feet giving the holds a sheen all too evident on the popular climbs, but when the duo first climbed it there was much grass and vegetation.

With the Easter break now over Menlove returned to Liverpool to work while Noyce stayed on in Wales eager for the following Sunday when he could at last climb on Clogwyn du'r Arddu. Menlove took him and Major Bradley up Chimney Route climbed in nailed boots and not rubbers the normal footwear associated with harder climbs. He was clearly climbing well and his immense strength allowed him to hang on to holds that would leave lesser mortals quaking. In May he took Major Bradley and two female companions up Longlands Climb on Cloggy, the first women to climb the route, and again he chose to climb in nailed boots and he even believed that the route would 'go' in the wet.

Menlove's work was progressing well and he made frequent trips to Wales throughout the summer, occasionally climbing a new route on some obscure crag like Drws Nodded in the shadow of Tryfan. In July he climbed two superb routes on Carreg Wastad in the Llanberis Pass that are still very popular today, Shadow Wall (Very Severe) is a steep little climb progressively harder the higher one climbs and with the crux move right at the top. Crackstone Rib is probably the most photographed route in the whole valley and while quite an amenable 'Severe' was at the time considered harder than Shadow Wall – probably on account of the exposure encountered on the second pitch where one traverses out towards the arête with the ground sweeping away beneath your heels.

At the end of July one of Menloves relationships with an unknown man ended and he seemed to seek solace upon the water again as he wrote to an old friend, Alec Keith, proposing a trip from the east coast of Scotland to Norway. Alec put him in touch with a couple of people who were selling a boat though he protested about such a venture as did his friends. Undeterred he ordered supplies and loaded them onto the boat, which was in no state for such a voyage with rotting bows and a design which was not made for single handed sailing. Menlove sailed out of Aberdeen and was sighted the next morning twelve miles out from Rattray Head. The Peterhead steam drifter Golden Dawn offered to assist him back to the mainland though he refused point blank any assistance and fully intended to carry out his plan. In the end the captain rammed the boat breaking its rudder and forcing Menlove back to shore whereupon the boat promptly sank. Menlove was furious and demanded to know who was responsible for spoiling his plans though he never found out and eventually calmed down.

Late in August Menlove met up with Wilfrid Noyce again in the Lake District and they climbed on Pillar Rock and Scafell making an ascent of the Central Buttress climb. This was an impressive feets for young Noyce who was only seventeen at the time.

Menloves swansong for the year was an audacious effort on water.

A few days after Christmas, Menlove travelled by night train to Achnasheen in the Scottish highlands and then caught a bus to Gairloch where he picked up a previously arranged boat. He rowed the boat from Gairloch across to the island of Harris in the Outer Hebrides, landing on a deserted beach where he made camp and spent three days before re-crossing to the mainland. He was swept off course on the way back and was forced to put into Gruinard Island. The crossing of the Minch, the 40-mile-wide channel between wester Ross and the Outer Hebrides, took him 28 hours to Lewis and 24 coming back. It was a truly preposterous adventure. The Minch is much wider than the English Channel and only on very clear days can one discern the islands, to row out into these waters is to face the full force of the Atlantic, to do so alone and in mid winter says something of the fragile state of Menloves mind.

Menlove started an article on this episode but it remained unfinished and makes painful reading in that it was offering a window into his innermost thoughts and feelings and perhaps that is why it was never completed for fear of giving too much away. A short report was printed in the Liverpool Daily Post:-

Adventure on water seems to be the spice of life for Dr J. M. Edwards of Rodney Street, Liverpool.

The doctor has just been on holiday at Gairloch, Ross-shire. He took out a small 12-ft rowing boat and accomplished the feat of rowing across the Minch from Gairloch to the island of Lewis and back – a distance of 100 miles. The doctor was carried off his course and it was seven days before he was able to return to the mainland.

Attired in a lounge suit, he hired the rowing boat and gave the owner a cheque with the remark, 'this is in case I don't come back'. When experienced boatmen learned of his proposed expedition they advised him to abandon it because no-one else had ever accomplished the hazardous crossing.

The doctor, however, was determined to succeed, and stocked his boat with a good supply of food and water. He had neither sail nor auxiliary motor.

Nothing was heard of him for two days and seafaring folk became anxious. A postcard was received at Gairloch the following day saying he had arrived safely. Several times the small craft narrowly escaped foundering, and he was carried off his course on the return journey, and it was exactly seven days from the start that he landed at Gruinard Bay on the mainland. Owing to a violent gale springing up he had to send the boat back to its owner by motor-lorry.

This would prove to be the last of his marine adventures for several years.

In 1936 the Climbers Club published the new Cwm Idwal guidebook written by Menlove and it proved to be very well received and is considered by some to be the finest rock-climbing guide ever written. Its success made the Climbers Club ask Menlove to produce another guide to the grand and shapely peak of Tryfan, Menlove chose Wilfrid Noyce to act as collaborator. A relationship had developed between the two men and the opportunity to work on a guidebook for the summer assured Menlove some much needed company and affection.

One well known incident took place in July on the magnificent East face of Tryfan that shook British climbing almost to its core. A visiting party of German climbers, one of whom was Max Sedlmayer who would later die on the North Face of the Eiger, put up a new route called Munich Climb. However they placed two pegs for protection, which was common practice among the mountains of the Alps but not in the UK. The members of the Climbers Club were outraged and Menlove later climbed the route without the pegs and removed them so that British honour could be restored. Munich Climb is still a good Hard Very Severe though not easy at the grade.

Wilfrid Noyce returned from the Alps in August and he and Menlove went high up into Cwm Tryfan, pitched their tent and worked every day checking routes, making the occasional new climb and even having an 'off' day when they visited another cliff outside of their guidebook area. On one such occasion they climbed Lot's Groove on Glyder Fach and on another they made their way to Cloggy to climb Great Slab which in the intervening years had become a lot cleaner and more popular. However b

September the rains began and they beat a retreat to Helyg and ultimately back to Birkenhead where Menlove now lived.

Noyce went from Charterhouse onto Cambridge and Menlove felt a distance develop between them that could not accounted for in mere miles, Noyce was now moving in the higher and more elite circles where Menlove felt uncomfortable. Matters were not helped at Christmas when Menlove joined Noyce in the Lake District to stay at a large house with his professor and some other university friends. The professor was happy to indulge Wilfrid and on his birthday, which was on New Year's Eve, bought him a top of the range Leica camera complete with many lenses and cleaning materials. Menlove gave Noyce his present which was another Leica camera but a cheaper version, what Menlove felt is not known but his feelings of inadequacy must surely have been difficult to hide.

A new guidebook was needed for Lliwedd, the large brooding cliff near Snowdon, and Menlove was again given the task to bring it up to date, he asked Noyce to act again as a collaborator and one must assume that this was an act on his part to try and keep them together.

The end of July saw Menlove and Noyce trying to solve the 'last great problem' on Lliwedd Central Gully Direct. The route had defeated a German party the year before, it was to prove too much for them both and they had to leave it unfinished. Noyce went to the Alps shortly thereafter with his professor and Menlove continued to work on the guide, climbing with anyone he could find.

Menlove met up with Alec Keith again in the summer and they planned a trip to Norway where they hoped to traverse a fjord in the Bindal region. It was a difficult trip not eased by the spartan diet provided by Menlove, eventually the terrain proved too difficult and they had to head to Bindal on recognised paths. Menlove was in a hurry as he wanted to be back in Wales as he had arranged to climb with Wilfid Noyce who had had a very good alpine season. Staying at Helyg the weather was dismal and they did out a little climbing though they did arrange to meet in the Lake District in September when Noyce would be staying with the professor again.

A fine day dawned on the 21st September and Menlove with Noyce made their way to the steep East Buttress of Scafell intending to climb Colin Kirkus route Mickledore Grooves. Noyce led the first pitch and Menlove the second, the third pitch involved a long run out with no real protection and given that the rock was wet in places both climbers were climbing in socks which afforded a better grip on the greasy holds. Noyce had run out 90ft of rope and was stood on a small sod of turf only a few moves from safety when suddenly the turf gave way and he fell 180ft. It was only by the quick action of Menlove who managed to take in some of the rope that Noyce avoided hitting the screes below. He was badly injured though Menlove was able to lower him to the ground and roped himself down to him where he tended his wounds and in essence saved his life. Friends later said that if Noyce had been climbing with anyone else he would have died that day. Menlove stayed at his bedside for three days willing him to live, he eventually came round but the injuries would leave a visible scar for the rest of his life.

Menlove was becoming dissatisfied with his work around this time and had unsuccessfully applied for a post in Birmingham to be near Alec Keith. Menlove was very good at his practical psychology but his real desire lay in research and he felt unable to persuade those that mattered that his theories were worthy of further research.

After the accident Menlove only climbed once again in 1937 where he climbed Primitive Route on Lliwedd with Alec Keith and Bill Stallybrass on a bitterly cold December day where the climb was more of true winter ascent than a rock climb with snow and ice in abundance.

Most weekends on the Welsh hills during 1938 were spent on Lliwedd with a variety of partners repeating routes for the new guidebook which would eventually appear in 1939 to some criticism due to its literary style. Lliwedd is a large and complex cliff and if ever somewhere needed a clear and concise guidebook it was Lliwedd that required it. The guide bore Wilfrid's name upon it but save for only a handful of occasions when he climbed with Menlove he took no real part in its compilation. It began to dawn on Menlove, clearer than ever, that their love affair was over.

Menlove did little climbing during 1939 and when war broke out he intended to register as a conscientious objector, his research work was not going as well as he had hoped and a feeling of deep despair was looming over him. At Christmas 1939 he went to Helyg but only did one short climb however he seemed to enjoy the break and in 1940 he began to take more of an interest in climbing again.

At Easter 1940 he went to Helyg to be met by some old friends and the rain, the weather did not stop them visiting Lliwedd to climb Rocker Route and the better weather of Easter Sunday saw a large party in Cwm Idwal. On Easter Monday Menlove and Colin Kirkus climbed together for the last time, there were no new routes climbed but they went up Hope on the

Idwal slabs and made their way over to the wonderful Cneifion Arete before finishing the day walking over the Glyderau and back to Helyg for tea. It is rather poignant that these two men, probably the best two climbers of their day, would have such an easy and enjoyable day in the mountains. There was nothing to prove to each other or anyone else and they climbed for the sheer joy of movement on rough rock over terrain they knew probably better than anyone else.

With the war escalating most of Menlove's friends were enlisted in the forces and while his pacifism, homosexuality and high idealism prevented him from seriously considering joining up it added to his sense of loneliness and isolation. In June 1940 he registered as a conscientious objector before going to Harlech to spend time with his sister and her family as well as working on a farm hay-harvesting. In the August he managed two new climbs in the Llanberis Pass, Brant and Slape on Clogwyn Y Grochan and today these two popular climbs are considered good value and graded Very Severe. Menlove climbed them in a fine drizzle and so, with the occasional loose rock, would have been much harder for him to climb than they are today.

The next time Menlove climbed was in October when with John Barford he climbed Horseman's Route on Dinas Cromlech, overall it is a poor climb by today's standards but the top pitch is worthwhile. Late autumn saw Menlove appointed Chief Psychiatrist at the Liverpool Child Guidance Clinic which increased his workload to the detriment of his research and consultancy work. Air raids were now a frequent part of Liverpool life and twice Menlove narrowly escaped injury, ultimately he moved into his consulting rooms in Rodney Street while his mother went to stay with his brother and family near Hereford.

In April 1941 Menlove was called to appear before a tribunal to adjudicate on his status as a conscientious objector. Menlove made his claim on his Christian beliefs, even though he was no longer practicing, and on his utter conviction of pacifist principals. In 1941 for a man to hold these ideals while the rest of the country were fighting was not popular and in many ways increased his isolation. Menlove refused to even consider a role in the army as a psychiatrist for wounded soldiers so strong where his beliefs. Menlove was spending 12-14 hours a week carrying out humanitarian work, was on fire watch duties and on call most nights of the week – he just could not kill another man. The tribunal rejected his application and Menlove lodged an appeal before taking himself off to

Wales for a week to get away from it all, but even while he was there at 1.30am on Whit Saturday some German planes managed to drop their bombs in the valley thus heightening his anxiety and sense of persecution.

On Whit Sunday Menlove with Jim Joyce went to Cloggy where they attempted to make a girdle traverse of the formidable west Buttress, an audacious undertaking given that Menlove had done very little climbing at such a high standard for a while. Menlove was not climbing at his best and they had to finish up Great Slab though the next day ambitions were still high when they made their way round to the Suicide Wall area of the Idwal Slabs. He climbed the hardest technical part of what was to become Suicide Wall Route One but could see no way up unless he was prepared to use pitons and so he retreated. The route was later climbed by a traverse out to the right and then straight up.

A few days later Menlove met up with Alec Keith, who had been posted to Chester, and they went climbing on Helsby, a week later they went to Wales where on the Sunday they could be found walking up to Cloggy to attempt a new climb without success. They returned to Helyg only to be asked to take part in a rescue on Holly Tree Wall which delayed their return to Birkenhead.

Menlove had a successful appeal and was now registered as a conscientious objector though work was now collapsing around him due to the war and his clinic was shut down. This did allow Menlove a chance to pursue his research work in earnest and he hired a small lonely cottage in Wales, Hafod Owen, from his friend Colin Kirkus.

In early August Menlove made the move from Liverpool to Hafod Owen and spent the first two weeks of the month getting the cottage habitable. He then went climbing again at first on Idwal Slabs and then in the Llanberis Pass where he climbed the beautiful Nea with Nea Morin, this climb is still one of the best Very Severe climbs in the whole of North Wales. A couple of days later Menlove with John Barford and Nea Morin went up to Cloggy again to prospect for new climbs, they thought they had made one climb but were disappointed to note that it had been climbed before by Maurice Linnell and was called Narrow Slab.

This was the last climb Menlove would do for over a year as he settled into the life of an ascetic recluse in lonely Hafod Owen. He chose to live as such as he believed that a pacifist should not be dependent upon a society whose values he did not share and that he should be self-supporting whenever possible. He gave away his clothing and sweet rations and settled down into a routine of deep and rigorous academic work.

This lonely existence, broken only occasionally by visits from friends and the occasional letter can only have heightened Menlove's feeling of isolation and rejection. It was a hard existence at the cottage, water had to be brought from a nearby stream which was doubly exhausting in the winter of 1942 which was harsh. He caught fish in a nearby lake and ate nettles but chose to give butter and sugar to any visitors who called on him. Wilfrid Noyce came to visit him on a couple of occasions though they never climbed together, Menlove said he needed to spend time on his research and climbing would be a distraction after which it would be days before he could get back into a routine where his work could find meaning within him. Although it was hard Menlove seemed to find a peacefulness from the, at times, difficult existence. John Barford also called on him and together they wrote the first ever guide book to Clogwyn Du'r Arddu. In the summer of 1942 he started to apply for jobs and fellowships however, even given his experience and excellent references nothing but rejection came his way.

Menlove met up with 'Nully' Kretschmner and they managed to fit in a couple of days climbing on the slabs of Idwal and an obscure Carneddau cliff before news reached Menlove that an old friend had died when the ship he was on was bombed off Cornwall. Worse news was to follow when news reached him about the missing Colin Kirkus and suddenly Hafod Owen seemed a haunted place to him. In the second week of October 1942 he left and moved to London to try and secure some voluntary work and in time paid employment. Menlove felt that his time at Hafod Owen was good as far as his research work went but he lamented that much more time would be needed to make a success of it.

In January 1943 he managed to secure two jobs that would afford him an income of £200 a year but he hoped that he could ultimately secure a paid research position. He missed the countryside however and frequently wrote of his longing for Wales, a two week holiday in Cornwall during the summer helped and he met up with A W Andrews, a Climbers Club stalwart, for some climbing. Menlove particularly enjoyed swimming in the big Atlantic waves, often he would allow the waves to carry him high up onto the rocks where he would cling on and scramble out of reach of the next wave. The Atlantic is extremely powerful and to anyone other than a superbly strong swimmer and climber such actions would be deemed almost suicidal.

Menlove returned to London somewhat refreshed for a time though he became increasingly frustrated at the lack of opportunity to continue with his research work, Alec Keith offered to put him in touch with an eminent uncle but it was a forlorn hope especially when another author brought out a published work broadly similar to what Menlove had been working on in relation to fear, the over–rigidity of centralized social systems, public schools, attitude of the working masses towards the aristocracy etc, in essence the rug had been taken from under his feet and it was a bitter blow.

Menlove now began to show the first tangible signs of schizophrenia and slowly started to lose his intellectual control as his letters to friends and family, as well as his prose [Menlove wrote poetry frequently] began to exhibit a certain degree of duplicity. To escape Menlove went once again to Helyg and though he was there for two weeks he only managed to climb on two days, inter alia repeating Colin Kirkus magnificent Pinnacle Wall on Craig Yr Ysfa one day and the next a pleasant easy day on Lliwedd.

He now began to openly criticise those within his profession, feeling that 'they' were ganging up on him. He felt as though he was being tested by his superiors who were sending him young boys as though to ascertain his sexual orientation. Then the V1 doodlebug's started to fall on London which made Menlove even more anxious. To try and escape he went to Skye to climb, walk and row a boat across to the isles Rhum and Canna spending a total of eighteen hours out at sea in squally weather.

By the autumn his mental deterioration had became a cause for major concern and so his brother Stephen came to London from County Durham, where he was a minister, to see him and as he arrived at the station Menlove was waiting for him despite not knowing what time he would be arriving. One look was all it needed and save for a quick journey back to Menlove's flat to collect some personal belongings the two of them headed back up north and with this chain of events Menlove's professional career was now over.

Initially Menlove adapted to life in a country vicarage though whenever a plane flew overhead he could scream that 'they' were watching him. He took a job in the local forestry and was liked by the villagers though at the vicarage conversation was never easy and Menlove was easily irritated. Winter came and Stephen asked if Menlove would like to go for a walk but, as usual, was rebuffed though ten minutes later Stephen heard the front door slam shut. Hours passed by and nothing was heard so Stephen went to the police station and a search was mounted but nothing could be found. They turned around half a mile from where Menlove was lying unconscious in a hedge, his face burnt by the chloroform-soaked pad he had bound around his nose and mouth.

Menlove came to and fell in the river which revived his senses and he knocked at a local farmhouse for help which duly came, he was then taken to a local hospital. Stephen was called and was told that if Menlove was kept under close supervision and that he would attend a mental institution for further care then no further action would be taken. One must remember that attempted suicide was a crime in Britain until 1961.

Two days later Menlove tried to throw himself out of a window and survived as the snow cushioned his fall. The hospital refused to care for Menlove any longer and he was taken to a mental hospital where he was to spend three long and necessary months under their care.

Menlove needed a fresh start, he withdrew his name from the list of conscientious objectors as he felt that having to live up to an ideal was part of his undoing, he accepted the defeat in the natural order of things. He left the mental hospital in March 1945 against his doctor's wishes though he did abide by the doctors request not to spend any great length of time at Stephen's house and so it was arranged for him to spend time with friends on the Wirral which worked well for a short while but the old hurt re-surfaced soon enough. Menlove would denunciate his old colleagues or anyone who did not agree with him and his ideas. In the end he went to stay with Wilfrid Noyce in Cambridge for a while, which was probably not the best place for him, then he moved onto his sister's house 'The Towers' near Ashford in Kent which was to be his home for the rest of his life.

Menlove sought help wherever he could and his friends rallied round in trying to get his research work analysed and recognised however eminent authorities, while thinking it interesting, dismissed it as amateurish as it had not been tested. Menlove had not received any practical training and as a consequence that side of his research would be lacking but he had hoped his ideas alone may secure some funding to allow such research to be carried out. Together with his sexual inclinations he found himself isolated, lonely and out of favour with the general thinking and attitude of the time.

Menlove did try to resurrect his medical career and saw a psychiatrist but it was a lost cause and so he settled into life at the Towers where he kept a small market garden and was paid a weekly allowance by her sister's husband, Hewlett Johnson for maintaining the much larger garden, this would be the only paid work he would have until he died.

Time passed slowly for Menlove now, he tried to get his poems published, without any real success, and on quiet evenings at the Towers he could be seen scribbling his research notes still holding onto the faintest of hopes that some renowned academic may take an interest and see them published.

In the spring of 1947 Menlove went climbing with John Barford and Nea Morin on the sandstone walls of Harrison's Rocks near Tunbridge Wells. Nea noted that although Menlove had not climbed for so long he had such immense strength that invariably he would get to the top of everything they tried. He also put up a difficult new climb Edward's Effort which no-one else could manage.

In the summer Menlove went with his sister and family to Harlech for a couple of weeks and she noted that he now seemed more relaxed and at ease with himself. The family spent the holiday walking in the local mountains and playing in the sea and when Nowell and the children went home Menlove made his way to Helyg in the hope of doing some climbing. He met a young Mike Ward, who was later the medical officer on the successful British Everest expedition of 1953, and they spent a day climbing in Idwal before venturing onto Cloggy where they found an alternative finish to the classic Longland's Climb. Menlove's family were hopeful of him making a full recovery and when an opportunity arose to take young people climbing in the newly found Outward Bound centre in the Lake District they were clearly pleased however Menlove only lasted a day, after years of isolation and loneliness he was unable to face the closeness of youth and his fellow men.

Menlove continued to try and secure some sort of work that his experience and qualifications could do justice to, however he was clearly deluding himself that he could cope with the stresses of such work and so he continued looking after the garden at the Towers and caring for his mother who had moved in with them. The summer of 1948 was a poor one and Menlove managed just a little climbing on Gallt Yr Ogof and in the Llanberis Pass adding the classic 'Rift Wall' to Craig Du which sadly nearly always appears to be wet. Come August he was back home but he was not happy and by October he was back in Wales staying at Cwm Glas cottage in the Llanberis Pass, were it not for a group of Sandhurst Cadets walking into the cottage and finding Menlove in a coma after a drug overdose his pain may have ended there and then. As it was an ambulance was called and he was taken to hospital and then sectioned at the mental hospital in Denbigh where he was to spend the next four months.

Menlove was discharged in the February 1949 and the doctor told his sister Nowell that he had suffered irreparable brain damage and that Menlove's suicide was inevitable sooner or later. She had to live with that thought for another eight years.

After his discharge Menlove went to work on a friends farm not far from Hafod Owen and despite the harsh and at times debilitating treatment he had received at Denbigh Menlove proved his prodigious strength by moving a half ton boulder off the drive and up the hillside with nothing more than a crowbar.

For the next few years Menlove made occasional trips to Wales where he repeated the occasional classic climb or put up a new one which he typically under-graded. One particular climb called 'Route of Knobs' was graded by Menlove as Hard Severe, the next known ascent of the climb was by the legendary Joe Brown who thought it more like a Hard Very Severe and quite committing at that.

A trip to Cornwall with Nea Morin and others was less successful though Menlove managed a few new climbs and some hair raising swims in the rough seas. Sadly Menlove's mental stability was clearly in further decline. He became more argumentative, his correspondence with friends though became more reflective and he still climbed once or twice a year making the trip to Wales on a motorbike that he now owned.

One such sighting of him is climbing down the classic Very Severe Belle Vue Bastion on Tryfan in a pair of battered old boots. His last new climb was a direct ascent of the waterfall in the Devil's Kitchen high up in Cwm Idwal at Very Severe in 1957. On the way home to the Towers he suffered an accident on his motorbike when a young boy riding a pushbike cut across his path and they collided, Menlove sustained some serious injuries but the poor boy died.

There was an inquest in which Menlove was exonerated of all blame but the accident affected him greatly and over the coming months Menlove went into a gradual and serious decline. He constantly believed that his family, his co-workers in London during the war and even his friends had conspired against him, his letters to friends were cutting and cruel but he was beyond all ordinary human concern at this point and on the 2nd February 1958 he swallowed potassium cyanide and the end finally came.

He was cremated later that month and his ashes were scattered on the hillside above Hafod Owen, perhaps the last place where he had known some true peace.

On his death all his research material was destroyed and so we can never truly know what was going through his mind and what he hoped to discover or understand about the human psyche.

His climbs are many and very distinct from those climbed by Colin Kirkus, Menlove seemed to seek unfrequented places and was not afraid to deal with loose, damp or vegetated rock if the end result was a good climb that others could enjoy.

It would be wrong to assume that Colin and Menlove were the only climbers from Merseyside making great routes during the 1930's and one man and one climb in particular stand out. Graham Balcombe from Southport climbed a route in the Lake District in the June of 1934 that was not repeated for nearly twenty years. Engineers Slabs, still a tough Very Severe today, lies high up on Great Gable and the top pitch, which takes an eternity to dry, involved six hours of cleaning on its first ascent and still causes modern leaders hearts to flutter. He returned again later in his holiday and added a different finish before leading Central Buttress on Scafell in less than ideal conditions. As if this was not enough he added a different and more direct finish to this climb, in the wet, and climbing in socks. This alternative finish is now the accepted way of climbing this classic route.

Great Changes

During the Second World War the hills and mountains of Britain fell largely quiet with only the occasional climber venturing out into the wild and near empty mountains. The British military soon realised however that our mountains and sea cliffs would prove an ideal training ground for newly recruited British troops and a fair number of our best climbers found work teaching the newly formed Commandos how to climb and abseil. The cliffs of North Wales and Cornwall were very popular and often used for cliff-assault practice.

Equipment improved as a consequence with the classic rubber soled Vibram boot replacing nailed boots, which had polished many of the holds on the classic climbs to a high sheen, and karabiners became more widely available due to mass production. Nylon ropes began to appear replacing the stiff and heavy hemp ropes that had hardly changed in nearly 100 years. Nylon ropes stretched when loaded by a fall and could absorb the shock much better than a hemp one which could snap unexpectedly. A Liverpool climber, Ken Tarbuck, developed a special knot for tying onto the rope that helped reduce friction in a fall, he suggested tying the nylon rope to a karabiner which was attached to a 'belt' of hemp rope tied around the waist. This neatly avoided the problem of nylon to nylon heat generation which could seriously weaken a rope and was in fact the first, albeit rudimentary, climbing harness.

The usage of piton's, always a debatable and contentious issue, became more widespread with a general acceptance that if no other protection could be found then one could be used to safeguard progress or retreat but any excessive use would bring criticism and much scorn on the climber concerned. Pebbles, sometimes gathered from the foot of the cliff, would be inserted into a crack on a climb with a loop of rope around them and with a karabiner they could then be attached to the climbing rope as a running belay, drilled out 'Worthington' nuts were also used in a similar way and they can still sometimes be seen wedged deep into cracks rusting away.

All of this helped give climbers greater confidence and it was inevitable that standards in climbing would rise when the war ended.

Many social changes took place after the war which enabled a new breed of climber to get away from the towns and cities at the weekend.

The advent of the Welfare State, better working conditions & pay with shorter hours and more holidays for the workers meant that it was much easier to get away into the hills and mountains of Britain. The hills of the Peak District were very popular, given the proximity of the large cities of Manchester and Sheffield, and with legislation doing away with the need to seek a permit to visit them many thousands of people discovered the outdoors for the first time. The Gritstone edges of the Peak District made it easier for many to take up rock climbing, although of no great height, the nature of the climbing meant that standards rose at a much greater rate than on the big mountain crags and in time these standards would be transferred to the bigger cliffs of North Wales and elsewhere. Two men in particular helped advance standards to such a degree that they are considered true legends in mountaineering and climbing circles. Joe Brown and Don Whillans were two working class lads from Manchester who put up so many climbs of such an audacious nature that it took a fair few years for the rest of the climbing community to take stock and catch up. Their climbs and the club they helped form, The Rock & Ice Club, were at the forefront of British climbing for most of the 1950's, an aura of extreme difficulty had built up around their climbs

One Liverpool man who did catch up and repeat many of Joe and Don's climbs, as well as putting up a fair number of his own was Hugh Banner from Crosby.

Hugh was educated at Merchant Taylor's school before going to study at Bristol University and while he was there he began to climb, as his father had forbid him to do so when he was in Liverpool. In 1952 / 53 he was involved in the first ascents of three major climbs in the impressive Avon Gorge, Central Buttress, Great Central and Desperation, in addition he made the first ascent of Sceptre in the awesome Cheddar Gorge. These climbs were originally graded as mere Very Severe's however in modern guidebooks they are considered quite bold Extremely Severe's. When at home in Liverpool Hugh began to climb regularly at Helsby, completing most of the classic and hard climbs while developing his strength and technique for the harder climbs to come. Hugh fell into what some people called the trap of repeating the climbs of the Rock & Ice club, making second or very early ascents of climbs such as Cenotaph Corner on Dinas Cromlech, Diglyph and White Slab on Cloggy or The Grooves on Cyrn Las, Hugh believed he had lost two years of possible new climbs by repeating the routes of others rather than concentrating on putting up his own.

However in 1958 he started his new route campaign in earnest by putting up some brilliant climbs in the Llanberis Pass, which was now one of the most popular places to climb in North Wales, indeed as it still is today. Rackstone Crib on Carreg Wastad was a mere aperitif for in May Hugh, with another Merseyside climber Jim O'Neill, climbed The High Level Girdle and the sensational Overhanging Arete on the steep north facing cliff of Cyrn Las. In August and again with Jim O'Neill and Bob Beesley he climbed the steep and poorly protected Karwendal Wall on Clogwyn Y Grochan

However it was on Clogwyn Du'r Arddu where the Rock & Ice seemed to hold the greatest sway though in 1959 Hugh began to change all that and climbed the impressive Gecko Groove for the first time with Bob Beesley who was climbing in an old battered pair of kletter-shoes held together with a leather strap, the route was so-named as 'one would need the adhesive toes of a Gecko to get up it'. Next Hugh added his brilliant and most coveted wall climb The Troach to the cliff later that year. This was a big breakthrough as they were the first real climbs done on the cliff by someone outside the Rock & Ice club, the following year Hugh added the wonderfully steep and exposed Hand Traverse to the Pinnacle Face of the cliff.

Hugh then went to work away for a while and made infrequent trips to the mountains of North Wales though nearer to his new home in Northumberland he made many impressive ascents including Thunder Crack and The Trouser Legs. In 1963 he co-wrote the minimalist guide to Cloggy with Peter Crew which did much to dispel the myth of the difficulty of the Rock & Ice routes on the cliff.

In 1965 Hugh made a further contribution to Welsh climbing with the first ascent of Rake End Wall a sadly neglected, though very good climb, in the Ogwen valley. Hugh returned back to Merseyside in the 1970's and teamed up with Derek Walker to climb regularly on Helsby, the Gritstone Edges and Wales. When approaching fifty he climbed The Nose on El Capitan in Yosemite, it was clear that despite advancing years he had not lost any of his real ability and in 1988 he moved to North Wales to establish 'HB Climbing Equipment' which quickly became renowned for its innovative and world-class climbing protection. Hugh continued to climb the easier extremes well into his sixties though a bad motorcycle accident in 2000, when he lost a leg, curtailed his climbing activities. In 2007 he passed away shortly after being diagnosed with an inoperable brain tumour.

Sir Charles Evans was born in Liverpool in 1918 and after reaching Oxford University to read medicine he took up climbing and fast became one of the country's best young alpinists before the Second World War cut his climbing short. After the war he resumed his studies and climbing and in 1952 he was deputy leader on the 1952 Everest training expedition to Cho Oyu. On the successful 1953 Everest expedition he was appointed deputy leader alongside Col. John Hunt and were it not for a faulty, leaking oxygen set he may well have been the first man, along with Tom Bourdillion, to reach the summit. As it was they had climbed higher than anyone else in reaching the south Summit.

In 1955 he was leader of the successful expedition to Kanchenjunga, the third highest mountain in the world and it is widely accepted that the organisation of this expedition to such a complex and often attempted peak was a master-class. In 1957 he climbed Annapurna IV (7525m), got married and was settling down to life as Principal of Bangor University when he was diagnosed with Multiple Sclerosis, his climbing began to slowly come to an end though he devoted himself to his job and family overseeing the expansion of the University and retiring in 1984. He died peacefully in a nursing home, within view of his beloved Welsh mountains, in 1995.

Alan Rouse

Alan Paul Rouse was born on 19th December 1951 in Wallasey and from an early age he developed a wanderlust that would stay with him for the rest of his life. Academically he was very bright and won a scholarship to Birkenhead School and then a place at Emmanuel College, Cambridge to eventually gain a degree in mathematics.

Inspired by books from the school library and having had a taste of the outdoors on a couple of family walking holidays he decided to give rock climbing a go after seeing some climbers at a local sandstone quarry in Wallasey called The Breck. The quarry was only 100yds from where he lived at 12 Knaresborough Road and with a friend he would go several times a week watching how the older climbers would manage the various problems and traverses and then they would copy them. It was here that Alan met a couple of climbers who invited the two young schoolboys along to their newly formed climbing club, Gwydyr Mountain Club which despite its Welsh name actually met on the Wirral.

There was a foot and mouth outbreak in the Lake District and North Wales so trips to the mountains were not possible therefore Alan's first proper climbs were at Helsby in January 1968. A few weeks later the restrictions were lifted and a trip to North Wales with John Huxley from the Gwydyr club afforded them an opportunity to do some real climbs. Although there was still snow on the ground they managed a few easy routes in the Ogwen Valley and the climbing bug had truly bitten.

In June 1968, after four months of regular climbing at the Breck and Helsby, where he had begun to do some of the classic climbs like Flake Crack, Alan went to Tremadog with his regular partner Nick Parry and polished off three classic Very Severes at Tremadog, a delightful series of cliffs overlooking Porthmadog.

Alan climbed most days at the Breck with his friends and soon became very proficient at some of the harder problems. Alan was a good chess player and he seemed to be able to treat the short technical problems like a vertical chess game and figure out the moves that needed to be made in advance. In August Alan was in the Llanberis Pass and had just done Colin Kirkus climb, the Direct Route on Dinas Mot and Menlove Edwards superb route Sabre Cut on Dinas Cromlech when he saw a leader take a big fall on the classic Cemetery Gates (E1, 5b). Alan asked if he could have a go and promptly led the difficult climb originally climbed by Joe Brown and Don Whillans in the fifties. The classic Joe Brown climb, Vector (E2, 5c) at Tremadog followed in the October of that year and at the end of October The Plum (E1, 5b), Leg Slip (E1, 5b) and First Slip (E1, 5c) were also climbed though a nasty fall on the latter route slowed Alan and his ambitions for a while.

That winter Alan had his first taste of winter climbing on Snowdon and the wonderful ridge of Crib Goch with members of the Gwydyr club who now had a hut in Llanrwst. Alan had to spend a lot of time preparing for his A-Levels at the beginning of 1969 so there were not too many trips to the mountains however he did work on a difficult traverse at the Breck whenever he could. The Bluebell Wall in the quarry is severely undercut in places and the low level traverse is certainly quite stiff at [only] 5c grade, Alan was the first to successfully cross it and not before long he was able to do a double crossing.

Alan continued to climb regularly at the Breck and Helsby and when his A-Levels were over he made his first visit to the Alps with some members of the Gwydyr Club, he climbed the Menegaux Route on the

Aiguille de L'M and the Requin from the Mer De Glace before witnessing a terribly sobering accident where a party of English climbers were killed, this deeply affected the party and while they did some more easier climbs their heart was not in it though they were certainly impressed by the Alps. It was perhaps here that Alan began to think beyond mere rock climbing and look toward the bigger mountains for excitement.

Once he had his A-level results and knew he had secured a place at Emmanuel College, Cambridge he had a few months of much longed for freedom. Alan passed his driving test first time after just one professional lesson, his parents though began to doubt their wisdom as he borrowed the family car at almost every opportunity. Alan spent a lot of time driving from one social engagement to another and perhaps an accident was almost inevitable, and so it proved when he crashed the car into the wall of the Birkenhead Girls School. This increased his reputation amongst his friends though failed to do so with his parents, in later life Alan said that he would never be so irresponsible as to lend a car to an eighteen year old.

Rock climbing was increasingly important though and Alan progressed through the grades with amazing speed and together with Nick Parry, Fred Heywood and a group from the Vagabond Mountaineering Club he polished off a significant number of the hard Welsh classic climbs.

From 1970 Alan Rouse began to climb more and more with the Vagabond's who had, and still have, a cottage in the Llanberis Pass which was handy for the climbs and even handier for the pub which was fast becoming as much of a focus of attention as the cliffs themselves. Alan led his first new route on Cloggy Gemini (E4,5c) not a bad effort for a nineteen year old on only his second visit to this dramatic cliff.

As well as leading some of the hardest climbs of the day Alan began to take up soloing, after a chance meeting with Eric Jones who had given him a lift while hitch hiking out to Wales. In one weekend he soloed Suicide Wall (E2,5c) and Suicide Groove(E1,5b) in Cwm Idwal on the Saturday and on the Sunday he amazed everyone and announced himself to the climbing world in a big way by soloing the impressive The Boldest (E4,5c) on Cloggy. This last climb was considered one of the hardest on the cliff and also North Wales, it was an audacious effort and one that elevated him to the top echelons of climbers operating in Britain at that time.

Almost every weekend Alan was away climbing and partying in North Wales, there was a very active core of hard climbers based in Llanberis, as there is today, and after a hard days climbing there invariably followed a hard night's partying back at someone's house after the pubs had closed. Wild tales were told, relationships with the opposite sex were won and lost and many climbing trips planned around the world in a drunken haze. The next morning over breakfast in Wendy's Cafe (now the ever popular Pete's Eats) the day's objective would be decided upon by the severely hung-over, or still drunk, climbers and then they'd depart for the crags at high speed eager not to miss a moment on the rock.

Later that summer Alan made a second trip to the French Alps and attempted the difficult south face of the Fou with Leo Dickinson but they had to retreat for various reasons, they also had to retreat from the 90m deidre on the west face of the impressive Dru with Geoff Tabner. Thankfully the trip was not a failure as he did manage to climb the north ridge of the Peigne in a fast time as well as the west face of the Blatiere which he did with Geoff Birtles though not without incident as they narrowly escaped the storm, that was to kill fifteen climbers that night, over Mont Blanc as they made their way back down to Chamonix.

Alan went to Cambridge University in the October and immersed himself into student life, even leaving his climbing gear at home intending to concentrate on his studies. However after only a few days he could be found at the Cambridge University Mountaineering Club (CUMC) stand at the Societies Fair making himself known and thoroughly intending to keep his climbing going for as long as possible. He took to wearing his mothers old fur coat to lectures, grew his hair even longer and became a typical student of the time. The CUMC had many meets mainly to Derbyshire which could be reached in a long day and Alan worked his way through the classic hard lines and much soloing. In early 1971 he managed the first ever lead and solo of The Beatnick (E5,6a) at Helsby, this classic Jim O'Neill problem still stops many leaders today in their tracks and is rarely led, most climbers preferring the assurance of a top-rope.

At the university Alan teamed up with another student, Mick Geddes, who introduced him to the delights of extreme Scottish winter climbing and on one CUMC trip to the CIC hut on Ben Nevis they climbed the formidable Point Five gully in very good time. The CIC hut lies beneath the imposing north face of Ben Nevis and it was while on one meet here in March 1971 that the CUMC introduced the annual *'Standing Outside in the Nude in a Blizzard Competition'* – it is not known how well Alan did in this. However Alan did improve his winter climbing abilities and claimed a number of coveted second ascents of the classic winter lines, this is more impressive when one considers how far he and his fellow CUMC members had to travel compared to the Scottish locals.

After the winter Alan got back into his rock climbing and made the first ascent of, on that most imposing of sea cliffs Craig Gogarth, Positron (E5,6a) which has now achieved legendary status and is one of the most desired routes for its grade in the country. He continued to solo a lot soloing the classic Vector (E2, 5C) at Tremadog and making the first ascent of Sheaf Direct (E3,5c) on Cloggy.

Later that summer Alan again went to the Alps and soloed the forbidding north ridge of Piz Cengalo in Switzerland then he climbed the west face of the Dru and the north face of the Triolet with Pete Minks from the Vagabonds. While attempting to solo the south face of the Fou which had previously defeated him, Alan broke his ankle in a fall when a piton failed and he needed to make a difficult diagonal abseil to reach a gully and down climb some 300ft to reach his rescuers. Not to be put off Alan was climbing and soloing again by the following October and in December he led the Joe Brown classic on Craig Gogarth, Rat Race (E2,5c)

In the winter of 1972 Alan was back on Ben Nevis with Mick Geddes from the CUMC and together they made the second ascent of the Orion face direct as well as a couple of other difficult winter climbs and a first ascent of south Pillar of Creag Meaghaidh. Later that summer Alan went back to the Alps to climb the famous Walker Spur on the Grandes Jorasses. Following this Alpine season he travelled to the Yosemite Valley where he again broke his ankle in a short fall on the north face direct of Half Dome when yet another peg failed, this was quite a complicated fracture and it took a long time to heal.

In 1973 Alan went on the International Meet at the Ecole Nationale in Chamonix, he then, with Rab Carrington, went to Patagonia where a number of bureaucratic hold ups limited their time in the mountains though they did manage a climb on east side of Mojon Rojo and tried the magnificent looking west face of Fitzroy but time was against them. However this trip did lay a seed in Alan's mind for a future long 'super' trip to south America. Later on that year, Alan was back in the Alps and made the second ascent of the Zappelli / Bertone route on Mont Maudit a mountain adjacent to Mont Blanc and nearly as high, with Mick Geddes.

After returning from south America in 1974 Alan lived in a cottage near Bangor in North Wales and continued to climb whenever he could, for

Alan climbing was proving to be everything and even though he had passed his degree (just) at Cambridge it was clear that, for a while at least, the call of climbing and the mountains would override any desire to obtain a more secure existence.

Money was never easy to come by and clearly to fund his lifestyle something had to be done and so a variety of jobs were undertaken as and when required. Having a degree helped to secure a number of supply teaching posts near to where they lived at the time.

In 1975 Alan made his first visit in winter to the Alps with Rab Carrington, he had secured an apartment in the small village of Argentiere near Chamonix for the winter which was supposed to sleep four but often held many times that number, with visiting guests being invited to contribute to the rent it proved an affordable way to spend the winter. While there they climbed the stunning Gervasutti Pillar with two bivouacs after they had failed on the Super Couloir of Mont Blanc Du Tacul, they then made the first winter ascent of the stunning Rebuffat / Terray route on the Auguille des Pelerins which is now considered a classic winter climb. Much partying was done with Alan totally immersing himself in the life of a Chamoniard, skiing or climbing by day and drinking / partying to the early hours every night. Back in the UK later that year Alan made an early ascent of the difficult Leech on Cloggy and resumed his climbing and stop start supply teaching career.

1976 was to be a busy year largely devoted to organising the 'super-trip' to south America where Alan and Rab Carrington felt that they had a score to settle from their disastrous 1974 trip when they had a lot of difficulty in getting their climbing equipment away from the customs officers in Buenos Aires. Before leaving the UK though Alan and Rab made a fine first winter ascent of the Left Edge Route on Gardyloo Buttress on Ben Nevis, rarely in good winter condition this very good grade 5 winter climb is still much sought after by modern climbers.

Late in 1976 Alan, Rab Carrington with several other climbers and accompanying girlfriends went to south America for the best part of a whole year. Again Alan & Rab's primary aim was the west face of Fitzroy (3441m), a towering spire of rock and ice that is fully exposed to the ferocious winds and frequent storms so prevalent in Patagonia.

By January 1977 they were both at their previously gained highpoint bivouac from 1974 and Alan confidently talked through with Rab the route they would take to the summit and dismissed it in a mere sentence or two as being something of a dawdle. The reality was far from the case and the next day they began a rising traverse on steep unstable rock to a large corner which proved much harder than it appeared the night before. Rab noticed some bad weather coming in quickly and they had to descend, eleven difficult abseils later saw them back at the bivouac site from the night before and with no improvement in the weather they descended to base camp to wait for better weather.

A week later the weather came good and they both climbed quickly up to their previous high point when the weather began to look ominous again however they climbed on up the corner and onto a snow slope where they dug a poor snow cave and cowered in their sleeping bags waiting for the storm to abate and hopefully allow them another chance to continue. Dawn came but they were to be denied further progress as the rocks were covered in a thick veneer of verglas which would make any attempt to go higher futile. Alan reckoned another two days of good weather would have seen them up the route which was not climbed until 1983 by a Czech team utilising fixed ropes and taking nearly six weeks to complete the ascent. Alan & Rab headed back to base camp and looked for another objective to satisfy their hunger.

They decided upon the west face of a neighbouring peak Poincenot, the ascent of which was duly despatched in a single day by a new route, they reached the base of the peak just as a big storm came in to envelop them. It was a superb ascent but they were both frustrated by their inability to climb Fitzroy.

The party then headed over the border to Chile in the hope of getting some climbing in the Paine region but eight days of continuous rain put paid to their aspirations and so they made their way to the impressive Rondoy west face (5870m). Joe Brown had refused to set foot on the face and the legendary Italian climber Walter Bonatti failed to find a way up. A British team did finally climb the mountain using 'siege' tactics and fixed ropes but their line of ascent was to be Alan & Rab's descent route.

Alan had decided that a 'warm-up' climb was needed and suggested Nevado Rasac Principal (6040m), Rab agreed and three hard days later they were back in base camp having reached the summit. Days were spent watching the west face of Rondoy to see where the avalanches were falling in an effort to find the safest route. One afternoon they were staring at the mountain when all of a sudden a huge avalanche came down the central section of the face they were hoping to climb, this forced the climbers to accept the left side of the west face as the safest and most logical line on the mountain.

Alan and Rab set out early the next morning and were faced with some difficult mixed climbing on snow and rock, they intended to reach a couloir where they hoped to find a bivouac site which they eventually did in an icy cave. The terrain was especially hazardous and they both knew that retreat was not possible as they were carrying minimal equipment in the hope that they would move fast and be safer. They climbed all through the next day on steep ice and as it began to grow dark they became more anxious about finding somewhere to spend the night as no ledges or caves were visible. Eventually Rab punched a hole in some snow and he was able to enlarge it into a small ledge where they could both sit down for the night clipped into their ice pegs, not a comfortable prospect but at least it was a rest from the difficult climbing.

The next morning they climbed higher but the snow became much softer and granular making for increasingly precarious climbing, they finally reached the notch between the north and south summits and instinctively headed for the slightly lower north summit which looked safer and easier. After they left the summit the ridge became a nightmare to descend as they were faced with snow that had the consistency of polystyrene granules, it took an eternity to kick a step in the soft snow that would be able to hold their weight and frequently they poked their axes through the snow to suddenly find that they were on a cornice with a view of the glacier visible through the hole made by the axe. Eventually they found their descent route which was technically easier but more tiring given the length of time spent on the route. After four days hard climbing they made it back to base camp where they could relax.

After this climb they had a long rest before climbing the south face of Yerupaja (6635m), the second highest peak in Peru before Rab and the others went home and Alan went to the USA with his girlfriend to do some guiding.

This was a hugely successful trip and one that really opened Alan's eyes as to what he could achieve in mountaineering, clearly the Himalaya's would be the next logical step and after sending applications to the Nepalese and Indian governments, by April 1978 permission had been received from the Nepalese for Jannu in the post monsoon (autumn) period of that year.

Jannu (7710m)

This difficult peak, which is a western outlier of Kanchenjunga, the third highest mountain in the world, had only been climbed on three previous occasions. It was this present expeditions intention to climb the mountain alpine style. That would mean eschewing all siege tactics as used on previous expeditions to the mighty Himalayan peaks and climbing as one would in the Alps with the climbers operating self sufficiently carrying their own food and equipment and not utilising porters or sherpas on the mountain. There would be no oxygen and no safety in numbers but this type of climbing has benefits of its own in that one could climb the mountain quicker, there would be less need to repeatedly climb dangerous sections of a route carrying supplies and perhaps just as important it was cheaper to climb this way.

The expedition did not have long to get ready and the need for money was never more apparent and so sponsors needed to be found. One sponsor was the brewer Bass Charrington who provided much needed funds as well as lots of beer which Alan and the others eagerly devoured while packing.

The party consisting of Alan, Rab, Brian Hall and another climbing friend Roger Baxter Jones left the UK on 15 August 1978 and after the usual problems with Indian & Nepalese customs found themselves in the Nepalese capital, Kathmandu. They decided to travel like the locals and took the overloaded bus to Dharan Bazaar, Himalayan bus journeys are even today, considered as dangerous and stressful as the actual climbing of a big peak. Such are the poor state of the roads, the vehicles and the usual mad driving of the bus drivers, who on occasion fall asleep at the wheel or collapse due to too much hashish, death by bus is one of the more common causes of death in Nepal.

The trek in to Jannu began from Dharan and all the climbers suffered from the heat, leeches and the local Chang which they consumed in ever increasing quantities aware that there would be no more beer till they were back from the mountain. Eventually they reached the summer settlement of Ramshey where the party were granted their first view of Jannu, it looked a daunting prospect. They were hoping to climb the east face of Jannu which from the glacier near base camp looked a tormented mass of rock walls, ice slopes and hanging glaciers all leading to a final 600m high wall of steep, icy granite.

Base camp was at an altitude of 4800m and lay on a grassy terrace opposite the massive east face, there was no doubt the climbing would be difficult and dangerous and their early forays proved this to be the case. Tempers became fraught and the party divided, Alan & Rab favoured the east face while Roger and Brian thought they should cut their losses and repeat the French route on the south west side of the mountain.

They both spent the rest of the week reconnoitring their respective routes and met again at base camp to decide how best to proceed. They decided to give the east face one more try and if that were not successful then they would concentrate on the French route. On the 7th October the monsoon ended and the weather improved, they headed back up to the face full of hope. As they climbed higher the snow conditions worsened but for four days they climbed on and eventually reached the col where they could look up at the rest of their climb. It was hopeless as another full week of sustained effort would be needed to complete the route and so a descent was made back to base camp and a walk around the mountain to the French route.

On the 17th October the four climbers were loaded down with heavy sacks as they made their way through the ice fall onto the glacier beneath the south west face. Although this route had been climbed back in 1961 it was still to prove a tough undertaking especially as the climbers would have no support, fixed ropes or oxygen. They climbed as two separate pairs of climbers swapping leads as required to break trail and sharing the hard pitches. They reached a good bivouac site at 19000ft and the next day the real climbing started, for the following two days they climbed on the most difficult and dangerous snow any of them had ever encountered. A long and complicated snow-ridge led to a giant snow gendarme blocking the rest of the route, they had to find a way around this obstacle and the steep snow slopes led to an area of giant unstable mushrooms of soft bottomless snow with no belays, a fall would probably have been fatal though they made it safely to another bivouac site at 21000ft.

The next day Brian Hall fell into a crevasse and the remaining three had to haul him out before climbing a steep snow flute, the walls of which came ever closer until it constricted so tightly they had to force a way out onto a vertical wall of snow. As they climbed higher the snow conditions worsened and the slopes threatened to avalanche at any moment but they climbed on almost swimming through waist deep snow. They were becoming worried about how they would be able to descend such treacherous snow and considered retreating while they could, food and gas were running low and they were all close to calling it a day when Roger disappeared round a corner and found some better snow in an old avalanche runnel which they climbed to reach another bivouac site at 21650ft. The ground was flatter now but there was no shelter from the wind, in an effort to reduce weight they had not brought a tent only their sleeping bags and bivouac sacks. The next morning they crossed a plateau to find a better, more sheltered, site for a bivouac from which they hoped to make for the summit they next day.

They rose just after midnight and began to cook a breakfast of tea and cereal, at this altitude there is no water and snow had to be melted for everything which takes an eternity. A further 2300ft lay between them and the summit and so leaving their rucksacks, stove and sleeping equipment they left the bivouac at 3.30am and by the light of their head-torches climbed upwards into the ever increasing wind. The snow conditions worsened but by 11.30am they had reached the summit and after taking a few photographs headed back down to their last bivouac site to crawl exhausted into sleeping bags. The rest of the descent took four days hard graft, two without food, before they finally reached base camp where they could eat, drink and sleep to their heart's content.

Alan had finally summited a difficult Himalayan peak in impressive style and it was clear to him now that this was the life he wanted to lead while he could. How many more expeditions would there be to these magnificent mountains he could not say but with this ascent he had come to greater prominence in the mountaineering community and surely more trips would come his way. Climbing in the Himalaya in the 1970's and early 80's was vastly different from today as there were few, if any, commercial guiding companies and those wishing to visit the Himalaya to climb high mountains had to essentially organise everything themselves.

On his return from the Himalaya it was not long before Alan was back in the mountains when he made the first winter ascent of the Pointe Du Domino in the French Alps. Then followed a summer trip to south America with Brian Hall and the Frenchman Nicholas Jaeger where together they made the first ascent of the west face of Tscara Grande Oeste and the south west ridge of Trapecio. He also climbed the west ridge of Ninashanka (5607m) with Brian Hall.

Nuptse (7861m)

Alan had been invited by Doug Scott, the first British climber to summit Mount Everest, on an expedition to Nuptse. They intended to climb the north face direct from the western Cwm but Everest was also on the agenda with a hope of an ascent of the stunningly difficult west ridge.

Alan, Brian Hall & Rab Carrington went for a climb on a smaller peak first, Kangtega (6782m) but failed to reach the summit due to poor snow conditions and threatening bad weather. It was on this climb that Alan and Rab had a major falling out the full reasons for which are hardly known though it was in all probability a desire in both of them to go a different direction in life. Rab was married and beginning to settle down whereas Alan just seemed content to climb, he had a girlfriend but did not want or need a serious relationship or commitment.

Doug, Alan, Brian and Frenchman Georges Bettembourg all met at base camp where Alan and Brian were unwell as the previous day they had gone from 18000ft to 22000ft up the Khumbi Icefall and were clearly not fully acclimatised yet. A couple of rest days later the party of four made their way through the treacherous icefall to camp in the western Cwm, so named by George Mallory on the early Everest expeditions of the 1920's when he looked down into it from the nearby Lho La pass. Nuptse had been climbed previously but never by the imposing north face and the idea of climbing it originally struck Doug when on his ascent of the Everest south Face in 1975, despite a number of opportunities a chance to 'rub noses' with the face had only now finally materialised.

A brief reconnoitre proved the face to be in good condition and on the descent back to camp two hopes were running high for a successful ascent. The next day they left camp with four days supplies and climbed onto the face and by early afternoon they reached a bergschrund which they could fashion into a comfortable and safe sleeping place. All four were not fully acclimatised and so the opportunity of an early finish, good food and comfortable sleeping place seemed too good an opportunity to waste. The following morning, feeling as refreshed as one can at over 23000ft they climbed on upwards in near perfect snow conditions where one could kick a small step rather than rely upon ones crampon front points which tire the legs so much. They were climbing a shallow subsidiary ridge on the north face and where it ran into the north ridge proper they ran into some rocks, Alan & Doug decided to dig an ice cave while Brian and Georges ran out a good length of rope so that a good start could be made in the morning.

There was just over 1000ft to go now to the summit and so, as on Jannu, the party dispensed with anything unnecessary to the actual climbing and went for the summit. Alan and Brian took the lead kicking steps and finding the route while Doug and Georges followed closely behind. With 400ft to go they swopped leads and the weather began to show ominous signs of changing however they climbed on and after surmounting a difficult cornice they all reached the summit on the 20 October 1979. Actually they had to stop a few feet away from the summit due to the poor snow which made the highest point a cornice, on which it would have been unwise to tread.

With huge whale-back lenticular clouds threatening the climbers descended back to the last ice cave and the following morning made it all the way back to camp two in the western Cwm. Doug thought it only a couple of hours from there back to base camp however there had been some upheaval in the Khumbu Icefall and a much more difficult descent awaited them involving nine hours of difficult, dangerous and precarious climbing amongst the fragile seracs and crevasses before they finally made it back to base camp and a proper, much needed, rest.

The plan to attempt Everest by the west ridge was shelved as Georges wanted to go home, Alan had permission for Everest the following winter and Brian had slight frostbite. All the four climbers accepted that they had had a great climb on Nuptse, with winter coming Everest would have been too much and with no regrets they quit while they were ahead.

For Alan this was yet another successful visit, the falling out with Rab Carrington aside, to the Himalaya and was a vindication in his belief in the lightweight alpine style approach. His next three expeditions would not quite go to plan however and these trips would be all the more frustrating for him.

In early 1980 Alan joined up with the legendary Chris Bonington et al for a short reconnaissance trip to the formidable looking Mount Kongur (7719m) in China with a view to staging a full scale expedition the following year. While on reconnaissance they climbed Sarakyaguqi (6200m) for the first time.

Everest (8848m)

Late in 1979 Alan had received permission for the west ridge of Everest in winter, in summer the temperatures on the high Himalayan summits are cold and the wind can often reach frightening strengths however in winter things are often much worse. Winter climbing in the Himalaya was something of which little was really known, true, the Poles had climbed Everest in February 1980 by the south col route but the west ridge was to be a different prospect altogether. It was longer, much more technical and critically exposed to the jet-stream winds which descend upon the mountain in winter.

Despite a lot of financial support from various companies and institutions the expedition was run as cheaply as possible. The alpine style approach of a summer expedition was simply not possible during a winter expedition so there would be load carrying responsibilities for the climbers and the need to establish fixed camps and ropes along the ridge. All the expedition members were from the elite of British mountaineering with an impressive array of successful expeditions in the Himalaya, south America and Alaska. If anyone had dropped out there were few if any who could replace them at short notice

Between the 1st and 5th December all the expedition members arrived at Everest base camp in mild winter weather where there was only five degrees of frost at midday. No time was wasted in establishing camp one at the Lho La (20000ft) where Brian Hall, Joe Tasker and Paul Nunn cut out an ice cave, which in time became two caves as more climbers moved up. The Burgess twins, Paul Nunn and Joe Tasker pushed the fixed ropes out onto the west ridge proper and progress was gradual but steady until Christmas. Most expedition members came down with the usual stomach and chest ailments though Alan took longer to recover no doubt due to the extra responsibility of leading the expedition.

On the 23rd December the temperature dropped ten degrees at base camp and the high altitude all in one down suits were donned by everyone just to keep warm. Christmas Day was spent at base camp where a sumptuous meal was enjoyed together with a liberal smattering of Brandy & Whisky though Joe Tasker was keen to still push the route despite the atrocious weather and he moved up alone to the ice caves on the Lho La late on Christmas Day.

The climbers continued to push the route as best they could and eventually established camp two at 6700m where a near indestructible Whillans Box tent was erected. Meanwhile the climbers continued to ferry loads as high as possible to make sure the camps were properly stocked. Eventually the weather took a further turn for the worse and all the climbers had to retreat to the ice caves at the Lho La where they could escape the constant noise of the wind.

In a short period of good weather during mid January the climbers managed to push the route a bit higher and established camp three (23000ft) in a deep crevasse. The temperature inside camp three never rose any higher than -20 degrees and despite periodic short breaks in the bad weather there was no real opportunity to force the route higher.

All the climbers lost weight, Alan lost two stone in all, and the continued time above 17000ft made the climbers more susceptible to illness and infection and in the end the general consensus was that the expedition would not reach the summit within the time allocated by its permit and that there was a very real chance that someone could find themselves cut off for days at a time at one of the high camps and no-one would be able to help them.

In the end the expedition was called off, much to the chagrin of some members who thought a chance still existed however the chosen route, the weather and extreme conditions proved too much for such a small team and failure was inevitable. Alan was bitterly disappointed by this failure but he would be returning to the Himalaya soon enough to hopefully rectify matters.

Mount Kongur (7719m)

In the early summer of 1981, only a couple of months after his return from Everest, Alan went to China with Chris Bonington on an expedition to climb Mount Kongur, one of the highest unclimbed mountains in the world at that time. The team selected by the climbing leader Chris Bonington was only small, besides Chris and Alan there would only be two other climbers, Joe Tasker and Peter Boardman as well as a doctor and Michael Ward who was to be the overall leader of the expedition. Michael Ward was the doctor on the successful British expedition to Everest in 1953 and had climbed extensively in the Himalaya. Alan was now moving in rather high circles of the mountaineering establishment as his previous big climbs had brought him to some prominence and his desire now was to make a living from mountaineering if at all possible. To climb with the right people and get invited onto the big expeditions would raise his profile and thus it would be easier to fill theatres when lecturing and there are always books to be written.

On the reconnaissance the previous year Alan thought that Mount Kongur looked an easy climb, he always seemed to dismiss many climbs as easy and only rarely changed his mind for fear that word would get out that he found something hard. On arrival in China the team spent a few days sight-seeing, giving lectures and attending official banquets before they travelled by truck to their base camp near the Karokol Lakes, they could not see Kongur from there as a small peak hid it from sight though the climbers made several training climbs on nearby peaks to gain a better view and see what they had taken on.

On the 4th June the team established an advance base camp on the glacier and two days later they set out for the south ridge intent on seeing how difficult it would prove before trying the south west rib which also looked a viable proposition. Alan favoured the south west rib but was out-voted and the south ridge was where they would direct their energies. The weather was very mixed and they rarely had two good consecutive days of decent weather, given that they reckoned on needing four or five good days to make the ascent the party became increasingly concerned whether they would get a chance to even have a proper go at the mountain. The weather turned bad on this initial foray and so the climbers bid a hasty retreat back to base camp in a white out.

A few days later an attempt was made on the south west rib but this was stalled due to the weather and poor snow conditions that threatened to avalanche at any time and so another descent to base camp followed. The climbers now decided that the only viable route up Kongur lay on the south ridge and so they diverted all their energies to that.

They climbed up to their previous high point on the ridge and were faced with a huge tower of rock which they managed to skirt round to the right and then followed a nightmarish ridge of poor snow where a fall could not have been stopped. They pitched camp in a sheltered nook and prepared their evening meal but unfortunately Chris mistook some lemonade powder for curry powder and the resulting meal was hardly to anyone's liking. At this altitude the brain is slow to react and mistakes are easily made, food is hard to digest at the best of times and if one fails to eat strength rapidly fades leaving the climber susceptible to injury or worse. The next day they climbed on over pinnacles of rock and treacherous snow ridges to finally dig a snow cave by Junction Peak in which to spend the night, the summit still seemed a long way off and they decided to leave their sleeping bags in the hope that they could make a quick dash for the summit.

They were all hungry now and eager to get up and back down to base camp where good food and British beer awaited them. Climbing up on loose rock and poor snow they eventually came to a place not far from where another snow cave could probably be dug however with no sleeping bags and the wind increasing to spend a night at this extreme altitude would be more than foolish. Peter wanted to push on but the other three decided against it and a retreat was made to their old snow cave and then back down to base camp. As they walked back along the glacier they glanced up to see Kongur's summit clad in a dense cloud and they knew they had made the right decision.

The descent down the south ridge proved harder than anticipated and so the climbers focused their attention on the south west rib again which proved to be in better condition now and eventually they reached their old snow cave by the Junction Peak, so called as it lay at the junction of the south ridge and south west rib. The climbing remained difficult and dangerous though they finally reached a large snow bank where they hoped to dig a snow cave from where they could launch their final summit bid. Unfortunately the snow was not as deep as they had hoped and so they could only dig some deep slots, snow coffins as Chris Bonington called them, for each climber. They did not know it at the time but they would have to spend three days in these coffins as the weather took a turn for the worse yet again and they were too weak to force the route in anything but decent weather.

On the 12th July the weather improved and the four climbers were galvanized into action. Peter had developed frostbite in his fingers and climbing was painful, they climbed 150 metres in five hours but now the summit lay before them and they could walk rather than climb to gain height. The wind grew strong but they were not to be defeated now despite their suffering and all four reached the summit where they lingered for only ten minutes as the day was progressing and the need to descend put paid to any procrastination. Two new snow caves had to be dug and at 2.00am they finally lay down to sleep after Alan's hardest and most physically demanding climb to date.

The next day the descent continued and it was four very weary climbers that finally found their snow cave at the Junction Peak where another night was spent before carrying on down the mountain to base camp the next day.

Within a year Peter Boardman and Joe Tasker were to die on the north east ridge of Everest on an expedition led by Chris Bonington. Alan was very disappointed in not being invited on this expedition and thought it incredulous that he was not there. A pattern was developing in his life now where every year he would be away for month's at a time climbing amongst the highest mountains of the world.

Ogre 2 (6960m)

In early July 1982, Alan was again en-route to the Himalaya with Paul Nunn, Andy Parkin & Brian Hall to attempt a small but very difficult mountain, Ogre 2 in the Karakoram region. It had only been attempted twice before and no-one had successfully made the summit.

A small un-named Aiguille was attempted as a practice climb and when above all the major difficulties the party bivouacked in the hope of finishing the climb the next day however the weather prevented them from doing so and they bid a quick retreat back to base camp satisfied that they had at least started to get acclimatised.

On the 28th July the team set off and by 10.30am they had reached a shoulder on the north ridge of the Ogre which allowed them the luxury of an early finish and a decent snow cave. Their chosen route looked too difficult and so they elected to cross below a band of tottering seracs, the next morning they crossed the rocks beneath them and reached a relatively safe point where another ice cave could be dug in a bergshrund while Alan and Andy prospected the route ahead which looked a formidable undertaking.

The next morning the party moved on over difficult ground, so steep was the rock that it proved near impossible to climb with a rucksack on one's back and so they had to be hauled up after each pitch was climbed, exhausting work at altitude. Eventually the angle eased and the climbers re-grouped to discuss the way forward when suddenly an avalanche of ice missiles fell on them and they were forced to seek shelter from the barrage, when it finally stopped a unanimous decision was reached and they descended quickly due to their being no safe place in which to camp. They reached their ice cave and realised that to descend the way they had come would be foolish and an alternative descent had to be and was found down the seemingly notorious 'Death Alley'. This was a broad couloir full of threatening seracs which looked like they could fall any minute. There was no choice however and the four of them descended as quickly as possible without incurring any injury though all expressed a desire never to enter the place ever again.

The party made their way round to the south Face but the ascent looked hopeless from there as well however Alan espied a couloir coming down from the south west ridge and they decided that they would concentrate on that when Brian Hall suffered a dislocated shoulder and forced him to retire from the expedition.

Alan, Andy Parkin and Paul Nunn made their way up the ice gully leading to the couloir and found a precarious bivouac site beneath some looming cornices. The following morning the three of them set off only to be confronted with another disaster when Paul Nunn broke a crampon and it was not possible for him to go on. He tried to persuade Alan & Andy to continue but their heart was not in it and they descended back to base camp. They had all recently lost two good friends on Everest and throughout the entire expedition their deaths seemed to cast a cloud over their climbing.

An attempt was made to climb back up via Death Alley but an avalanche of falling seracs while near the top put paid to those ambitions and the expedition was over.

K2 (8611m) & Broad Peak (8051m)

In 1983 Alan was invited to join an international expedition with the ultimate aim of trying to climb K2, the second highest mountain in the world, by the south ridge direct. On the expedition would be Doug Scott from Nuptse and the legendary Don Whillans who now looked anything unlike a hardened mountaineer but one whose experience would doubtless prove useful at some point.

K2 is certainly the most difficult mountain of all the 8000m peaks and it has received fewer ascents than any other of the world's highest mountains.

The expedition began with an ascent of Biale One which had never been climbed before and Alan, Greg Child, Andy Parkin & Pete Thexton got to within thirty feet of the summit before having to turn back because of bad weather. To have continued would have meant an enforced bivouac with no equipment which at best would have meant for an uncomfortable night. Alan & Andy Parkin then tried the west face of Lobsang but failed while only a few hundred feet from the summit, again because of poor weather.

Their next objective though would certainly be more successful as on the 25th June Alan, Andy Parkin, Roger Baxter Jones & Jean Afanassieff made a fast alpine style ascent of Broad Peak, the twelfth highest mountain in the world and one of the coveted fourteen 8000m peaks.

The expedition suffered a great tragedy a few days later as Pete Thexton died of Pulmonary Odema at 7650m while descending from making his own attempt on Broad Peak.

Alan stayed on to try K2 with Andy Parkin however the weather remained bad with barely more than two or three days good weather in succession. They reached a height of just under 8000m and so the mountain had still yet to receive a British ascent.

Alan had now seemingly become pre-occupied with Himalayan mountaineering however for the next couple of years he re-focused on his rock climbing and put up a number of new routes in the Peak District and Jersey. His climbs in Jersey are now considered 'must do' classics to anyone visiting the island. In 1984 Alan went to Pakistan with Chris Bonington to attempt an ascent of Karun Koh (7350m) which they had espied from the summit of Kongur back in 1981. The only way they could get permission to this remote mountain was to agree to climb with two, to them, unknown Pakistani climbers. They proved to be somewhat inexperienced but immensely keen and had a great love of the mountains, in addition they proved to be delightful company.

The approach march to the peak could have been done in a day but local porter regulations stipulated three days. Alan & Chris 'negotiated' them down to a day and a half but still had to pay for three days porters labour. On arrival at base camp there awaited an array of unclimbed and unexplored peaks of around 6000m, their peak looked no push-over as they had hoped it would be from the photographs they had seen. They decided that the west ridge offered the best chance of success but hard compact rock and much ice would prove to be a serious obstacle and largely precluded an alpine style push with two inexperienced climbers. After Chris had explained to them the difficulties of the climb they were happy to allow Alan & Chris to climb the peak alone and while the initial part of the ridge was not hard it was nerve wracking with brittle ice and little protection. They both reached the same conclusion and decided that there must be a better way and a quick retreat was made back to base camp. Alan and Chris decided to have a look at the other side of the mountain but to no avail as, if anything, the east side looked even harder. There then followed a storm which lasted for ten days and with their time running out and with commitments back home Alan & Chris called it a day and abandoned the expedition.

Alan had plans to return to K2 in 1986 and so most of 1985 was spent in organizing the expedition however he did make a visit to New Zealand on a lecture tour and managed to get some climbing done in the magnificent New Zealand Alps. Alan also became the Vice President of the British Mountaineering Council, respectability was beckoning and he felt a certain pressure to add K2 to his mountaineering CV and cement his reputation as one of the country's foremost Himalayan mountaineers.

K2 – The Savage Mountain

Alan had received permission to attempt the unclimbed north west ridge of K2 and together with John Barry, the Burgess twins, John Porter, Jim Hargreaves, Phil Burke, Brian Hall, Jim Curran, Dave Wilkinson and Bev Holt they left the UK in late April heading for Islamabad and the long march to K2. The weather on the walk in was not kind and more often than not was very bad however they arrived at base camp on the 22nd May in the hope that things would improve.

A week later on the 29th May the climbers arrived at camp one at the start of the main difficulties. On the first day of establishing the route proper a small avalanche broke on Alan & John Porter narrowly missing them as they reached the safety of a rock buttress. Ahead the route looked even more difficult and dangerous, another three weeks of concerted effort, often hampered by the weather saw the establishment of camp two at 6700m on the ridge proper. Brian Hall had to leave the expedition with a damaged knee ligament which reduced their numbers and with the weather proving particularly atrocious the best they could hope for was one good day at a time.

The expedition was not being carried out in true alpine style as favoured by Alan as the route was complex and unknown. The only way they could climb the route would be by establishing fixed camps along the way and fixing ropes, really an anathema to Alan.

By mid June the weather improved briefly and they could push the route out a bit further. Alan and John Porter climbed up to camp two with heavy loads, loads that were needed to stock the camp sufficiently with supplies to enable climbers to move further up the mountain. For two days Alan and John enjoyed perfect weather as they pushed the route out up to 7400m, Alan started to believe that they could make a push for the summit however he had started to develop a typical high altitude cough and when John Porter suggested descending to camp one for a good rest before going for the summit Alan agreed.

That decision perhaps saved his life as a massive storm enveloped the mountain for the next three weeks and eventually all the climbers had to return to base camp as it was not possible to recuperate at the higher camps.

During this period, and unbeknown to the expedition, other expeditions attempting the normal route on K2, the Abruzzi spur, were having their own difficulties. Ordinarily the Pakistan authorities would only allow one or two expeditions a season on a big Himalayan peak but in 1986 there were to be ten large expeditions attempting various routes to the summit of K2. The consequences of this would not be appreciated until later in the summer when the full tragedy of what happened came to light.

After nearly two months of continuous bad weather Alan was on the verge of calling the expedition to a halt though he did consider attempting an ascent of the normal Abruzzi route even though they did not have permission. An attempt was made but abandoned after only a day due to the continual bad weather.

At base camp morale was low, already this summer six people had died on K2, and the majority of the British expedition wanted to go home. Alan still wanted K2 and together with his good friend and expedition cameraman, Jim Curran, he decided to move base camp nearer the international base camp populated by the teams attempting the Abruzzi Spur in the hope of joining up with one of those expeditions and getting his chance to summit. The remaining expedition members went home, some struggled to make the decision but with the weather being as it was that summer it was not a hard decision to see through once made.

Abruzzi Spur

Alan had taken the failure of his expedition to the north west ridge quite hard and was anxious to salvage something for himself, even if it was to be just the first British ascent of K2. The Abruzzi Spur while technically the easiest way up K2 is not an easy climb and there are limited places in which to site a camp, platforms are not large and often only two or three tents can be pitched at each site. This year a complication would arise with the sheer number of people climbing this route that would bring a lot of pressure to bear on the climbers while in extremis. Alan decided to team up with Mrufka Wolf, a female Polish mountaineer, who was originally on the Polish south west ridge expedition but had decided to climb with Alan as she felt this gave her a better chance of the summit.

Towards the end of July the weather seemed to finally settle down and on the evening of the 29th July Alan with Mrufka Wolf set out from base camp intending to reach advance base camp for a brief rest before pressing straight on for camp one. On the 2nd August Alan & Mrufka made it to camp four and squeezed themselves into a tiny two man tent. However a team of descending Austrian climbers who had failed to summit found themselves without a tent and after pleading with the tent's occupants one of the exhausted Austrians got into Alan's & Mrufka's tent which became so cramped Alan elected to sleep half in the tent and half in the porch. For some reason, probably extreme exhaustion, Alan and Mrufka decided to take a rest day, a fatal decision at 8000m as the body simply cannot recover or rest at that altitude. Many climbers call the region above 8000m 'The Death Zone' and for good reason, the weather continued to remain perfect and maybe the climbers thought it would continue for a while yet.

On the 4th August Alan and Mrufka set out followed by a party of Austrians and the legendary Kurt Diemberger with his climbing partner, the female British mountaineer Julie Tullis. The snow was very soft and Alan broke trail nearly all the way to the summit before being overtaken by two of the Austrians. At about 3.20pm Alan stood on the summit of K2 he was the first British mountaineer to reach this point though Julie Tullis was only a few hours behind him. As Alan began to descend he noticed the skies darkening and it must have been clear to him that the weather was changing. He passed Mrufka Wolf who had struggled vainly all day and persuaded her to descend with him, they finally made it back to camp four on the shoulder of the mountain. Julie Tullis and Kurt Diemberger did not make it back to the camp that night and endured a horrific bivouac at 8400m in the open before finally reaching the tents late the following morning in a near white-out.

All the climbers were exhausted and no-one moved down the mountain that day, by the evening of the 5th August a huge storm hit the mountain with seven climbers trapped in three tents that soon became two as one was destroyed by the wind. Julie Tullis was slipping in and out of consciousness and the night she died she spoke to one of the Austrians in whose tent she was staying and said 'Willi, get Kurt down safely'. She then closed her eyes and never spoke again. Kurt was devastated and Alan did all he could do to console him, Alan was a tower of strength for the trapped climbers frequently getting out of the tent to clear the snow away and making drinks but when the gas ran out on the 8th August he was the first to succumb, the effect of staying too high for too long was now becoming apparent but there was nothing he could do for himself.

The next night Alan was delirious, begging for water and mumbling incoherently and by the 10th August the surviving climbers had to move or they would surely die, the three Austrians, Kurt Diemberger and Mrufka Wolf all prepared to descend. Kurt had to make the horrible decision to leave Alan, who was still drifting in and out of consciousness and mumbling to himself, but there was nothing that could be done for him. He found a dry sleeping bag and tried to make him comfortable and then the remaining five climbers began the long and tortuous descent, a descent where only two of them would survive.

The summer of 1986 was a particularly tragic season with a total of thirteen climbers dying on the mountain. When the news of the death of Alan and Julie broke there was much sadness in the mountaineering community and many memorial services were held. Alan had been living in Sheffield for a number of years and there is now, housed within the city library, a specialist mountaineering library named after him which houses one of the largest collections of mountaineering literature, maps and expedition reports in the country.

Epilogue

Many years ago, while giving a lecture, Bill Tilman was asked by a young man how he could go on an expedition. Bill, paused for a moment and then gave a reply which seemed to sum up his whole approach to life, he said 'Just put on your boots and go'.

We now live in an age where the highest mountains of the world are within reach of anyone with big enough wallets and there is certainly less exclusivity in going to the Himalaya or other far flung region, so for a budding adventurer, it would appear that there is little left to do.

However, true adventures can still be sought out by even the most impecunious of individuals. We are most fortunate in living in a roughly central position in the UK. Snowdonia, the Lake & Peak Districts can all be reached in less than two hours and with a bit more driving we have the incomparable Scottish peaks at our disposal. I've often pitied our southern mountaineering friends, whose weekend begins and ends with a long drive.

I have never forgotten my first time walking with my father, I'd acquired a cheap pair of walking boots from the old Coates Army & Navy stores, a shop now sadly long gone. We went up Snowdon via the Miner's track and came down the PYG track in glorious late afternoon sunshine, though we were denied any views from the summit as it had remained in cloud for most of the day. I can still taste the powdered chicken soup cooked on an old Camping Gaz stove just off the path in a little hollow and the whole day seemed to be one of pure adventure.

We had no tent and knew nothing of clubs and so slept in our old Ford Cortina estate in the Pen Y Pass car park. The next morning, all stiff and cold we made our way up Tryfan though the summit proved to be beyond our abilities and we descended back down to Ogwen Cottage. Many more weekends followed and before long we were good strong walkers and even managed to find the confidence to venture onto the easier scrambles such as the impressively pinnacled crest of Crib Goch. We acquired the necessary camping equipment and took to walking the long distance paths before my burgeoning ambition to go rock climbing led me to joining a local club and well the rest, as they say, is history.

For nearly thirty years I've made some great friends and had days so incredible that they are etched forever into my memory.

By joining a club you will meet many like minded individuals of varying abilities who get out most weekends, sharing cars, sometimes camping and sometimes staying in the many club 'huts' throughout the country's mountainous regions.

Even those of us who seem to have little time at the weekends can find much fun at the local climbing walls or, on warm summer evenings, the local outcrops of Helsby, Frodsham and the incomparable Pex Hill where a novice will find many a climber more than willing to offer advice and encouragement.

And so, why don't you put on your boots and go and have some fun ....you'll never regret it.

GLOSSARY

There are throughout the book a number of words and expressions which the casual reader may not be familiar with, I hope this brief glossary will help !

Abseil – A method of descending down a rope quickly.

Aiguille - A rock peak or needle.

Arête – An sharp edge / ridge of rock.

Bergshrund – A crevasse where one side of the crevice is higher than the other, usually found where a glacier abuts against a buttress of rock.

Col – A pass, a French name in common use amongst mountaineers.

Cornice – A projecting mass of snow on a snow ridge, generally formed by a prevailing wind.

Crampons – A steel / alloy frame with projecting spikes which fit onto the sole of a boot which facilitate the climbing of steep ice or snow without the need to cut steps with an ice axe.

Crevasse – A crevice or fissure in a glacier, ranging in width from a few inches to many feet.

Cwm- A Welsh word for valley, though courtesy of Mallory using the word on Everest it has become used by mountaineers all over the world.

Gendarme – A tower or pillar of rock on a ridge that has resisted shattering from frost.

Glacier – A field or river of ice, sometimes the lower part of a glacier may be covered in stones and all the ice may be hidden underneath.

Glissade – A method of descent used by mountaineers to slide down a safe snow slope, can be done either sitting or standing.

Karabiner – An oblong metal ring with a spring clip used for attaching a running rope to a piton or some other piece of protection

Moraine – Stones and debris carried down by a glacier and collected into a heap on each side.

Nullah – A small gully or ravine

Pemmican - Lean dried meat pounded fine and mixed with melted fat. It can keep for many years without refrigeration and thus is easy to carry and a good source of protein.

Piton – A small metal spike hammered into a crack in to the rock to aid progress or secure a difficult move by inserting a Karabiner through its eye and clipping the rope into it.

Rock Climbing Grades – These are the grades given to rock climbing routes in the UK. Climbs are graded from Moderate through to Hard Very Severe. The harder or Extremely Severe climbs are numbered from E1 through to (at the moment) E11. The 'E' grade takes into account a multitude of factors such as length of climb, loose rock, poor protection etc. The rock climbs are further graded to denote the technical difficulty of the hardest move on the route. These grades go from 4a (easy) to 8c (hard!).

Scree – Slopes of loose stones found at the bottom of rock faces.

Serac - A tower or pinnacle of ice, occasionally unstable and then hazardous to encounter.

Snow Bridges – Arches joining the two sides of a crevasse formed by the remnants of snow which formerly covered the crevasse.

Verglas – A thin glassy coating of ice on rock, treacherous when encountered and hard to see.

Whillan's Box – A near indestructible box shaped tent popular in high altitude mountaineering before the advent of modern Geodesic tents.

SELECT BIBLIOGRAPHY

I have leant heavily on the resources of the Local Record Office at the Liverpool and Birkenhead Libraries as well as the various journals of the Alpine Club, Fell and Rock Climbing Club, Climbers Club and Wayfarer's Club.

J. R. L. Anderson – High Mountains & Cold Seas 'A biography of H. W. Tilman'

Herbert Carr – The Irvine Diaries

Ronald Clark - The Victorian Mountaineers

Elizabeth & Nicholas Clinch – Through a Land of Extremes 'The Littledales of Central Asia'

A superbly researched book on two largely and previously unknown explorers and travellers

Jim Curran - K2, The Story of the Savage Mountain

Steve Dean - Hands of a Climber 'A biography of Colin Kirkus'

Joan Evans - The Conways 'A History of Three Generations'

Fergus Flemming - Killing Dragons

Quite simply one of the most under-rated books on early alpine mountaineering

Florence Craufurd Grove – The Frosty Caucasus

The story of the first ascent of Mount Elbrus

John Huxley – The Gwydyr

Tim Madge - Bill Tilman, The Last Hero

Geoff Milburn (Edt) - Alan Rouse, A Mountaineers Life

Jim Perrin - Menlove

Julie Summers - Fearless on Everest 'The Quest for Sandy Irvine'

H. W. 'Bill' Tilman - Snow on the Equator, The Ascent of Nanda Devi, When Men and Mountains Meet, Everest 1938, Two Mountains and a River, China to Chitral, Nepal Himalaya, Mischief in Patagonia, Mischief among the Penguins, Mischief in Greenland, Mostly Mischief, Mischief Goes South, In Mischief's Wake, Ice with Everything, Triumph and Tribulation.

All of Bill Tilman's books are worth reading and they are available in modern compilation editions.

MERSEYSIDE & NEARBY WALKING AND CLIMBING CLUBS

Gwydyr Mountain Club
www.gwydyrmc.co.uk

Merseyside Mountaineering Club
www.merseysidemc.org

Vagabonds Mountaineering Club
www.vagabondmc.com

Wayfarer's Club
www.wayfarersclub.org.uk

Liverpool Ramblers
www.liverpoolramblers.co.uk

Chester Mountaineering Club
www.chestermc.org

Clwyd Mountaineering Club
www.clwydmc.co.uk

St Helens Mountaineering Club
www.sthelensmc.org

NOTES :

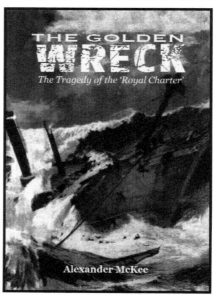

JUST NUISANCE AB - HIS FULL STORY

by Terence Sisson

The amazing but true story of the only dog that was officially enlisted into the British Royal Navy, a Great Dane whose name was Nuisance, his official rank and name was AB Just Nuisance. Famed for his preference for the company of navy ratings (he wasn't too keen on Officers) in and around the famous World War II naval base of Simonstown, South Africa, Nuisance helped many a sailor rejoin his ship after a night on the town.

Today his own statue overlooking the bay off the Cape of Good Hope commemorates AB Just Nuisance.

£10.50

THETIS - THE ADMIRALTY REGRETS
- THE DISASTER IN LIVERPOOL BAY

by C.Warren & J.Benson

The definitive minute by minute account of this terrible tragedy in 1939 when 99 men lost their lives as the Birkenhead built HM Submarine *Thetis* undertook her first and only dive. It was the worst submarine disaster in British history....only four men escaped.

With new photographs and previously unpublished documents as well as a new foreword by survivor's son Derek Arnold, and a new postscript by maritime historian David Roberts.

Why didn't anyone cut open the submarine?
Why was there no urgency in the Admiralty's rescue system?
Did the Admiralty **really** regret?

ISBN 0 9521020 8 0   £14.50

HMS THETIS - SECRETS AND SCANDAL - AFTERMATH OF A DISASTER

by David Roberts

The truth behind the cover-up of this terrible submarine disaster and the shameful treatment of those left behind. Contains interviews with relatives of victims and survivors; Sons, daughters, brothers, sisters and those very rare ladies, living *'Thetis'* widows.

Why did the Official Inquiry blame nobody, explaining it away as 'an unfortunate sequence of events'? Why did the civil action on behalf of the widows fail? Did the Admiralty cover it up? How much did Churchill know?

A huge publicly subscribed disaster fund was collected for the relatives. How was this managed and distributed? Who got what and why? What ever happened to the money that was left?
Why do a handful of living widows still today get just £9.62 per month from the fund, in one case LESS TAX !

'The Hillsborough of its day' .....- BBC Radio Merseyside
'Exposes how 'The Establishment' closed ranks' - Liverpool Daily Post
'A book that shocks' - Sea Breezes

ISBN 0 9521020 0 5 £14.50

FORGOTTEN EMPRESS
- The Tragedy of the Empress of Ireland
- by David Zeni

Tells the fascinating story of the Canadian Pacific Passenger liner RMS *Empress of Ireland*. On her way home to Liverpool from Canada, she was sunk in a collision on the St. Lawrence River. Two years after the *Titanic*, it was, in terms of passenger fatalities, an even greater tragedy. These two ships, along with the *Lusitania*, form a triumvirate of maritime tragedies, all within a three-year period, that sent shock waves around the world.

Yet whilst *Titanic* and *Lusitania* seem to be almost household names, the disaster that befell the *Empress of Ireland* has until now always been shrouded in the cloak of history, as impenetrable as the fog that brought about her total loss, along with 1,012 lives, on 29th May 1914. With a chilling connection to the 'Crippen Murders' and containing never-before-published material, Forgotten Empress grips the reader in such a way it is hard to put aside... a thoroughly excellent book.

'*...dubbed 'The 'Forgotten Empress'...the second in a shocking trio of tragedies at sea...sandwiched in between the disasters of the Titanic and the Lusitania, ...it was a sudden death... that sent Liverpool into mourning...*
Liverpool Echo

' *Zeni brings a fresh, moment by moment urgency to this real life tragic drama*
Winnipeg Free Press

LIFE AT LAIRDS
- MEMORIES OF WORKING SHIPYARD MEN

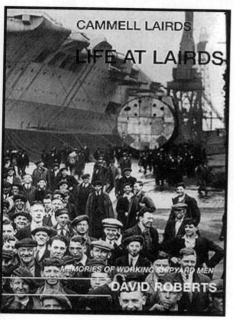

by David Roberts

'The time may not be far off when young people will ask, What did they do there, what were they like? This book answers the questions......'

Sea Breezes

'A book full of anecdotes and rich in humanity...a piece of social History...'

Liverpool Echo

ISBN 0 9521020 1 3   £10.00

CAMMELL LAIRD - THE GOLDEN YEARS

David Roberts - Foreword by Frank Field M. P.

by David Roberts

With a foreword by Frank Field MP

'Captures life in the prosperous years at the historic Birkenhead shipyard......'

Liverpool Echo

'Puts into perspective ... the strikes... the Polaris contract... and those who worked at the yard...' Sea Breezes

**ISBN 0 9521020 2 1
£10.00.**

A GUIDED TOUR OF MERSEYSIDE WILDLIFE AND NATURAL HISTORY

by Bob 'The Birdman' Hughes

Merseyside Wildlife is perhaps not a term you would asocciate with the region yet local naturalist Bob Hughes and his team of intrepid observers show us that the areas wildlife is surprisingly very much alive and well if you know where to look.

A book that gives us a snapshot of the 'real' Merseyside in the early 21st century.

ISBN 978-1-902964-24-9 £10.00

A HISTORY OF THE SCALA CINEMA - PRESTATYN
by Fred Hobbs

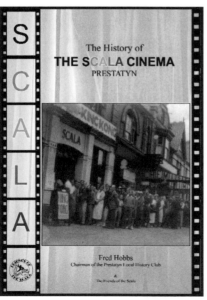

The 'Pictures', the 'Flicks', the 'Talkies' and the 'Movies', have made all of us laugh and cry, sometimes at the same time. The Scala was one of the earliest cinemas in the country opening on the very eve of the First World War in 1913. Despite closing down in 2000 in need of major restoration, the people of the town organised themselves to raise awareness and funds to get the Scala re-opened. The result, a refurbished cutting-edge totally digital cinema (the first one in Wales), an arts centre, performance space, café bar and meeting rooms was reborn in 2009.

This is the history of that small local cinema, the Scala, and it's journey, 'Back to the Future'.

ISBN 978-1-902964-09-6 £10.00

RUNCORN - A TOWN NOT SO NEW

by H.F. Starkey

A pictorial record of a town which has undergone profound change. The archive photographs recall forgotten vistas as well as traditional customs and practices of times past together with vanished industries, rural landscapes and buildings which may now be beyond the memories of even the oldest Runcornians.

ISBN 978 - 1- 902964 -08- 9

£12.50

BLUE FUNNEL - VOYAGE EAST
by Richard Woodman

What was life like aboard a British vessel in the last great days of the Merchant Navy? *Blue Funnel - Voyage East* takes us in one of the Holt Line's 'China Boats' on a typical trip out of the Mersey, to the Far East and back again by way of Suez. The time is the 1960s and it is a style of seafaring now totally lost among today's container ships and roll on - roll off ferries.

We keep the long watches of the night, observe officers and men, sea and weather, in every mood. We learn about the transvestites of Singapore and the almond-eyed whores of Hong Kong, as well as the intricacies of derricks and cargo stowage - human hair and hog bristle from China, liquid latex and palm oil from Malaya. We can puzzle over the mysteries of navigation, what motivates the First Mate and why any sane man should go to sea, far from home and the love of good women.

The author draws on his many years service in Blue Funnel cargo liners to capture the sights, smells, enormous satisfactions and aching sadness that attended the 'carriage of general cargo in open stows'.

'This is life at sea, warts and all, and a better book because of it.'.... 'The story of an adventurous way of life offered to the sons of a once great seafaring nation...'

'Sea Breezes'

ISBN 978-1-902964-04-1   £15.50

ON D V D

BLUE FUNNEL - VOYAGES AND VOICES *VOLUMES I & II*
Produced and narrated by David Roberts

Compiled with the help of never before published film taken all over the world by some of those men who actually sailed with 'Blueys' on many of their well-known vessels.
Contains some of the sights and sounds of typical Blue Funnel voyages; leaving the home shores of the UK, sailing through both the Suez and Panama canals, the legendary gilly gilly man, Hong Kong, Singapore, Kobe, Tokyo, and other 'exotic' ports.
We also see and hear the thoughts and memories of some of those who actually sailed with 'Blueys' over their working lives, from Able Seaman to Captain, Steward to Engineer.

'... a must for anyone who sailed with 'Blueys' or who sailed in the merchant navy of old...'   Sea Breezes
£17.95 each

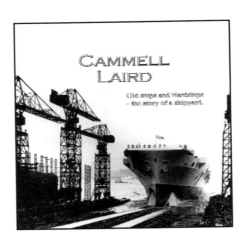

CAMMELL LAIRD
- OLD SHIPS AND HARDSHIPS

THE STORY OF A SHIPYARD

Produced and narrated by David Roberts

A film history of this world famous shipyard.
How Cammell Laird served the nation through two World
Wars, up to the tragic day in 1993 when Lairds was shut down.

The story of the yard is also told through the voices of the men
who worked at Lairds; Welders, Cranedrivers, Electricians and
Plumbers, they tell of the hardships of building ships in all
weathers and the lighter moments that came from some of the
'characters' of the yard.

£17.95